Reading Power

FOURTH EDITION

James I. Brown
University of Minnesota

D. C. HEATH AND COMPANY
Lexington, Massachusetts   Toronto

Acquisitions Editor:	Paul Smith
Developmental Editor:	Holt Johnson
Production Editor:	Renée M. Mary
Designer:	Sally Steele
Production Coordinator:	Charles Dutton
Text Permissions Editor:	Margaret Roll

Cover design by Linda Manley-Wade.

To the Student

What's most worth knowing? If you don't answer that all-important question right now, you can't begin to use your time to best advantage. After all, you're feeling the full force of a knowledge explosion of unbelievable magnitude. Books, for example, now pour from the world presses at almost a thousand a day! If you read only one today, you're already 999 books behind in your effort to keep informed. Now add newspapers and magazines, including almost 100,000 scientific journals! Overwhelming, isn't it? And—*you're* the one who's living in this print-filled world of fantastic change. With knowledge doubling every twenty months, you're probably in a state of shock—"future shock," as Toffler once called it.

Well—what *is* most worth knowing? The answer? Knowing how to read! That was apparently the answer back in the last century. Remember the three R's? Reading stood first, and that's still the answer today. A nationwide survey published in the *Phi Delta Kappan* lists developing "skills in reading, writing, speaking, and listening" as the number one goal of education. Again, reading comes first. Barbara Bush adds that there are presently an estimated twenty-three million Americans who have problems with literacy—with reading. What's most worth knowing? Knowing how to read!

Makes sense, doesn't it? For everyone, keeping up is all-important. Do you want that essential information coming at 100 words-per-minute— or 250 wpm? Remember—the average classroom lecture brings you information at about 100 words a minute. The average reader gets information at about 250 wpm—over twice as fast. This means that you hear about 4,000 words in a forty-minute lecture, as compared with getting 10,000 words in forty minutes of reading. But—best of all—by concentrated effort with this text, you should at least double your present rate—getting not 10,000 but 20,000 words in forty minutes of reading.

If reading comes first, what comes next? To find out, begin by putting this page so close to your face that your nose actually touches it. Then try to read the entire page. Go ahead. Try it!

See? To read even one page, you need one more thing of key importance—perspective. You need to get back far enough to see the whole, not just a small fragment.

Perspective is, in a word, the key to this book, as it is to life. We have to view the present within the frame of both past and future. For example, this book helps you look back to those early days in America when we put on rubber tires and sprouted wings. And it helps you look ahead to our need to manage waste and save the life-preserving ozone layer. It focuses on what's serious and what's humorous, what's entertaining and what's useful, what's work and what's leisure. And since all work and no play means lack of perspective, selections touch not only on how to make a speech and how best to apply for a job but also on the amazing first balloon ascension and the first sensational breaking of the sound barrier. In short, the thirty-four selections provide wide-ranging glimpses of life, from the practical to the exciting.

Furthermore, all selections fit into a broader perspective; they let you explore important rate and comprehension relationships. In short, they give you an ideal opportunity to apply newly learned reading skills in a variety of reading situations, including essential college textbook reading.

The very heart of reading—understanding—must also reflect desired perspective. It's not enough just to get the facts. You want to see both the trees *and* the forest—the facts as well as the main ideas, the literal as well as the reflective. You'll find both in this book, laid out in gradual steps, bringing both facts and meaning into balance. You must learn to crawl before you walk. In the same way, you must learn to get facts accurately before you can build complete comprehension. The first fourteen selections focus on getting the facts; the last twenty focus on getting both facts and meaning.

And what about vocabulary? Here too you need perspective. It's easy to focus on context and overlook word parts—or on the dictionary and overlook context. The exercises in this text focus on all three—context, word parts, and dictionary.

At times, context—even very limited context—practically defines a strange word for you; at other times it provides little or no help. In the following exercises, the very brief contexts in "Part A, Leaning on Context," reflect this varying degree of helpfulness and lay the groundwork for desired habits of attention to whatever clues are present. Add the heightened awareness of word parts, resulting from "Part B, Leaning on Parts," and you'll be even better prepared to unravel word meanings. Finally, in "Part C, Making the Words Yours," you'll find new sentence contexts, more conversational in nature, where you can fit the new words into place, making them indeed yours. This threefold attack on words ends, as it should, with application and use. As you know, best results come from doing—from actively using what you've learned.

Finally, remember that reviewing plays an essential role in learning. To expedite that step, you'll find mini-reviews of all prefix, root, and suffix elements covered in Part B, plus an important mini-review of twenty other useful prefix shortcuts. You'll also find a description of the LDE formula—a formula that will let you deal with literally thousands of additional word parts. Last, you'll find a simplified pronunciation guide to help you with words that might pose a pronunciation problem.

So, as you work through this book, be assured you're using an approach that will bring a greatly improved vocabulary and that reading skill most worth having. In addition, you'll find increased awareness of how to fit what you read into better perspective. It's a challenge worthy of your best efforts.

To the Instructor

As with previous editions, my goals for writing this fourth edition of *Reading Power* are:

1. To stimulate heightened student interest in reading and vocabulary development.
2. To provide a practical classroom-tested program for achieving maximum reading proficiency and vocabulary growth.
3. To provide help in applying a wide range of specific reading and study techniques for better and more flexible management of textbook reading.
4. To fit reading into a broad framework, establishing it as an activity of prime importance both in and out of school.

Teachers and students alike need a textbook that is both stimulating and practical. To provide that has been my hope. This text has grown out of my firsthand teaching experience with more than 6,000 students of reading at the University of Minnesota. Add other users of previous editions and I would like to think this text has helped over 150,000 students with their reading problems.

As in all subject matter areas, results tend to be unsatisfactory without high student interest. For that reason, I have continued to make interest a matter of prime concern in writing this book. That means using an informal style in the instructional articles to encourage easy reading. That means drawing from bestsellers and popular magazines and including well-known names among the authors. As a new feature for this edition, I have included eight passages from six currently and widely used college textbooks. But here, too, I have kept interest uppermost, selecting passages of particular appeal. As every teacher knows, strong student interest is imperative— insuring satisfactory progress.

I have chosen thirty-four entirely new selections for this edition, three more than in any previous edition. The added selections permit greater choice in making assignments. I have retained the same organizational format as before—a format well-accepted by previous users, encouraging, as it does, student development of metacognitive skills. Each of the fourteen instructional articles is followed by selections providing immediate opportunity to apply the techniques covered. This application step moves students quickly from theory into practice, accelerating growth.

The text is divided into five carefully structured parts, each advancing the student one step further toward development of full reading potential.

PART I, THE CHECK-UP, introduced by the instructional article, "Reading Power—Key to Personal Growth," focuses on diagnosis, providing initial explorations into the major factors of comprehension, rate, and word power. This opening part immediately involves the student and motivates increased effort, matters of key importance. You will probably want to supplement these informal explorations by using a standardized reading text. Test scores provide more accurate indications of ability and permit specific group comparisons.

Two selections follow this first instructional article. The first comes from Fulghum's bestseller—*All I Really Need to Know I Learned in Kindergarten*—a fascinating account of the first exploration of space—by balloon! The second selection—"Breaking the Sound Barrier"—comes from Yeager's autobiography—another bestseller—and describes the first flight faster than the speed of sound.

PART II, THE BUILD-UP, does two things—starts the student along 1) the vocabulary improvement road and 2) the reading-for-facts road, to build a solid foundation for the subsequent move into in-depth comprehension.

The vocabulary approach reflects significant research done by Holmes and Singer. Their research pinpoints factors of most importance in reading comprehension and speed. They discovered that *vocabulary in context* was the single most important first-order factor contributing to comprehension—39%—considerably more than *intelligence*, a 27% contribution. In addition to those figures for first-order factors, second- and third-order factors provide additional evidence—*vocabulary in isolation* contributing 47%, *prefixes* 11%, and *suffixes* 10%. In short, to improve comprehension, word study would seem the best path.

The vocabulary exercises in this text are solidly based on the Holmes-Singer research. Students are led gradually from *vocabulary in isolation* with minimal context to an informal *vocabulary in context* and, finally, to vocabulary in the full context of the article being read.

Before reading a selection, then, students work through an exercise— "Leaning on Context"—built around ten troublesome words drawn from that selection, words with minimal context. Such exercises uncover words that pose difficulties. Students are encouraged to resolve any difficulties by consulting their dictionary. The next exercise—"Making the Words Yours"—provides ten complete informal contexts except for missing key words—the ten just studied. Students must supply the appropriate word to fit each sentence context—an important reinforcing step. Now the student is properly prepared to read the article, ready to deal with the words in full context. This approach minimizes potential word blocks to understanding.

In addition, the vocabulary exercises, "Leaning on Parts," which also precede each selection, show students exactly how to make more effective use of word parts—prefixes, roots, and suffixes.

The second instructional reading—"How Do You Best Get the Facts?"—begins to lay a strong foundation for complete comprehension. Readers must be able to get facts accurately if they are to draw correct conclusions. Judgments or inferences based on a faulty or incomplete grasp of details are of necessity inaccurate. For that reason, the first twenty-one readings work to establish a solid foundation of factual accuracy.

PART III, THE SPEED-UP, concentrates on a matter of particular student concern. Almost all students have major problems covering the required reading. This part focuses on helping students manage their study time better by knowing and using such study techniques as surveying, skimming, and scanning, and by learning how to increase reading speed without losing comprehension—valuable aids in achieving academic success.

PART IV, THE WORK-UP, makes the all-important transition from factual to in-depth comprehension. "Reading for Meaning" starts the process. That and all the remaining selections—twenty-seven in all—have comprehension tests balancing factual with inferential, judgmental, and critical questions. Concentrated attention is given to reading words, paragraphs, and entire selections more effectively, an ordering to encourage metacognitive skills development. Techniques for getting better grades and developing special interests in varied academic areas conclude this part.

Finally, PART V, THE ROUND-UP, provides the opportunity to pull together all the newly developed reading and vocabulary suggestions—all the separate strands of content—for final application and reinforcement. Of the eight selections in this part, the first four come directly from college textbooks—samples of the reading students must do effectively to succeed in school. The last four come from books and magazines—general reading. This twofold division serves as a reminder that reading remains of prime importance both in and out of school.

The selections following each instructional article are ordered, insofar as possible, from easy to difficult, from shorter to longer. The average difficulty approximates the Standard English level on the Flesch Reading Ease scale. Exact reading ease figures are given for each of the selections on page 381 of the Appendix, a new feature with this edition. The selections touch a wide variety of subjects: serious and humorous, personal and social concerns, speaking, writing, listening, job-hunting, pollution, adventure, becoming educated, short stories, personal narratives, literacy, and creativity. The selections "Lincoln at Gettysburg" and "Biographies Bring New Companions" relate specifically to cultural literacy.

The Appendix, in addition to the index according to difficulty, contains progress record charts to help students visualize improvement, a conversion table for changing reading time to word-per-minute rate, and answers for all the exercises and comprehension tests to provide immediate feedback.

In short, this book is eminently practical, emphasizing both reading and study procedures. Flexibility is a central concept, with specialized techniques, different kinds of comprehension questions, and a wide variety of short, highly interesting articles and stories contributing to that objective. The book leads the student in a step-by-step progression toward achieving his or her full potential as a reader.

I wish to thank Vicki Fishco, Coordinator of the University's Communication Skills Center, Kentucky State University, for help in making a closer connection between text and current concerns. I also wish to thank the following individuals who reviewed the manuscript and made helpful suggestions for improving the text: Lois Hassan, Henry Ford Community College; Louise S. Haugh, Pima Community College; Clare E. Hite, University of South Florida; Vickie Kelly, Louisiana State University—Alexandria; Judith Little, Community College of Allegheny County; Barbara Risser, Onondaga Community College; and Westa W. Wood, Virginia State University. Especially do I wish to thank my wife, Ruth, who went over every page of the manuscript, making valuable suggestions and perceptive criticisms during its preparation. Her training and experience as a certified tutor and teacher of reading provided valuable insights.

J. I. B
Prescott, Arizona

Contents

Appendix

I

The Check-up

Getting Ready for Words

Now for your first step toward greater word power! It's the first of forty-eight such word power workouts, each with an in-depth coverage of ten of the most difficult words from the selection that follows. Complete all forty-eight; make your vocabulary 480 words richer.

At first in every exercise you'll meet each word in the briefest of contexts exactly as found in the selection to be read. Sometimes that context supplies no more than an indication of part of speech. You match words and definitions with context help. Next you make the words yours by turning to the longer sentence-length contexts, approximating the English you yourself might use. Fit each word into its appropriate sentence. Then repeat the sentence a time or so to make it seem natural. These steps sharpen your awareness of meaning and provide useful reinforcement before you meet the word for the third time as you read it in its full, complete context.

To make a word yours, use it three times. Once isn't enough. That's only a good beginning. Twice and it's almost within your grasp. It's the third time that does the trick—that makes it rememberable. That's the rationale behind these exercises.

To be sure, you already know some of those 480 words. Even so, the exercises will bring such words closer to the tip of your tongue or pen for easier use. That's called fluency—a very important facet of word power. After all, you don't want to waste time groping for words. You want them ready for immediate use.

In addition, starting with Selection 4, you'll find other vocabulary exercises over all-important prefix, root, and suffix elements—shortcuts to the meanings of over 15,000 words of desk dictionary size.

In short, when you finish this book, your vocabulary should be over 15,480 words stronger. That includes new words, new meanings for old words, old words raised to a more fluent level—plus some dramatically useful shortcuts to word meanings. That all adds up to increased confidence and satisfaction with your improved ability to communicate—in reading, writing, speaking, and listening.

So—do each exercise carefully, checking your answers with the key. Clear up any word difficulties before reading on. If needed, get additional help from your dictionary. Always get a total word power score for yourself.

1 Reading Power—Key to Personal Growth

WORD POWER WORKOUT

A. Leaning on Context

In each of the blanks provided, place the letter that precedes the best definition of the underlined word in context to the left.

FOR EXAMPLE:

   0. _k_ must <u>rely</u> on knowledge   k. depend

Words in Context	Definitions
1. ___ that <u>dependable</u> car	a. shocking, emotionally
2. ___ reading power <u>generates</u> learning power	b. supreme; special
3. ___ lying as in magic <u>preservation</u>	c. reliable
4. ___ know your <u>potential</u>	d. essential
5. ___ a recent comprehensive <u>survey</u>	e. detailed study; investigation
6. ___ an <u>avid</u> reader	f. unchanged condition
7. ___ not nearly so <u>traumatic</u> or unsettling	g. produces
8. ___ of <u>crucial</u> importance	h. capabilities; capacity
9. ___ serves as a <u>catalyst</u>	i. enthusiastic
10. ___ make himself genuinely <u>indispensable</u>	j. way of hastening a result

---

Check your answers with the Key on page 391 before going on.
Review any that you have missed. See the dictionary for further help.

Pronunciation aids: 6. av′id; 7. traw mat′ik; 8. krōō′shul; 9. cat′uh list.
KEY: add, āce; end, ēven; it, īce; odd, ōpen; pōōl; up.

B. Leaning on Parts (begins with Selection 4)

C. Making the Words Yours

In each blank below, enter the most appropriate word from the ten words in context in the first exercise, substituting it for the word(s) in parentheses. Use these words: *avid, catalyst, crucial, dependable, generates, indispensable, potential, preservation, survey, traumatic.*

FOR EXAMPLE:

0. Can we (depend) __rely__ on him?

---

1. Quick freezing keeps the food in perfect (unchanged condition) _____.

2. Being bitten by a snake can be quite (shocking, emotionally) _____.

3. He's an (enthusiastic) _____ baseball fan.

4. Use this chemical as a (way of speeding up reaction time) _____.

5. Fastening your seat belt is of (special) _____ importance as a safety measure.

6. He's the most (reliable) _____ pass receiver we have.

7. You should make a (detailed study) _____ of the job opportunities in that field.

8. This motor (produces) _____ how much horsepower?

9. You should certainly know your (capabilities) _____.

10. Salt is a(n) (essential) _____ ingredient in cooking.

How Well Do You Read?

If you decide to make a trip by car, the first thing you usually do is to get out a map and figure out your best route. It's the same with reading. First, you have to see where you are, decide where you want to go, then lay out the best route for getting there.

As you start your reading improvement program, you have three all-important questions to ask yourself. (1) How fast do I now read? (2) How much do I comprehend? (3) How much word power do I now have?

Those are the big three. Once you know the answers to those questions, you can see more clearly the best route to follow for maximum improvement. Obviously, you can't know when you've doubled your reading rate unless you know what your present rate is. And you can't know when you've improved comprehension or vocabulary unless you also know what they now are.

You'll find all kinds of combinations. After all, it's not only our fingerprints that are distinctively different. Some read fast and comprehend little; others read fast and comprehend much. With some, vocabulary is well developed; with others it is in need of major attention. What is exactly true of you? What are your own strong points and weak points?

These next few pages will begin to give you some answers. On the next page, you will find a selection which you are now to read. Use a stop watch or clock with a sweep second hand so that you can see exactly how long it takes you to read the entire 1,000-word selection. Read it once only—the way you normally read. Don't try to read either faster or slower than usual. When you have read the very last word, check to see how many minutes and seconds it took you. Then turn to page 385 to determine your word-per-minute reading rate.

Your next step is to take the ten-item test on the page following the selection to check comprehension. Don't look back at the selection. You want to know how much you comprehend with one reading, without further review or looking back.

After the comprehension check, you'll find a twenty-five item vocabulary test to check the third big question—how much word power do I have?

Now get ready to time yourself as you read the following selection—an exact timing. That's important if you are to have an accurate beginning rate score.

1

Reading Power—Key to Personal Growth

Begin Timing

Power! Could you get through a single normal day without using some? Take electrical power. Without it, your TV and radio would be soundless. And you might as well not own an electric refrigerator, toaster, mixer, or stove, not to mention a telephone or doorbell. And that dependable car of yours, minus a storage battery, is dead—utterly and completely. We're indeed heavily dependent on power, whether it be electric, gasoline, water, or nuclear.

Most people, however, overlook the most important power of all—reading power. Through reading we get knowledge; and according to Bacon, "Knowledge itself *is* power." Voltaire agreed. He said, "Books rule the world." Engineers, for example, must rely on knowledge to plan, build, and maintain all varieties of power systems.

But here's the important question. What can reading power do for you personally, now and for the rest of your life?

Reading Power = Learning Power

First, reading power generates learning power. As Carlyle said: "All that mankind has done, thought, gained or been: it is lying as in magic preservation in the pages of books." Reading provides the key.

Reading will help you know yourself better. You'll know your potential better—your strengths and weaknesses, including those in the area of reading. A recent comprehensive survey of 418 institutions of higher education was most revealing. From 64 to 95 percent of the students had trouble with their reading. That means that when you take steps to improve your reading, you soon gain a distinct advantage over those who don't.

Reading will also help you know others better. Back in 1926, Tunney challenged Dempsey, world heavyweight boxing champion, to a match. Tunney, an avid reader, read everything he could about his formidable opponent. He discovered that Dempsey's fists were once clocked at 135 miles an hour. To minimize Dempsey's hammerlike blows, Tunney practiced running backwards. Soon he ran as lightly and surely backwards as forwards. And it paid off. Tunney won. He became the new world champion. Knowing others helps you win friends and influence people as well as win championships—extremely valuable knowledge.

Finally, reading helps you understand past, present, and future more clearly. "Cultures which see no further than themselves bear the seeds of their own destruction." Similarly, individuals who see no further than themselves bear the seeds of their own difficulties. The past provides perspective for both present and future. "Future shock" is not nearly so traumatic or unsettling.

In those three areas—knowing self, others, and the broad sweep of time—reading power brings you added learning power. You can understand and cope more effectively with the sum total of life.

Reading Power = Earning Power

Your reading power activates a second power of crucial importance—your earning power. The move from learning power to earning power is easy to understand. An individual with know-how is obviously worth more than one without know-how. Suppose you have car trouble. You'll certainly want a technician who has read the various detailed instructional manuals. He should be able to solve your car problems quickly and efficiently.

Reading power helps in two ways. It helps you get a better job. And it helps you succeed better on the job.

William Anderson, Navy submarine officer, was called in for an interview with Rickover, Admiral of the Navy, about a special hush-hush assignment. During the interview, Rickover said, "Anderson, name the books and their authors that you have read in the last two years."

Anderson was struck completely dumb by this unexpected question. He couldn't remember a single title. Finally he stammered out the name of one book that came to mind, but he couldn't remember the author. Rickover frowned, then said with finality, "Goodbye."

When Anderson got home, he told his wife about the interview. He added, "I don't know what job he had in mind, but I do know I will never get it."

Later, he wandered into his library. He then began jotting down titles of the books he remembered reading. Just so Rickover wouldn't think him too easy-going and not sufficiently concerned with personal growth through reading, Anderson mailed him the list of twenty-four books.

Apparently Rickover had all but rejected him. But when he received his reading list, Rickover "changed his mind," Anderson says. So— Anderson got the position—commander of the world's first nuclear-powered submarine.

Reading contributes equally well to improved on-the-job performance. You'll find pertinent manuals, texts, and articles to help with any job. Technical information pours out at a rate of 60 million pages a year. Obviously, it takes a good reader to keep abreast of developments and make himself genuinely indispensable.

Reading Power = Yearning Power

Getting or keeping a job may not be as important as making your own job. That takes some not-so-impossible dreaming—some yearning, so to speak. That's still another benefit from reading. Reading serves well as a catalyst for creativity.

Reading can actually make you a billionaire. You'll see how. Just read on. You'll discover exactly where to find millions in gold and silver that you have a legal right to. The figures are from Rachel Carson's book *The Sea Around Us*. In every cubic mile of sea water you'll find about $93,000,000 in gold and $8,500,000 in silver. There it waits. Of course, you'll have to do some more reading to develop sufficient know-how to get it. But you can be certain that one of these days, some purposeful reader will work out the necessary details. He'll make himself a fortune. It's like buried treasure. It's waiting for the right person to move from yearning to earning.

In short, don't overlook the role reading power can play in your life from now on. In school, use it to achieve heightened scholastic success. Afterwards, use it to bring on-the-job success.

In fact, probably everything you do can be done somewhat better by some appropriate reading. So, make reading power your key to learning, earning, and yearning power. Make it your key to personal growth and achievement.

Reading Time: _____
See Conversion Table, Page 385.
Enter WPM Rate on the Progress
Record Chart on Page 382.

1 Reading Power–Key to Personal Growth

COMPREHENSION CHECK

1. What kind of power is *not* specifically mentioned? (a) earning power, (b) atomic power, (c) electrical power, (d) nuclear power.

   1. ___

2. Specific mention is made of whom? (a) Hitler, (b) Bacon, (c) Churchill, (d) Shakespeare.

   2. ___

3. The survey mentioned is of (a) junior colleges, (b) private colleges, (c) secondary schools, (d) institutions of higher learning.

   3. ___

4. What did Tunney practice? (a) running backwards, (b) ducking, (c) side-stepping, (d) making lightning jabs.

   4. ___

5. Dempsey's fists were clocked at (a) 60 mph, (b) 85 mph, (c) 100 mph, (d) 135 mph.

   5. ___

6. "Cultures which see no further than themselves bear the seeds of their own . . . " what? (a) death, (b) dominance, (c) destruction, (d) stability.

   6. ___

7. Rickover is spoken of as (a) a Navy Captain, (b) Admiral of the Navy, (c) Secretary of War, (d) a General.

   7. ___

8. Anderson (a) was demoted, (b) got a tentative appointment only, (c) did not get the job, (d) got the job.

   8. ___

9. Technical information pours out at a rate of how many million pages a year? (a) 20, (b) 40, (c) 60, (d) 80.

   9. ___

10. A single cubic mile of sea water contains about how much money in gold? (a) $120,000,000, (b) $93,000,000, (c) $28,000,000, (d) $8,500,000.

    10. ___

10 Off for Each Mistake
Comprehension Score: _____
Answer Key on Page 400.
Enter the Results on the Progress
Record Chart on Page 382.

Words in Isolation Vocabulary Test

The following test measures what might be called a basic knowledge of words. You have nothing to help you arrive at meaning but the word itself. Take the test without help from your dictionary. See how many of these words you know right now, without further study.

1. affronted   (a) met, (b) frightened, (c) offended,   1. ___
(d) asserted, (e) affected

2. intruding   (a) invading, (b) digging in, (c) begging,   2. ___
(d) asking, (e) visiting

3. scant   (a) limited, (b) rapid, (c) frightening,   3. ___
(d) colorful, (e) designed

4. fervor   (a) search, (b) intensity, (c) charm,   4. ___
(d) sickness, (e) fear

5. verdant   (a) sloping, (b) populated, (c) golden,   5. ___
(d) verbal, (e) green

6. propensity   (a) liking, (b) scheme, (c) propellent,   6. ___
(d) hatred, (e) expression

7. sundry   (a) bright, (b) various, (c) costly,   7. ___
(d) warm, (e) sullen

8. restive   (a) subdued, (b) limited, (c) nervous,   8. ___
(d) respected, (e) happy

9. impetuously   (a) rudely, (b) furiously, (c) impassively,   9. ___
(d) imperfectly, (e) plainly

10. belligerent   (a) overweight, (b) defeated, (c) hostile,   10. ___
(d) belittling, (e) hospitable

11. formidable   (a) deserted, (b) effective, (c) formal,   11. ___
(d) definite task, (e) hard to handle

12. nuances   (a) shades, (b) strings, (c) annoyances,   12. ___
(d) numbers, (e) proofs

13. arrogance   (a) height, (b) fracture, (c) pride,   13. ___
(d) arrangement, (e) style

14. malingering   (a) waiting, (b) lying, (c) pretending illness,   14. ___
(d) delaying, (e) harming

15. potentate   (a) ruler, (b) potentiality, (c) statesman,   15. ___
(d) messenger, (e) regulation

16. derogatory	(a) elevating, (b) disordered, (c) ruinous, (d) loud, (e) abusive	16. ___
17. amorphous	(a) desirable, (b) loving, (c) fiscal, (d) sensational, (e) shapeless	17. ___
18. epitomizes	(a) delays, (b) makes equal, (c) sums up, (d) contradicts, (e) writes	18. ___
19. evoke	(a) conquer, (b) put out, (c) shout, (d) call forth, (e) revoke	19. ___
20. pending	(a) brushing, (b) waiting, (c) yielding to, (d) waving, (e) capturing	20. ___
21. codify	(a) pamper, (b) study, (c) classify, (d) adjust, (e) talk about	21. ___
22. artifices	(a) tricks, (b) missiles, (c) artists, (d) fires, (e) fashions	22. ___
23. atrophy	(a) assail, (b) fasten, (c) repel, (d) waste away, (e) enchant	23. ___
24. avidly	(a) eagerly, (b) viciously, (c) helpfully, (d) reluctantly, (e) truly	24. ___
25. capitulation	(a) comparison, (b) repulsion, (c) impulse, (d) surrender, (e) captivation	25. ___

4 Off for Each Mistake.
Answer Key on Page 400.
Vocabulary Test Score: _____

Making the Application

This is the time to bring together your scores in the three areas checked—rate, comprehension, and word power. Enter them on the blanks below.

1. Word-per-minute (wpm) reading rate: _____ (from page 8)
2. Comprehension score: _____ (from page 9)
   (Enter your rate and comprehension scores on the progress record charts on pages 382 and 383 as instructed)
3. Vocabulary score: _____ (from page 11)

Use these scores to set up a target for yourself. Take aim at either rate improvement, comprehension improvement, or word power improvement. Or take aim at all three! The lower your score in any of the three major areas, the more room you have for improvement. A sharp, clear focus on what most needs your attention should do much to speed your progress.

Furthermore, no matter how good you are in any area, you still have room for improvement. A comprehension score of 70 percent is good, but a move up to 80, 90, or 100 percent is much better. A wpm reading rate of 250 wpm is good, but increasing your rate to 500 wpm is obviously much better.

A vocabulary (word power) score of 72 percent is good, but with special attention you can raise that to 80, 92, or 100 percent. In so doing, you help yourself in two ways: you increase your reading speed—for unknown words will no longer slow you down—and you improve your comprehension. One word often makes the difference between understanding and misunderstanding. For example, suppose you're planning a trip to the town of Lakeland and read that the climate there is *enervating*. Does that mean it's stimulating or weakening? Of the college graduates tested, 51 percent said *enervating* meant "stimulating." It really means "weakening," the very opposite. One word can make a tremendous difference.

Remember, the better you read, the better you feel about yourself. Traces of uncertainty or inferiority will disappear, to be replaced by feelings of self-confidence and assurance. To be sure, it takes effort. But a blood, sweat, and tears approach soon brings improved skill, success—and smiles. It does pay off.

Finally, to apply properly what you have learned about the organization of the book, follow this step-by-step procedure.

1. WORD POWER WORKOUT: Complete this step *before* reading the selection which follows. This should help you resolve major word problems before you read the selection which follows. Actually, for you, there are only two kinds of words—those you know and those you don't. Use these exercises to move as many as possible from the don't-know into the do-know category. And remember—words are much like muscles. If you don't use them, you lose them. So, even if

it's a word you already know, use it again; don't lose it. And if it's a word you don't know, use it again and again to move it firmly into your active vocabulary.

On the first page of each Word Power Workout (Part A), you will find simplified pronunciation respellings and markings for those words most likely to present difficulties. For this simplified system, no diacritical markings are used to indicate short vowels, as in *add*, *end*, *it*, *odd*, and *up*; long marks are used to indicate the sounds in *āce*, *ēven*, *īce*, *ōpen*, and *po͞ol*. For additional help refer to your own dictionary, which should have a system of diacritical markings you are best acquainted with. Remember also that dictionaries are like watches—they don't always agree.

2. INSTRUCTION SELECTION: Read this selection, timing yourself to get an accurate word-per-minute reading rate.

3. COMPREHENSION CHECK: Next complete the 10-item comprehension check, without looking back at the selection. Use the Answer Key on page 400 to get a comprehension score.

4. CONVERSION TABLE: To convert reading time into word-per-minute rate, use the Conversion Tables on pages 385–389.

5. PROGRESS RECORD CHART: Enter both word-per-minute rate and comprehension scores on the Progress Record Charts, pages 382–384.

6. MAKING THE APPLICATION: Work through these pages, which will suggest ways of applying techniques and principles covered in the instructional selection.

7. Follow the same steps with the two practice reading selections that follow, again consciously trying to apply your newly learned techniques.

2 Instrument of Evil!

WORD POWER WORKOUT

A. Leaning on Context

In each of the blanks provided, place the letter that precedes the best definition of the underlined word in context to the left.

Words in Context	Definitions
1. ___ <u>tethered</u> above	a. restless
2. ___ a huge <u>taffeta</u> bag	b. orderly
3. ___ cut from its <u>moorings</u>	c. fastened
4. ___ and the <u>bifocals</u>	d. forerunner
5. ___ the memorable <u>retort</u>	e. ropes or cables
6. ___ a <u>harbinger</u> of great evil	f. light-weight fabric
7. ___ a brilliant and <u>impatient</u> man	g. lived
8. ___ more <u>methodical</u> brother	h. dropped
9. ___ all <u>survived</u>	i. reply
10. ___ <u>plummeted</u> from the sky	j. pair of glasses

Check your answers with the Key before going on. Review any that you have missed.

Pronunciation aids: 2. taf′uh tuh; 6. har′bin jer; 10. plum′it′d.

KEY: add, āce; end, ēven; it, īce; odd, ōpen; pool; up.

B. Leaning on Parts (begins with Selection 4)

C. Making the Words Yours

In each blank below, enter the most appropriate word from the ten words in context in the first exercise, substituting it for the word(s) in parentheses. Use these words: *bifocals, harbinger, impatient, methodical, moorings, plummeted, retort, survived, taffeta, tethered*.

1. For some, the first robin seems like a (forerunner) _____ of spring.

2. How many people (lived) _____ after the tornado demolished their apartment?

3. Following (orderly) _____ procedures usually insures success.

4. While results aren't immediate, don't be (restless) _____; they'll soon be yours to enjoy.

5. I want to read. Have you seen my (pair of glasses) _____ anywhere?

6. The speaker's clever (reply) _____ made everyone laugh.

7. The plane (dropped) _____ to the ground after the loss of a wing.

8. Be sure the boat (ropes or cables) _____ will hold up under the heavy wave action.

9. The cowboys (fastened) _____ their horses close to camp every night.

10. The costume was made of a brightly colored (light-weight fabric)

    _____.

2

Instrument of Evil!

Robert Fulghum

*Read about a most exciting first—the very first step into space.
That's back when people thought the sky contained poisonous
gases. No one could prove it wasn't so! No one had ever gone up
into the sky. By the way, you'll also discover what Einstein
thought was more important than information.*

Begin Timing

The fourth day of the month of June, 1783—more than two hundred years
ago. The market square of the French village of Annonay, not far from Paris.
On a raised platform, a smoky bonfire fed by wet straw and old wool rags.
Tethered above, straining at its lines, a huge taffeta bag—a *balon*—thirty-
three feet in diameter.

    In the presence of a "respectable assembly and a great many other
people," and accompanied by great cheering, the *machine de l'aerostat*
was cut from its moorings and set free to rise majestically into the noontide
sky. Six thousand feet into the air it went, and came to earth several miles
away in a field, where it was attacked by pitchfork-waving peasants and torn
to pieces as an instrument of evil. The first public ascent of a balloon, the
first step in the history of human flight.

    Old Ben Franklin was there, in France as the agent of the new Ameri-
can states. He of the key and the kite and the lightning and the bifocals and
the printing press. When a bystander asked what possible good this *balon*
thing could be, Franklin made the memorable retort: *"Eh, à quoi bon
l'enfant qui vient de naître?"* ("What good is a newborn baby?") A man of
such curiosity and imagination could provide an answer to his own question, and in his journal he wrote: "This balon will open the skies to
mankind." The peasants, too, were not far from wrong. It was also a
harbinger of great evil, in that Annonay would one day be leveled by bombs
falling from the sky. But I am getting ahead of myself.

    Some months before that June day, Joseph-Michel Montgolfier sat of
an evening staring into his fireplace, watching sparks and smoke rise up the
chimney from the evening fire. His imagination rose with the smoke. If

smoke floated into the sky, why not capture it and put it in a bag and see if the bag would rise, perhaps carrying something or someone with it?

In his mid-forties, the son of a prosperous paper maker, a believer in the great church that was Science in the eighteenth century, a brilliant and impatient man with time on his hands was Monsieur Montgolfier. And so, with his younger, more methodical brother, Etienne, and the resources of their father's factory, he set to. With paper bags, then silken ones and finally taffeta coated with resins. And *voilà*! Came a day when from the gardens at Versailles a balloon carrying a sheep, a rooster, and a duck went aloft. All survived, proving that there were no poisonous gases in the sky, as some had feared.

The most enthusiastic supporter of the brothers Montgolfier was a young chemist, Jean-François Pilâtre de Rozier. He didn't want to make balloons; he wanted to go up in one. The Montgolfiers' interest was in scientific experimentation. They were older, wiser groundlings. Pilâtre wanted to *fly*. He was full of the adventure of youth. And so, that fall, November 21, 1783, Jean-François Pilâtre de Rozier got his wish. In the garden of the royal palace at La Muette, in the Bois de Boulogne, at 1:54 P.M., in a magnificent balloon seven stories high, painted with signs of the zodiac and the king's monogram. Up, up, and away he went—higher than treetops and church steeples—coming down beyond the Seine, five miles away.

Joseph-Michel and Etienne Montgolfier lived long and productive scientific lives, and died in their beds, safe on the ground. Two years after his historic flight, trying to cross the English Channel west to east in a balloon, the young Jean-François Pilâtre de Rozier plummeted from the sky in flames to his death. But his great-great-grandson was later to become one of the first airplane pilots in France.

Well, what's all this about, anyway? It's about the power (and the price) of imagination. "Imagination is more important than information." Einstein said that, and he should know.

It's also a story about how people of imagination stand on one another's shoulders. From the ground to the balloon to the man in the balloon to the man on the moon. Yes. Some of us are ground crew—holding lines, building fires, dreaming dreams, letting go, watching the upward flight. Others of us are bound for the sky and the far edges of things. That's in the story, too.

These things come to mind at the time of year when children graduate to the next stage of things. From high school, from college, from the nest of the parent. What shall we give them on these occasions? Imagination, a shove out and up, a blessing.

Come over here, we say—to the edge, we say. I want to show you something, we say. We are afraid, they say; it's very exciting, they say. Come to the edge, we say, use your imagination. And they come. And they look. And we push. And they fly. We to stay and die in our beds. They to go and to die howsoever, inspiring those who come after them to come to their own edge. And fly.

These things come to mind, too, in this middle year of my own life. I, too, intend to live a long and useful life and die safe in my bed on the ground. But the anniversary of that little event in the village of Annonay just happens to be my birthday. And on its bicentennial I went up in a balloon, from a field near the small Skagit Valley village of La Conner.

It's *never* too late to fly!

Reading Time: _____
See Conversion Table.
Enter WPM Rate on the Progress Record Chart.

2 Instrument of Evil!

COMPREHENSION CHECK

1. The first balloon went up how many feet? (a) three   1. ___
   thousand, (b) four thousand, (c) five thousand,
   (d) six thousand.

2. In what French village did this take place? (a) Etamps,   2. ___
   (b) Auteuil, (c) Annonay, (d) Anet.

3. In his journal, Franklin wrote that the flight would   3. ___
   (a) make history, (b) open the skies to mankind,
   (c) let us compete with the birds, (d) be of no practical good.

4. The balloon was made of (a) paper bags, (b) silken   4. ___
   bags, (c) taffeta coated with resins, (d) rubberized
   taffeta.

5. Monsieur Montgolfier was the son of a prosperous   5. ___
   (a) wine maker, (b) baker, (c) paper maker, (d) cabinet
   maker.

6. The first manned flight was for what distance? (a) three   6. ___
   miles, (b) four miles, (c) five miles, (d) six miles.

7. One balloonist attempted to cross (a) the Alps, (b) the   7. ___
   English Channel, (c) the Mediterranean Sea, (d) the Seine
   Valley.

8. According to Einstein, what is more important than infor-   8. ___
   mation? (a) experience, (b) imagination, (c) intelligence,
   (d) interest.

9. One balloon was (a) four stories high, (b) five stories   9. ___
   high, (c) six stories high, (d) seven stories high.

10. The author concluded that (a) everyone should fly,   10. ___
    (b) it's never too late to fly, (c) only the young
    should fly, (d) flying raises your spirits.

10 Off for Each Mistake.
Comprehension Score: _____
Answer Key in Appendix.
Enter the Results on the Progress Record Chart.

3 Breaking the Sound Barrier

WORD POWER WORKOUT

A. Leaning on Context

In each of the blanks provided, place the letter that precedes the best definition of the underlined word in context to the left.

Words in Context	Definitions
1. ___ damage to my <u>ego</u>	a. sound
2. ___ the sound <u>barrier</u>	b. steadying
3. ___ really <u>bolstered</u>	c. swung back and forth
4. ___ my <u>morale</u>	d. self-image
5. ___ started to <u>stall</u>	e. wall or obstruction
6. ___ in rapid <u>sequence</u>	f. confidence
7. ___ began to <u>buffet</u>	g. stop
8. ___ the <u>stabilizing</u> switch	h. order, succession
9. ___ <u>fluctuated</u> off	i. tossed about
10. ___ my <u>sonic</u> boom	j. strengthened, supported

Check your answers with the Key before going on. Review any that you have missed.

Pronunciation aids: 3. bōl'sturd; 4. mor al'; 7. buf'et.

KEY: add, āce; end, ēven; it, īce; odd, ōpen; pōōl; up.

B. Leaning on Parts (begins with Selection 4)

C. Making the Words Yours

> In each blank below, enter the most appropriate word from the ten words in context in the first exercise, substituting it for the word(s) in parentheses. Use these words: *barrier, bolstered, buffet, ego, fluctuated, morale, sequence, sonic, stabilizer, stall.*

1. You need some successes to improve your (confidence) _____ .

2. The pilot changed the (steadying) _____ controls.

3. I looked up for the plane when I heard the (sound) _____ boom.

4. We slowed up as we approached the (wall or obstruction) _____ across the highway.

5. Unfortunately, some people are cursed by an overly inflated (self-image) _____ .

6. The shots came in rapid (order, succession) _____ .

7. Don't let the engine (stop) _____ on this steep slope.

8. The promotion really (strengthened, supported) _____ my morale.

9. The stock market (swung back and forth) _____ wildly because of the news report.

10. The wind began to (toss about) _____ the plane badly.

5 Off for Each Mistake.
Word Power Score: _____
Answer Key in Appendix.

3

Breaking the Sound Barrier

General Chuck Yeager and Leo Janos

What a far cry from that first step into space in an unmanned balloon to General Yeager's incredible first. As he said—"The bullet-shaped X-1 zoomed me into the history books by cracking through the sound barrier." And he did it painfully because of two cracked ribs—a secret he kept from the flight surgeon. Ride along with Yeager on that historic day—October 14, 1947.

Begin Timing

Glennis drove me to the base at six in the morning. She wasn't happy with my decision to fly, but she knew that Jack would never let me take off if he felt I would get into trouble. Hoover and Jack Russell, the X-1 crew chief, heard I was dumped off a horse at Pancho's, but thought the only damage was to my ego, and hit me with some "Hi-Ho Silver" crap, as well as a carrot, a pair of glasses, and a rope in a brown paper bag—my bucking bronco survival kit.

Around eight, I climbed aboard the mother ship. The flight plan called for me to reach .97 Mach. The way I felt that day, .97 would be enough. On that first rocket ride I had a tiger by the tail; but by this ninth flight, I felt I was in the driver's seat. I knew that airplane inside and out. I didn't think it would turn against me. Hell, there wasn't much I could do to hurt it; it was built to withstand three times as much stress as I could survive. I didn't think the sound barrier would destroy her, either. But the only way to prove it was to do it.

That moving tail really bolstered my morale, and I wanted to get to that sound barrier. I suppose there were advantages in creeping up on Mach 1, but my vote was to stop screwing around before we had some stupid accident that could cost us not only a mission, but the entire project. If this mission was successful, I was planning to really push for a sound barrier attempt on the very next flight.

Going down that damned ladder hurt. Jack was right behind me. As usual, I slid feet-first into the cabin. I picked up the broom handle and waited while Ridley pushed the door against the frame, then I slipped it into the door handle and raised it up into lock position. It worked perfectly.

Then I settled in to go over my checklist. Bob Cardenas, the B-29 driver, asked if I was ready.

"Hell, yes," I said. "Let's get it over with."

He dropped the X-1 at 20,000 feet, but his dive speed was once again too slow and the X-1 started to stall. I fought it with the control wheel for about five hundred feet, and finally got her nose down. The moment we picked up speed I fired all four rocket chambers in rapid sequence. We climbed at .88 Mach and began to buffet, so I flipped the stabilizer switch and changed the setting two degrees. We smoothed right out, and at 36,000 feet, I turned off two rocket chambers. At 40,000 feet, we were still climbing at a speed of .92 Mach. Leveling off at 42,000 feet, I had thirty percent of my fuel, so I turned on rocket chamber three and immediately reached .96 Mach. I noticed that the faster I got, the smoother the ride.

Suddenly the Mach needle began to fluctuate. It went up to .965 Mach—then tipped right off the scale. I thought I was seeing things! We were flying supersonic! And it was as smooth as a baby's bottom: Grandma could be sitting up there sipping lemonade. I kept the speed off the scale for about twenty seconds, then raised the nose to slow down.

I was thunderstruck. After all the anxiety, breaking the sound barrier turned out to be a perfectly paved speedway. I radioed Jack in the B-29. "Hey, Ridley, that Machmeter is acting screwy. It just went off the scale on me."

"Fluctuated off?"

"Yeah, at point nine-six-five."

"Son, you is imagining things."

"Must be. I'm still wearing my ears and nothing else fell off, neither."

The guys in the NACA tracking van interrupted to report that they heard what sounded like a distant rumble of thunder: my sonic boom! The first one by an airplane ever heard on earth. The X-1 was supposedly capable of reaching nearly twice the speed of sound, but the Machmeter aboard only registered to 1.0 Mach, which showed how much confidence they had; I estimated I had reached 1.05 Mach. (Later data showed it was 1.07 Mach—700 mph.)

And that was it. I sat up there feeling kind of numb, but elated. After all the anticipation to achieve this moment, it really was a let-down. It took a damned instrument meter to tell me what I'd done. There should've been a bump on the road, something to let you know you had just punched a nice clean hole through that sonic barrier. The Ughknown was a poke through Jello. Later on, I realized that this mission had to end in a let-down, because the real barrier wasn't in the sky, but in our knowledge and experience of supersonic flight.

I landed tired, but relieved to have hacked the program. There is always strain in research flying. It's the same as flying in combat, where you never can be sure of the outcome. You try not to think about possible disasters, but fear is churning around inside whether you think of it consciously or not. I thought now that I'd reached the top of the mountain, the remainder of these X-1 experimental flights would be downhill. But having sailed me safely through the sonic barrier, the X-1 had plenty of white-knuckle flights in store over the next year. The real hero in the flight test business is a pilot who manages to survive.

And so I was a hero this day. As usual, the fire trucks raced out to where the ship had rolled to a stop on the lakebed. As usual, I hitched a ride back to the hangar with the fire chief. That warm desert sun really felt wonderful. My ribs ached.

Reading Time: _____
See Conversion Table.
Enter WPM Rate on the Progress Record Chart.

3 Breaking the Sound Barrier

COMPREHENSION CHECK

1. Yeager's wife, Glennis, took him to the base at (a) six A.M., (b) seven A.M., (c) eight A.M., (d) nine A.M.

   1. ___

2. The brown paper bag contained (a) a carrot, (b) a rope, (c) a pair of glasses, (d) all the preceding.

   2. ___

3. That day was Yeager's (a) third flight, (b) fifth flight, (c) seventh flight, (d) ninth flight.

   3. ___

4. What other plane beside the X-1 was mentioned? (a) the B-29, (b) the B-20, (c) the B-16, (d) the B-12.

   4. ___

5. The faster he went on the flight, (a) the rougher the ride, (b) the smoother the ride, (c) the more difficult the controls, (d) the more erratic the behavior.

   5. ___

6. He said at supersonic speed Grandma (a) could be sleeping, (b) could be knitting, (c) could be sipping lemonade, (d) could be rocking.

   6. ___

7. The first sonic boom was heard by the guys (a) in the radar crew, (b) in the base, (c) in the tracking van, (d) in the control tower.

   7. ___

8. The Machmeter registered only (a) 1.0 Mach, (b) 1.2 Mach, (c) 1.3 Mach, (d) 1.4 Mach.

   8. ___

9. His top speed on that flight was (a) 680 mph, (b) 700 mph, (c) 790 mph, (d) 820 mph.

   9. ___

10. Yeager likened the sound barrier to (a) cotton, (b) wispy clouds, (c) Jello, (d) yogurt.

    10. ___

10 Off for Each Mistake
Comprehension Score: _____
Answer Key in Appendix.
Enter the Results on the Progress Record Chart.

The Build-up

4 How Should You Build Up Your Vocabulary?

WORD POWER WORKOUT

A. Leaning on Context

In each of the blanks provided, place the letter that precedes the best definition of the underlined word in context to the left.

Words in Context	**Definitions**
1. ___ <u>consolidated</u> his findings	a. confirms; makes certain
2. ___ research <u>corroborates</u> that fact	b. hasten; speed up
3. ___ <u>discrimination</u> contributes more to speed of reading	c. preference
4. ___ strange words <u>hinder</u> comprehension	d. noting of differences
5. ___ <u>hybrid</u> corn combines the best qualities	e. prevent
6. ___ to <u>expedite</u> your use of word parts	f. interaction
7. ___ a <u>tentative</u> definition	g. surrounding words, phrases, and sentences
8. ___ a <u>predilection</u> for reading	h. mixed origin
9. ___ dynamic <u>interplay</u> of approaches	i. combined
10. ___ vocabulary in <u>context</u>	j. temporary

Check your answers with the Key before going on. Review any that
you have missed.

Pronunciation aids: 1. kun sol′uh dāt′d′; 2. kuh rob′uh rāts; 6. ek′spuh dīt′;
8. pred′uh lek′shun.

KEY: add, āce; end, ēven; it, īce; odd, ōpen; pōol; up.

B. Leaning on Parts

See how prefix meaning relates to word meaning by supplying the missing word or word part in each of the following sentences.

1. To heat "before" is to pre_____.

2. To make ready "beforehand" is to pre_____.

3. in our government, the one before all others is called pre_____.

4. The pre_____ pre- is a shortcut to the meanings of over 800 words.

5. To precede means to go _____ someone else.

C. Making the Words Yours

In each blank below, enter the most appropriate word from the ten words in context in the first exercise, substituting it for the word(s) in parentheses. Use these words: *consolidated, context, corroborated, discrimination, expedite, hybrid, hindered, interplay, predilection, tentative.*

1. In order to make a profit, the two companies were (combined) _____.

2. Most (mixed origin) _____ flowers are larger.

3. He tried to (hasten) _____ his trial.

4. His dishonesty (prevented) _____ him from receiving a promotion.

5. The lie detector (confirmed) _____ his guilt.

6. The group had a strong (preference) _____ for rock music.

7. The high team morale was due to the (interaction) _____ of many factors.

8. He made (temporary) _____ arrangements for his transportation.

9. The (noting of differences) _____ among synonyms can sometimes be troublesome.

10. A good reader uses (the surrounding words, phrases, and sentences) _____ to help understand an unknown word.

For the 25 Items on These Pages,
4 Off for Each Mistake.
Word Power Score: _____
Answer Key in Appendix.

4

How Should You Build Up Your Vocabulary?

Begin Timing

Exactly what do you do during a normal day? How do you spend your time? Paul T. Rankin very much wanted an answer to that question. To get it, he asked sixty-eight individuals to keep an accurate, detailed record of what they did every minute of their waking hours. When he consolidated his findings, he discovered that the average individual spent 70 percent of his waking time doing *one* thing only—*communicating*. That meant either reading, writing, speaking, or listening.

Put that evidence alongside of the research findings uncovered by the Human Engineering Laboratories. In exploring aptitudes and careers involving, among other things, data from 30,000 vocabulary tests given yearly, they discovered that big incomes and big vocabularies go together. Vocabulary, more than any other factor yet known, predicts financial success.

And it all fits. Each word you add to your vocabulary makes you a better reader, writer, speaker, and listener. Furthermore, linguistic scientists are quick to point out that we actually think with words. If that is so, new words make us better thinkers as well as communicators. No wonder more words are likely to mean more money. What better reason for beginning right now to extend your vocabulary?

Take reading. What exactly do you read? Common sense says you read words. Research corroborates that fact. "Vocabulary in context" contributes 39 percent to comprehension. That's more than any other factor isolated and studied—even more than intelligence. And "word discrimination" contributes more to speed of reading than any other factor—28 percent. In short, your efforts to improve vocabulary will pay off in both comprehension and speed.

Suppose, as you're reading along, you lumtebs across a strange word. Did you find yourself stopping for a closer look at *lumtebs*? Pardon the spelling slip. That's actually the word *stumble*. The letters just got mixed around. Obviously you now know that strange words do slow you down—or even stop you completely. Furthermore, strange words hinder comprehension. Which is easier to understand, "Eschew garrulity" or "Avoid talking too much"?

What you need is a vital, dynamic approach to vocabulary building. Hybrid corn combines the best qualities of several varieties to insure maximum productivity. A hybrid approach to vocabulary should, in the same way, insure maximum results. That's why you should use the CPD formula.

Through Context

When students in a college class were asked what should be done when they came across an unknown word in their reading, 84 percent said, "Look it up in the dictionary." If you do, however, you shortcircuit the very mental processes needed to make your efforts most productive.

But there's another reason. Suppose someone asks you what the word *fast* means. You answer, "speedy or swift." But does it mean that in such contexts as "*fast* color," "*fast* woman," or "*fast* friend"? And if a horse is fast, is it securely tied or galloping at top speed? It could be either. It all depends. On the dictionary? No, on context—on how the word is actually used. After all, there are over twenty different meanings for *fast* in the dictionary. But the dictionary doesn't tell you which meaning is intended. That's why it makes such good sense to begin with context.

Through Word Parts

Now for the next step. Often unfamiliar words contain one or more parts, which, if recognized, provide definite help with meaning. Suppose you read that someone "had a predilection for reading mysteries." The context certainly isn't too helpful. But do you see a prefix, suffix, or root that you know? Well, there's the familiar prefix *pre-*, meaning "before." Look back at the context and try inserting "before." Reading mysteries apparently comes "before" other kinds of reading. Yes, a pre-dilection—or *pre*ference—is something put "before" something else.

Or take the word *monolithic*. Try to isolate the parts. There's the prefix *mono-*, meaning "one," and the root *lith*, meaning "stone." Finally, there's the suffix *-ic*, meaning "consisting of." Those three parts add up to this definition: "consisting of one stone."

To expedite your use of word parts, you will be introduced to the fourteen most important words in the English language. The prefix and root elements in those few words are found in over 14,000 words of desk dictionary size. With those amazingly useful shortcuts, you can build vocabulary, not at a snail's pace, one word at a time, but in giant strides, up to a thousand words at a time.

Your second step, then, is to look for familiar word parts. If they do not give you exact meanings, they should at least bring you much closer.

Through the Dictionary

Now you can see why you should consult the dictionary last, not first. You've looked carefully at context. You've looked for familiar word parts. Now you play Sherlock Holmes—an exciting role. You hypothesize. In light of context or context and word parts, you try to solve a mystery. What exactly does that strange word mean? Only after you go through the mental gymnastics to come up with a tentative definition should you open the dictionary to see if you're right.

After all, those first two steps or approaches spark a stronger than usual interest in that dictionary definition. You're now personally involved. Did you figure out the word meaning? Your heightened interest will lead to better memory of both word and meaning. It also encourages your development of the habits needed to accelerate your progress. And when you see in black and white the definition you had expected, what a feeling of accomplishment is yours. In that way, the CPD Formula provides the exact dynamic interplay of approaches for maximum effectiveness.

Well, there it is, your new formula—Context, Parts, Dictionary. Use it! The exercises that follow will give you specific, step-by-step help in sharpening your awareness of contextual clues, learning the most useful word parts, and using the dictionary with increased accuracy and ease. The results will be like money in the bank.

Reading Time: _____
See Conversion Table.
Enter WPM Rate on the Progress Record Chart.

4 How Should You Build Up Your Vocabulary?

COMPREHENSION CHECK

1. What percent of the average person's waking time is spent in communication? (a) 30%, (b) 45%, (c) 60%, (d) 70%.

   1. ___

2. Specific reference is made to the (a) Scientific Energy Corporation, (b) Municipal Research Division, (c) Human Engineering Laboratories, (d) Human Resources Center.

   2. ___

3. With respect to comprehension, *vocabulary in context* contributes (a) less than intelligence, (b) the same as intelligence, (c) more than intelligence, (d) an unspecified amount.

   3. ___

4. "Eschew garrulity" means (a) stop shouting, (b) speak louder, (c) look up words, (d) avoid talking too much.

   4. ___

5. One of the words mentioned is said to have over how many different meanings? (a) 10, (b) 15, (c) 20, (d) 25.

   5. ___

6. As a shortcut to vocabulary, you will be introduced to how many important words? (a) 14, (b) 22, (c) 35, (d) 50.

   6. ___

7. To suggest the importance of context, which word is discussed? (a) fast, (b) slow, (c) sharp, (d) trip.

   7. ___

8. In the CPD Formula, the *C* stands for (a) confirm, (b) correct, (c) classification, (d) context.

   8. ___

9. Who is mentioned by name? (a) Einstein, (b) Tom Sawyer, (c) Johnny Cash, (d) Sherlock Holmes.

   9. ___

10. When you meet a strange word, you are told to consult your dictionary (a) first, (b) last, (c) as a second step, (d) at no set time.

    10. ___

10 Off for Each Mistake.
Comprehension Score: _____
Answer Key in Appendix.
Enter the Results on the Progress Record Chart.

Making the Application

Most of our English words, some 60 percent, are borrowings from the Latin or Greek. That means that you can learn words, not one at a time, but hundreds at a time, just by learning and using key elements.

Your Fourteen Master Words

The words in the table below contain twelve of the most important Latin roots, two of the most important Greek roots, and twenty of the most important prefixes. Why are they so important? Because over 14,000 relatively common words—words of desk dictionary size—contain one or more of those elements. They provide you with a truly remarkable shortcut to word power.

Words	Prefix	*Common Meaning*	Root	*Common Meaning*
precept	pre-	(before)	capere	(take, seize)
detain	de-	(away, from)	tenere	(hold, have)
intermittent	inter-	(between)	mittere	(send)
offer	ob-	(against)	ferre	(bear, carry)
insist	in-	(into)	stare	(stand)
monograph	mono-	(alone, one)	graphein	(write)
epilogue	epi-	(upon)	legein	(say, study of)
aspect	ad-	(to, toward)	specere	(see)
uncomplicated	un-	(not)	plicare	(fold)
	com-	(together with)		
nonextended	non-	(not)	tendere	(stretch)
	ex-	(out of)		
reproduction	re-	(back, again)	ducere	(lead)
	pro-	(forward)		
indisposed	in-	(not)	ponere	(put, place)
	dis-	(apart from)		
oversufficient	over-	(above)	facere	(make, do)
	sub-	(under)		
mistranscribe	mis-	(wrong)	scribere	(write)
	trans-	(across, beyond)		

How can you convert those fourteen words into keys to thousands of related words? Beginning with this selection, Selection 4, a new type of Word Power exercise is introduced, called Leaning on Parts. In the following selections these exercises will cover all twenty prefixes as well as the fourteen roots. They will help you master the keys to over 14,000 words of desk dictionary size.

In addition, follow the four steps below to speed your awareness of these elements. Take one of the fourteen words every other day for twenty-eight days.

1. *Look up the word in the dictionary.* Notice the relationships between prefix and root meaning and word meaning. The pieces don't always add up to the exact meaning of the word, although you can usually see a close relationship.

2. *Look up each prefix.* Note the meanings given and the various spellings.

3. *List at least ten words* that contain the prefix being studied. Check your list with the dictionary to avoid mistakes. Don't overlook the less common forms, as given in the dictionary prefix entry.

4. *List at least ten words* that contain the root being studied. Again, check your list with the dictionary to make certain you are right. Take *plicare*, as found in *complication*. It may be relatively easy to think of *application*, *implication*, or *duplication*. But did *duplication* suggest *duplex* and open the way to *perplex* and *complex*? Did *complex* suggest *comply*, *reply*, *imply*, and others? Did *ply* lead to *pliant*, *supple*, *deploy*, and *employ*?

To further expedite your mastery of these elements, use the Mini-Reviews on pages 231, 249, 332, and 348 and the additional helps on pages 43, 106, and 143, including the LDE Formula, which lets you deal more effectively with all such elements.

(To use color-coded cards to enhance the visualizing of elements found in over 50,000 English words of desk dictionary size, get the WORD POWER game, available from Telstar Productions, Inc., 10 North 10th Avenue, Hopkins, Minnesota 55343. This specially devised card game contains not 14 but 50 root cards, 22 prefix cards, 22 suffix cards, plus jokers and word-ending cards. You can play solitaire or games for two or more, such as Flash, Rote, Rummy, and the like. Write Telstar for details.)

5 How to Write a Personal Letter

WORD POWER WORKOUT

A. Leaning on Context

In each of the blanks provided, place the letter that precedes the best definition of the underlined word in context to the left.

Words in Context	**Definitions**
1. ___ <u>frankly</u>, we don't shine	a. event, happening
2. ___ escape from <u>anonymity</u>	b. close friend
3. ___ few letters are <u>obligatory</u>	c. in truth
4. ___ a <u>sensuous</u> line	d. brother or sister
5. ___ write the <u>salutation</u>	e. namelessness
6. ___ simple <u>declarative</u> sentence	f. making a statement
7. ___ end of one <u>episode</u>	g. required
8. ___ a <u>compadre</u>	h. pleasing to the senses
9. ___ a soul <u>sibling</u>	i. keepsake
10. ___ a precious <u>relic</u>	j. words serving as greeting

Check your answers with the Key before going on. Review any that you have missed.

Pronunciation aids: 2. an uh nim´i tē; 3. uh blig´uh tor´ē; 4. sen´shoo us;
8. kum pah´drä.

KEY: add, āce; end, ēven; it, īce; odd, ōpen; pool; up.

B. Leaning on Parts

The prefix *re-*, found in over 1,000 words, means "back or again." Supply the missing word or word part in each of the following blanks.

1. To turn back and read an article again is to re_____ it.

2. If you appear again, you can be said to re_____.

3. To go back home is to re_____ home.

4. To repair something is to put it _____ into good condition.

5. To rewrite a report is to write it _____.

C. Making the Words Yours

In each blank below, enter the most appropriate word from the ten words in context in the first exercise, substituting it for the word(s) in parentheses. Use these words: *anonymity, compadre, declarative, episode, frankly, obligatory, relic, salutation, sensuous, sibling.*

1. The artist's use of (pleasing to the senses) _____ curving lines added interest and appeal.

2. A letter from a (close friend) _____ is always most welcome.

3. The movie had one very striking (event, happening) _____.

4. Is attendance at the annual meeting (required) _____?

5. What (words serving as a greeting) _____ do you use in your business letters?

6. Instead of an interrogative sentence, change to a (making a statement) _____ sentence.

7. Do you have a (brother or sister) _____?

8. My friend had a (keepsake) _____ from Civil War days.

9. Well, (in truth) _____ I hope it doesn't rain during the game.

10. (Namelessness) _____ is a criminal's best disguise.

4 Off for Each Mistake.
Word Power Score: _____
Answer Key in Appendix.

5

How to Write a Personal Letter

Garrison Keillor

*We spend most of our waking hours doing one thing only—
communicating. Yes—we're either writing, reading, speaking, or
listening 70 percent of our waking time. If we don't communicate well, we have problems. The man from Lake Woebegon has
important things to say about writing personal letters.*

Begin Timing

We shy persons need to write a letter now and then, or else we'll dry up
and blow away. It's true. And I speak as one who loves to reach for the
phone, dial the number, and talk. I say, "Big Bopper here—what's shakin',
babes?" The telephone is to shyness what Hawaii is to February, it's a way
out of the woods, *and yet*: a letter is better.

Such a Sweet Gift

Such a sweet gift—a piece of handmade writing, in an envelope that is not a
bill, sitting in our friend's path when she trudges home from a long day
spent among wahoos and savages, a day our words will help repair. They
don't need to be immortal, just sincere. She can read them twice and again
tomorrow: *You're someone I care about, Corinne, and think of often and
every time I do you make me smile.*

We need to write, otherwise nobody will know who we are. They will
have only a vague impression of us as A Nice Person, because frankly, we
don't shine at conversation, we lack the confidence to thrust our faces forward and say, "Hi, I'm Heather Hooten, let me tell you about my week."
Mostly we say "Uh-huh" and "Oh really." People smile and look over our
shoulder, looking for someone else to talk to.

So a shy person sits down and writes a letter. To be known by
another person—to meet and talk freely on the page—to be close despite
distance. To escape from anonymity and be our own sweet selves and
express the music of our souls.

Same thing that moves a giant rock star to sing his heart out in front of 123,000 people moves us to take ballpoint in hand and write a few lines to our dear Aunt Eleanor. *We want to be known.* We want her to know that we have fallen in love, that we quit our job, that we're moving to New York, and we want to say a few things that might not get said in casual conversation: *thank you for what you've meant to me, I am very happy right now.*

Skip the Guilt

The first step in writing letters is to get over the guilt of *not* writing. You don't "owe" anybody a letter. Letters are a gift. The burning shame you feel when you see unanswered mail makes it harder to pick up a pen and n..kes for a cheerless letter when you finally do. *I feel bad about not writing, but I've been so busy,* etc. Skip this. Few letters are obligatory, and they are *Thanks for the wonderful gift* and *I am terribly sorry to hear about George's death* and *Yes, you're welcome to stay with us next month,* and not many more than that. Write those promptly if you want to keep your friends. Don't worry about the others, except love letters, of course. When your true love writes *Dear Light of My Life, Joy of My Heart, O Lovely Pulsating Core of My Sensate Life,* some response is called for. Some of the best letters are tossed off in a burst of inspiration, so keep your writing stuff in one place where you can sit down for a few minutes and *Dear Roy, I am in the middle of an essay for International Paper but thought I'd drop you a line. Hi to your sweetie too* dash off a note to a pal. Envelopes, stamps, address book, everything in a drawer so you can write fast when the pen is hot.

A blank white 8"×11" sheet can look as big as Montana if the pen's not so hot—try a smaller page and write boldly. Or use a note card with a piece of fine art on the front; if your letter ain't good, at least they get the Matisse. Get a pen that makes a sensuous line, get a comfortable typewriter, a friendly word processor—whichever feels easy to the hand.

Sit for a few minutes with the blank sheet in front of you, and meditate on the person you will write to, let your friend come to mind until you can almost see her or him in the room with you. Remember the last time you saw each other and how your friend looked and what you said and what perhaps was unsaid between you, and when your friend becomes real to you, start to write.

Tell Us What You're Doing

Write the salutation—*Dear You*—and take a deep breath and plunge in. A simple declarative sentence will do, followed by another and another and another. Tell us what you're doing and tell it like you were talking to us. Don't think about grammar, don't think about lit'ry style, don't try to write dramatically, just give us your news. Where did you go, who did you see, what did they say, what do you think?

If you don't know where to begin, start with the present moment: *I'm sitting at the kitchen table on a rainy Saturday morning. Everyone is gone and the house is quiet.* Let your simple description of the present moment lead to something else, let the letter drift gently along.

Take It Easy

The toughest letter to crank out is one that is meant to impress, as we all know from writing job applications; if it's hard work to slip off a letter to a friend, maybe you're trying too hard to be terrific. A letter is only a report to someone who already likes you for reasons other than your brilliance. Take it easy.

Don't worry about form. It's not a term paper. When you come to the end of one episode, just start a new paragraph. You can go from a few lines about the sad state of rock 'n roll to the fight with your mother to your fond memories of Mexico to your cat's urinary tract infection to a few thoughts on personal indebtedness to the kitchen sink and what's in it. The more you write, the easier it gets, and when you have a True True Friend to write to, a *compadre*, a soul sibling, then it's like driving a car down a country road, you just get behind the keyboard and press on the gas.

Don't tear up the page and start over when you write a bad line—try to write your way out of it. Make mistakes and plunge on. Let the letter cook along and let yourself be bold. Outrage, confusion, love—whatever is in your mind, let it find a way to the page. Writing is a means of discovery, always, and when you come to the end and write *Yours ever* or *Hugs and Kisses*, you'll know something you didn't when you wrote *Dear Pal*.

An Object of Art

Probably your friend will put your letter away, and it'll be read again a few years from now—and it will improve with age.

And forty years from now, your friend's grandkids will dig it out of the attic and read it, a sweet and precious relic of the ancient Eighties that gives them a sudden clear glimpse of you and her and the world we old-timers knew. You will then have created an object of art. Your simple lines about where you went, who you saw, what they said, will speak to those children and they will feel in their hearts the humanity of our times.

You can't pick up a phone and call the future and tell them about our times. You have to pick up a piece of paper.

Reading Time: _____
See Conversion Table.
Enter WPM Rate on the Progress Record Chart.

5 How to Write a Personal Letter

COMPREHENSION CHECK

1. Keillor spoke of himself as (a) awkward, (b) quiet,
   (c) shy, (d) antisocial.

   1. ___

2. The author mentioned (a) a giant rock star, (b) a
   humorist, (c) a well-known movie star, (d) a juggler.

   2. ___

3. According to Keillor, what letters must be written?
   (a) letters of apology, (b) thank-you letters, (c) letters
   of congratulations, (d) how-are-you-letters.

   3. ___

4. You were told to (a) use good bond paper, (b) keep your
   writing stuff in one place, (c) keep a "to answer" file,
   (d) use both pens and pencils.

   4. ___

5. Keillor mentioned (a) singing messages, (b) a copy
   machine, (c) a fax machine, (d) a word processor.

   5. ___

6. Keillor suggested (a) starting the letter immediately,
   (b) doing a rough copy first, (c) thinking about the
   person before starting, (d) re-reading the person's
   last letter.

   6. ___

7. The toughest letter to write, he said, was one (a) to
   a stranger, (b) asking for a favor, (c) meant to apologize,
   (d) meant to impress.

   7. ___

8. Keillor said a letter is not (a) a term paper, (b) an
   essay, (c) a news report, (d) a formality.

   8. ___

9. Writing to a true friend was likened to (a) sailing a
   kite, (b) swinging in a hammock, (c) driving a car on
   a country road, (d) drifting down a river in a boat.

   9. ___

10. Keillor suggests your letter may eventually be read by
    your friend's (a) children, (b) sisters and brothers,
    (c) relatives, (d) grandkids.

    10. ___

10 Off for Each Mistake.
Comprehension Score: _____
Answer Key in Appendix.
Enter the Results on the Progress Record Chart.

Shortcuts to Word Meanings

Vocabulary, like Rome, isn't built in a day. If you lived to the ripe old age of 80 and learned one new word every single day of your life, you would have a vocabulary of only 29,200 words—less than 14 percent of the 400,000 words found in our largest dictionary. That's why you need a shortcut, a way of learning words not one at a time but hundreds at a time. Prefix, root, and suffix elements—the building blocks for the bulk of our English vocabulary—provide just that.

Suppose someone speaks of a "precocious youngster." You can look *precocious* up in the dictionary and learn its meaning. Or, better yet, you can put a shortcut to work. Look up *precocious* but notice that *pre-* means "before." In that way, you'll learn not only the meaning of *precocious* but also the meanings of hundreds of other words with that prefix.

For example, you'll know that a reader with a PREdilection for mysteries prefers mysteries "before" other kinds of books. You'll know that someone with rare PREscience knows things "before" they happen (has foresight, as we'd say). One unabridged dictionary lists 2,791 words with the prefix *pre-*, in addition to defining 13 pages of other *pre-* words. *Pre-* is your amazing shortcut to all such words. While it may not always bring you the exact dictionary definition, it will bring you closer to meaning—a big advantage.

Take the prefix *com-* (also spelled *col-*, *cor-*, *con-*, or *co-*) meaning "together." That knowledge provides you with a shortcut to almost two thousand words of desk dictionary size. For example, when you COMpose a theme, you put your ideas "together," so says the prefix. If things are CONcatenated, you know from the prefix they're "together," or, as the dictionary says, "linked or joined together." If two things are CONcomitant, they happen "together."

So, beginning now, whenever you look up a word, notice any prefix, root, or suffix meanings. Turn each element into a useful shortcut for defining hundreds of related words besides the one you looked up. Start by memorizing the all-important elements in this text (see pages 231, 249, 332, and 348). Begin using them immediately in dealing with strange words.

6 Look! No Words!

WORD POWER WORKOUT

A. Leaning on Context

In each of the blanks provided, place the letter that precedes the best definition of the underlined word in context to the left.

Words in Context	Definitions
1. ___ <u>fancifully</u> labeled	a. without exception, always
2. ___ <u>nuances</u> of sound	b. changed
3. ___ someone <u>interjected</u> a comment	c. absorb, take in
4. ___ <u>invariably</u> that meant	d. imaginatively
5. ___ a skill that is not <u>acquired</u>	e. signs, indications
6. ___ can be <u>altered</u>	f. speaks
7. ___ becomes <u>vastly</u> complicated	g. inserted, introduced
8. ___ because of such <u>manifestations</u>	h. fine variations
9. ___ Every tone he <u>utters</u>	i. immensely
10. ___ more to <u>assimilate</u>	j. got, obtained

Check your answers with the Key before going on. Review any that you have missed.

Pronunciation aids: 2. noo′ahns′s; 4. in vair′ē uh blē; 8. man uh fes tā′shuns.

KEY: add, āce; end, ēven; it, īce; odd, ōpen; pool; up.

B. Leaning on Parts

The prefix *pro-* means "forward," as in *proceed*. Supply the missing word or word part in each of the following blanks.

1. For the parade, the marching band led the pro_____.

2. To show this film, you'll need a movie pro_____.

3. With proper diet and care you can pro_____ your life.

4. Motorboats are usually driven through the water by a pro_____.

5. If *regress* means to go back, *progress* should mean go _____.

C. Making the Words Yours

In each blank below, enter the most appropriate word from the ten words in context in the first exercise, substituting it for the word(s) in parentheses. Use these words: *acquired, altered, assimilated, fancifully, interjected, invariably, manifestations, nuances, utters, vastly.*

1. Her personality can be (changed) _____ as easily as her wardrobe.

2. Every word he (speaks) _____ conceals a secret meaning.

3. The heckler (inserted) _____ comments throughout the professor's speech.

4. She (got) _____ more information in her senior year than ever before.

5. Purifying our air and water becomes (immensely) _____ complicated.

6. The pigeons in his coop are (imaginatively) _____ named.

7. (Signs) _____ of advanced age are becoming apparent in his manner.

8. The student (always) _____ overslept and went without breakfast.

9. Has anybody noticed the (fine variations) _____ of behavior I'm attempting?

10. She is certain that she has (absorbed) _____ all the information in the course.

4 Off for Each Mistake.
Word Power Score: _____
Answer Key in Appendix.

6

Look! No Words!

Ralph G. Nichols
Leonard A. Stevens

All too often we pay attention only to what is said. What about all the nonverbal communicating that goes on? It's that side that deserves a much closer look, as you will soon discover.

Begin Timing

The French writer Victor Hugo said, "When a woman is speaking to you, listen to what she says with her eyes."

Victor Hugo was talking about what is now fancifully labeled "nonverbal communication."

When people talk, the words they utter are only a part of their effort to communicate. With the words come gestures from the talker's hands and from nearly every muscle in his body. Even the temperature of a person's body, as it shows in the color of his face or the moisture in the palms of his hands, says something about what he is putting into words or about the silence he maintains.

"Self-betrayal oozes from all our pores," said Sigmund Freud.

The pitch and timbre of a person's voice; the way he pauses between words; the rhythm with which the words flow from his mouth; oddities in pronunciation; the speed at which words are spoken—all of these things have something to say, over and above that which is being communicated by words alone.

Erle Stanley Gardner, the mystery writer, wrote the following in *Vogue* magazine recently.

"Voices," said Gardner, "betray other thoughts and emotions. The average man has not trained his ears to the fine nuances of sound so that he can appreciate these things. Animals have this ability. Your dog, with his delicately attuned ears, can tell so much about your emotions and thoughts from the simple sound of your voice that if he could speak to tell you what he has learned you'd be astounded. As it is, the dog shows by his actions something of what he has learned from listening to the tone of your voice.

"For many years," Gardner continues, "I was in partnership with an attorney who had been an expert court reporter; he had reported some famous cases and many important legislative inquiries.

"In those cases, and particularly in the legislative hearings, many persons took part, but if the reporter had looked up from his notes to see who was talking each time someone interjected a comment, he would have been far behind in his transcript. So my friend made a study of voices. I think if that man had ever heard a voice anywhere, he could instantly place that voice when he heard it again. He might not remember the man's face but he would remember his voice.

"This man had received a legal education and his experience in reporting hearings gave him a background of practical experience so it was an easy matter for him to pass the bar examination and enter the practice of law. During the years that he was my partner, when we were in court together, he made it a point not to look at the witness on the stand; he kept his eyes on a piece of paper, sometimes taking down what the witness was saying in shorthand, sometimes simply doodling, but always listening to the voice of the witness.

"At some stage in the examination my partner would nudge me with his elbow.

"Invariably that meant that the witness was either lying at that point in his testimony, or was trying to cover up something.

"My untrained ears were never able to detect these subtle changes of voice and tempo, but my partner could spot them with startling accuracy."

Gardner is talking about a skill that is not acquired through reading improvement courses. In print, a word is a word—black against white. When spoken, a word comes to life. It has everything from a facial expression to a stage setting all of its own.

The simple word "oh" says little as you see it printed here. But in spoken form, "oh" can acquire scores of meanings. According to the way in which it is spoken, "oh" can mean: "You surprised me"; or "I made a mistake"; or "You're a pain in the neck"; or "You make me so happy"; or "I'm bored"; or "I'm fascinated"; or "I understand"; or "I don't understand."

Definitions of this simple word can be altered by simple changes in voice or gestures, each of which give a new twist to the two letters.

As you may see from this simple example, the nonverbal messages that we receive as listeners reinforce, modify or even contradict the words that a talker speaks. Sometimes the nonverbal part of the communication received by the listener is far more important than the verbal part. This is certainly true when the word "oh" is employed.

The wordless language that accompanies what we hear becomes vastly complicated when we try to pin it down. All of our senses become involved, and possibly extrasensory perception plays a role.

Touch plays a part in nonverbal communication. What happens when you receive a hearty "how-do-you-do" but at the same time your hand receives a handshake that feels like a cold, wet towel?

Physical distance between speaker and listener has something to say for itself. There's the man who comes too close and the one who won't come close enough. Both of them modify what they have to say by the distance they keep.

The words we hear may be given additional meaning by the way a talker holds his cigarettes, or toys with his glasses at certain moments, or adjusts his belt, or bites at a fingernail, or squints his eyes, or adjusts his necktie.

A slip of the tongue or a fumble for words may say more than the smoothest portions of language that we hear. A change in tone of voice can betray a lump in the throat that has more meaning than the forthcoming words.

The way a talker wears his clothes, washes his face, combs his hair, keeps his desk, or arranges his furniture can all broadcast certain nonverbal messages that have their effect upon what the person speaks in words.

Because of such manifestations when he speaks, the talker is in a position where he is bound to give more of himself than is usually the case with the writer. Every tone he utters, every twitch of his muscles, every flick of his eye is likely to betray what he has on his mind.

Reading Time: _____
See Conversion Table.
Enter WPM Rate on the Progress Record Chart.

6 Look! No Words!

COMPREHENSION CHECK

1. Victor Hugo said to listen to what a woman says with   1. ___
   her (a) lips, (b) eyes, (c) legs, (d) head.

2. According to Freud, self-betrayal oozes from all our   2. ___
   (a) pores, (b) moves, (c) words, (d) body.

3. Erle Stanley Gardner wrote an article for (a) *Harper's*,   3. ___
   (b) *Court Reporter*, (c) *Vogue*, (d) *Atlantic*.

4. Gardner said his partner found it easy to (a) notice   4. ___
   mannerisms, (b) pass the bar exam, (c) take shorthand,
   (d) notice facial expressions.

5. In discussing verbal and nonverbal communication it   5. ___
   was said that (a) nonverbal was sometimes more important, (b) verbal was usually more important, (c) both
   were equally important, (d) no comparison could be made.

6. Specific reference was made to (a) a slap on the back,   6. ___
   (b) shifty eyes, (c) downward glances, (d) a handshake.

7. Mention was made of (a) physical distance, (b) ESP,   7. ___
   (c) mental telepathy, (d) word connotations.

8. What word was used as a special example? (a) *yes*, (b) *no*,   8. ___
   (c) *well*, (d) *oh*.

9. A change of tone can betray (a) a lump in the throat,   9. ___
   (b) an emotional upset, (c) rage, (d) relief.

10. It was said that words have added meaning by the way   10. ___
    the speaker (a) sits, (b) leans against a support, (c) bites
    at a fingernail, (d) stands.

7 How Do You Best Get the Facts?

WORD POWER WORKOUT

A. Leaning on Context

In each of the blanks provided, place the letter that precedes the best definition of the underlined word in context to the left.

Words in Context	Definitions
1. ___ <u>dominates</u> his every move	a. false, untrue
2. ___ <u>inevitably</u> suffer	b. theory, proposition
3. ___ comprehension was <u>abysmally</u> poor	c. extremely; immeasurably
4. ___ <u>fallacious</u> notion	d. certainly
5. ___ <u>blurred</u> . . . details	e. vocabulary, terms
6. ___ he knows . . . the <u>terminology</u>	f. actually
7. ___ <u>literally</u> invite your attention	g. rules
8. ___ case-solving <u>hypothesis</u>	h. suitable
9. ___ <u>appropriate</u> reading rate	i. the greatest possible
10. ___ brings <u>maximum</u> comprehension	j. hazy, unclear

Check your answers with the Key before going on. Review any that you have missed.

Pronunciation aids: 2. in ev'uh tuh blē; 3. uh biz'mul lē; 4. fuh lā'shus.
KEY: add, āce; end, ēven; it, īce; odd, ōpen; pōōl; up.

B. Leaning on Parts

Fill in the missing word or word part in each of the following blanks. Notice also how knowing the meaning of *inter-* helps with word meanings.

1. The highway going between states is known as the inter_____.

2. The period between acts of a play is called the inter_____.

3. If you mediate a problem, you become an inter_____or.

4. To break into someone's discussion or talk is to inter_____it.

5. An international agreement is an agreement _____ nations.

C. Making the Words Yours

In each blank below, enter the most appropriate word from the ten words in context in the first exercise, substituting it for the word(s) in parentheses. Use these words: *abysmally, appropriate, blurred, dominates, fallacious, hypothesis, inevitably, literally, maximum, terminology.*

1. One student constantly (rules) _____ the discussion.

2. The weather was (extremely) _____ poor during the whole vacation.

3. The class read at its (greatest possible) _____ speed.

4. Some people (actually) _____ do not know how to boil water.

5. The bigger team will almost (certainly) _____ win the football game.

6. The lack of description in the article left many (hazy) _____ ideas.

7. Those (false) _____ statements caused tension in the group.

8. My reading rate was (suitable) _____ for my grade level.

9. I found it impossible to prove my (theory) _____.

10. My friend knows the (vocabulary) _____ of football.

4 Off for Each Mistake.
Word Power Score: _____
Answer Key in Appendix.

7

How Do You Best Get the Facts?

Begin Timing

How do you get factual information? Well, one thing is certain. You're not born with it. You have to acquire it. John Locke explained the process in this way. Our mind is at birth like a blank sheet of paper. Gradually, everything we see, feel, taste, hear, and smell—our total sensory experience—writes on that blank sheet. That's what gives us mind and memory. That's how Locke focuses attention on the countless bits of reality called facts. In reading, how do we get them?

The Role of Factual Information

As a first step, look closely at the role of facts. They form the base or foundation half of comprehension. They're the raw material or ingredients, such as are used in making an angel food cake. If a single ingredient is missing, the end results may be disastrous. Similarly, in reading, missing a fact may make quite a difference.

Facts *are* important. But isn't what they add up to even more important? See the problem? Which is more important, the ingredients or the cake? How do you add 3 and another number if you don't know the other number? As a reader, how do you evaluate the facts if you don't get all of them? Apparently the place to start is with the facts.

Setting the Purpose

Next—establish purpose. A good hunter, for example, doesn't rush into the woods and start shooting blindly in all directions, hoping somehow to hit something. No! If he is hunting deer, that purpose dominates his every move. So it is with reading. Don't just open a book and begin. Without a crystal-clear purpose, your comprehension will inevitably suffer.

Let's restate in terms of purpose what was said about facts. One purpose is to get the facts, accurately and completely. That's perhaps the prime purpose in school as well as in much of life. The second purpose, very closely related, is to get an understanding of those facts—a move into depth. Sherlock Holmes was a genius at both noting details and adding them together into a case-solving hypothesis.

Exactly how does purpose affect end results? To see, try reading the following short passage. Your purpose? To find out exactly how many men stepped out of the elevator at the top floor. Read with that purpose uppermost.

Here's the passage: Six men and three women got into the waiting elevator at the bottom floor. At the next stop, four more men entered and two women got out. At the next stop, five men got out and three men entered. At the next stop, two men got out and three entered. At the top floor everyone got out. How many men got out?

Now—without rereading—do you know exactly how many women got out? And do you know how many stops the elevator made?

This should let you see for yourself the importance of setting purpose. It pays! You can also see that too specific a purpose may actually keep you from getting some facts. A more general purpose such as "get *all* the facts" should make it easier to answer *all* three questions. Always set purpose!

Setting Your Reading Rate

As a third step, set an appropriate reading rate.

With many things, the faster you do them, the worse the results. If a typist hurries too much, for example, accuracy suffers. From this, you might assume that the way to get all the facts is to read very slowly. Let's examine that idea.

In one of my classes, one student after two weeks showed almost no progress. His starting speed was 170 words per minute (wpm). His in-class reading had never gone beyond the 190 wpm mark. Furthermore, his comprehension was abysmally poor. Before class one day, I suggested that he step up his speed by 50 to 100 wpm. He looked at me sadly and shook his head. "I only get 30 to 40 percent comprehension when I read slowly. I wouldn't get anything if I went any faster." See? There's that fallacious notion, the slower the better.

"With reading," I said, "it's a bit different. Within limits, the faster you read, the better you comprehend. Try it." He did. He read the next article at 260 wpm—for him a breakneck speed. To his surprise and pleasure, his comprehension soared to an all-time high of 70.

Compare rapid reading with rapid driving and you'll understand why. When driving along a country lane at 20 miles an hour, you literally invite your attention to wander. Now step up briefly to 60 miles an hour on a freeway. See how that speed forces concentration on the road.

So it is with reading. The slower you read, the more you encourage your mind to wander. *Within limits*, faster reading forces improved concentration.

What are those limits? For most students, increasing speed from 50 to 175 wpm above their normal rate still means improved comprehension. Of course, you'll have to discover your own limits. When you have, you'll know exactly what rate brings maximum comprehension.

Building Improved Background

As a final step, plan mini-reading programs to improve weak background areas. For example, take an avid baseball fan. With his background, reading a news account of a game seems almost effortless. He knows the players by name, the teams, the leagues, the terminology. As he reads, the details form a sharp, clear picture.

By contrast, take someone who has never seen a game. He doesn't know what RBI or AB stand for. He doesn't know what players are on each team or what city to connect with, say, the White Sox. In short, when he reads the same account, he gets a fuzzy, out-of-focus picture. Why? He lacks background.

Well—there you are. To sharpen your ability to get the facts, just apply these suggestions. Set your purpose. Use an appropriate reading rate. Build improved backgrounds. Soon, with practice, blurred or missed details will begin to come through, sharp and clear.

Reading Time: _____
See Conversion Table.
Enter WPM Rate on the Progress Record Chart.

7 How Do You Best Get the Facts?

COMPREHENSION CHECK

1. Mention is made of (a) Walter Logan, (b) John Locke, (c) Thomas Hobbes, (d) Voltaire.   1. ___

2. Reference is made to what kind of cake? (a) fruit cake, (b) sponge cake, (c) angel food cake, (d) devil's food cake.   2. ___

3. For one illustration, mention is made of a (a) hunter, (b) fishermen, (c) scuba diver, (d) pianist.   3. ___

4. One purpose is to get the facts, the other is to (a) recall them, (b) understand them, (c) relate them, (d) combine them.   4. ___

5. One illustration is of (a) a bus, (b) an elevator, (c) a train, (d) an airplane.   5. ___

6. You are told always to (a) set purpose, (b) check carefully, (c) reread, (d) avoid distractions.   6. ___

7. The starting rate for the slow reader mentioned is (a) 100 wpm, (b) 140 wpm, (c) 170 wpm, (d) 190 wpm.   7. ___

8. That slow reader's comprehension is (a) poor, (b) average, (c) good, (d) not discussed or mentioned.   8. ___

9. Reading is compared to (a) eating, (b) speaking, (c) walking, (d) driving.   9. ___

10. In one illustration, reference is made to (a) football, (b) hockey, (c) baseball, (d) tennis.   10. ___

10 Off for Each Mistake.
Comprehension Score: _____
Answer Key in Appendix.
Enter the Results on the Progress Record Chart.

Making the Application

1. By this time you have probably taken comprehension tests over seven different selections, with a total of 70 questions. Why not see what kinds of facts come through well and what kinds you tend to miss? Some people can remember telephone numbers with almost no effort. Others have to rely on a directory or list of numbers frequently called.

Suppose we set up some categories to let you see if there is a definite pattern in your answers.

A. *Names of people* (such as John Locke, Abraham Lincoln, Bacon, etc.)
Number of errors:_____
B. *Names of places* (such as Brazil, Ohio, etc.)
Number of errors:_____
C. *Statements* (such as "our mind is like a blank sheet of paper")
Number of errors:_____
D. *Figures* (such as one student's starting figure for reading—170 wpm)
Number of errors:_____
E. *Details* (such as dates, colors, abbreviations, addresses, phone numbers, etc.)
Number of errors:_____
F. *Organizational facts* (such as number of points, main divisions, or subdivisions)
Number of errors:_____

Go back over the preceding seven comprehension tests to find two questions under each of the six categories indicated. Then tally the number of errors you have made in each category. As one expert said, a problem well-identified is a problem half-solved. If you know from this survey that you tend not to notice organizational facts, you will obviously be more aware of them in the readings that follow, and be more likely to improve in comprehending them.

2. Before reading Selections 8 and 9, set your purpose mentally, as clearly as possible. Take advantage of the survey you just made. In case you tended not to note organizational facts, set that as a special purpose before beginning to read. Note particularly anything that suggests major divisions or subdivisions. Or, if you tend to miss numbers, see if you can set your purpose to get more of them with accuracy.

3. To help improve your background, complete the following exercise:

A. List your most difficult subject:_____

B. Check the library to find three easy, popular books in that subject matter area. You can usually tell from the title whether it is a textbook or a popular book. For example, the title *Our Friend the Atom*, by Heinz Haber, lets you know that this is probably a popular, easily read book on atomic physics. List three books by title that should provide better background, yet be relatively easy readings in your difficult subject matter area. Your instructor may have a suggestion here.

_____

_____

_____

C. List three specific moves you can now make to improve your background further for this difficult subject.

_____

_____

_____

_____

8 How to Make a Speech

WORD POWER WORKOUT

A. Leaning on Context

In each of the blanks provided, place the letter that precedes the best definition of the underlined word in context to the left.

Words in Context	Definitions
1. ___ for the <u>uninitiated</u>	a. bundle
2. ___ able to <u>articulate</u>	b. raised platform
3. ___ four main <u>intents</u>	c. aims, purposes
4. ___ the final <u>exhortation</u>	d. inexperienced
5. ___ that most <u>embodies</u>	e. offensive, in-sincere
6. ___ thick <u>sheaf</u> of papers	f. put into words
7. ___ on the <u>lectern</u>	g. unrehearsed
8. ___ to sound <u>spontaneous</u>	h. stand to hold notes
9. ___ first remarks on the <u>dais</u>	i. earnest urging
10. ___ <u>fulsome</u> introduction	j. gives form to

Check your answers with the Key before going on. Review any that
you have missed.

Pronunciation aids: 2. ar tik′yuh lāt; 7. lek′turn; 9. dā′is.
KEY: add, āce; end, ēven; it, īce; odd, ōpen; pōol; up.

B. Leaning on Parts

The prefix *non-* means "not," as in *nonexistent*. Fill in the blanks in the following sentences with the appropriate word or word part.

1. Things that are not essential to life can be called non_____.

2. A person not conforming to accepted behavior is a non_____.

3. Books are often classified in two ways, as fiction or non_____.

4. If something is unbelievably foolish, call it utter non_____.

5. A nonresident is, of course, _____ a resident.

C. Making the Words Yours

In each blank below, enter the most appropriate word from the ten words in context in the first exercise, substituting it for the word(s) in parentheses. Use these words: *articulate, dais, embodies, exhortation, fulsome, intents, lectern, sheaf, spontaneous, uninitiated*.

1. In some classrooms the teacher's desk stands on a (raised platform) _____.

2. To the (inexperienced) _____, driving a big truck does pose problems.

3. The specific (aims, purposes) _____ of the new organization deserve careful consideration.

4. One critic gave the first night performance (offensive, insincere) _____ praise.

5. One student was able to (put into words) _____ the problem quite well.

6. The minister ended the sermon with a very forceful (earnest urging) _____.

7. Some students go around always carrying a big (bundle) _____ of papers.

8. The speaker spread his papers out on the (stand to hold notes) _____.

9. The detailed report (gives form to) _____ the ideas of all committee members.

10. Any comments you make that receive (unrehearsed) _____ applause give you great satisfaction.

4 Off for Each Mistake.
Word Power Score: _____
Answer Key in Appendix.

8

How to Make a Speech

George Plimpton

*Does it bother you to speak in public? You're not alone. "Fear of
public speaking" is cited in the* Book of Lists *as the number 1 fear
in the United States. What about fear of death? It ranks a distant seventh! That fact gives you a special reason to read the following article carefully. Get rid of some of that natural fear.*

Begin Timing

One of life's terrors for the uninitiated is to be asked to make a speech.

"Why me?" will probably be your first reaction. "I don't have anything
to say." It should be reassuring (though it rarely is) that since you were
asked, somebody must think you do. The fact is that each one of us has a
store of material which should be of interest to others. There is no reason
why it should not be adapted to a speech.

Why Know How to Speak?

Scary as it is, it's important for anyone to be able to speak in front of others,
whether twenty around a conference table or a hall filled with a thousand
faces.

Being able to speak can mean better grades in any class. It can mean
talking the town council out of increasing your property taxes. It can mean
talking top management into buying your plan.

How to Pick a Topic

You were probably asked to speak in the first place in the hope that you
would be able to articulate a topic that you know something about. Still, it
helps to find out about your audience first. Who are they? Why are they
there? What are they interested in? How much do they already know about
your subject? One kind of talk would be appropriate for the Women's Club

of Columbus, Ohio, and quite another for the guests at the Vince Lombardi dinner.

How to Plan What to Say

Here is where you must do your homework.

The more you sweat in advance, the less you'll have to sweat once you appear on stage. Research your topic thoroughly. Check the library for facts, quotes, books and timely magazine and newspaper articles on your subject. Get in touch with experts. Write to them, make phone calls, get interviews to help round out your material.

In short, gather—and learn—far more than you'll ever use. You can't imagine how much confidence that knowledge will inspire.

Now start organizing and writing. Most authorities suggest that a good speech breaks down into three basic parts—an introduction, the body of the speech, and the summation.

Introduction: An audience makes up its mind very quickly. Once the mood of an audience is set, it is difficult to change it, which is why introductions are important. If the speech is to be lighthearted in tone, the speaker can start off by telling a good-natured story about the subject or himself.

But be careful of jokes, especially the shaggy-dog variety. For some reason, the joke that convulses guests in a living room tends to suffer as it emerges through the amplifying system into a public gathering place.

Main body: There are four main intents in the body of the well-made speech. These are 1) to entertain, which is probably the hardest; 2) to instruct, which is the easiest if the speaker has done the research and knows the subject; 3) to persuade, which one does at a sales presentation, a political rally, or a town meeting; and finally, 4) to inspire, which is what the speaker emphasizes at a sales meeting, in a sermon, or at a pep rally. (Hurry-Up Yost, the onetime Michigan football coach, gave such an inspiration-filled half-time talk that he got carried away and at the final exhortation led his team on the run through the wrong locker-room door into the swimming pool.)

Summation: This is where you should "ask for the order." An ending should probably incorporate a sentence or two which sounds like an ending—a short summary of the main points of the speech, perhaps, or the repeat of a phrase that most embodies what the speaker has hoped to convey. It is valuable to think of the last sentence or two as something which might produce applause. Phrases which are perfectly appropriate to signal this are: "In closing . . ." or "I have one last thing to say . . ."

Once done—fully written, or the main points set down on 3" x 5" index cards—the next problem is the actual presentation of the speech. Ideally, a speech should not be read. At least it should never appear or sound as if you are reading it. An audience is dismayed to see a speaker peering down at a thick sheaf of papers on the lectern, wetting his thumb to turn to the next page.

How to Sound Spontaneous

The best speakers are those who make their words sound spontaneous even if memorized. I've found it's best to learn a speech point by point, not word for word. Careful preparation and a great deal of practicing are required to make it come together smoothly and easily. Mark Twain once said, "It takes three weeks to prepare a good ad-lib speech."

Don't be fooled when you rehearse. It takes longer to deliver a speech than to read it. Most speakers peg along at about 100 words a minute.

Brevity Is an Asset

A sensible plan, if you have been asked to speak to an exact limit, is to talk your speech into a mirror and stop at your allotted time; then cut the speech accordingly. The more familiar you become with your speech, the more confidently you can deliver it.

As anyone who listens to speeches knows, brevity is an asset. Twenty minutes are ideal. An hour is the limit an audience can listen comfortably.

In mentioning brevity, it is worth mentioning that the shortest inaugural address was George Washington's—just 135 words. The longest was William Henry Harrison's in 1841. He delivered a two-hour 9,000-word speech into the teeth of a freezing northeast wind. He came down with a cold the following day, and a month later he died of pneumonia.

Check Your Grammar

Consult a dictionary for proper meanings and pronunciations. Your audience won't know if you're a bad speller, but they will know if you use or pronounce a word improperly. In my first remarks on the dais, I used to thank people for their "fulsome introduction," until I discovered to my dismay that "fulsome" means *offensive* and *insincere*.

On the Podium

It help's one's nerves to pick out three or four people in the audience—preferably in different sectors so that the speaker is apparently giving his attention to the entire room—on whom to focus. Pick out people who seem to be having a good time.

How Questions Help

A question period at the end of a speech is a good notion. One would not ask questions following a tribute to the company treasurer on his retirement, say, but a technical talk or an informative speech can be enlivened with a question period.

The Crowd

The larger the crowd, the easier it is to speak, because the response is multiplied and increased. Most people do not believe this. They peek out from behind the curtain and if the auditorium is filled to the rafters they begin to moan softly in the back of their throats.

What About Stage Fright?

Very few speakers escape the so-called "butterflies." There does not seem to be any cure for them except to realize that they are beneficial rather than harmful, and never fatal. The tension usually means that the speaker, being keyed up, will do a better job. Edward R. Murrow called stage fright "the sweat of perfection." Mark Twain once comforted a fright-frozen friend about to speak: "Just remember they don't expect much." My own feeling is that with thought, preparation and faith in your ideas, you can go out there and expect a pleasant surprise.

And what a sensation it is—to hear applause. Invariably after it dies away, the speaker searches out the program chairman—just to make it known that he's available for next month's meeting.

Reading Time: _____
See Conversion Table.
Enter WPM Rate on the Progress Record Chart.

8 How to Make a Speech

COMPREHENSION CHECK

1. Mention was made of a hall filled with (a) 300 faces,
   (b) 500 faces, (c) 800 faces, (d) 1,000 faces.
   1. ___

2. Knowing how to speak was said to mean (a) better
   grades, (b) a job offer, (c) more income, (d) more
   prestige.
   2. ___

3. You were advised to (a) get help from a speech teacher,
   (b) write your speech out in full, (c) find out about
   your audience, (d) practice with a tape recorder.
   3. ___

4. Why research your topic thoroughly? (a) to insure accuracy, (b) to inspire confidence, (c) to fill the required
   time, (d) to make yourself an expert.
   4. ___

5. How many different speech intents were discussed?
   (a) only one, (b) two, (c) three, (d) four.
   5. ___

6. One football coach inspired his team to run into the
   (a) shower room, (b) gymnasium, (c) swimming pool,
   (d) opponent's locker room.
   6. ___

7. Mention was made of (a) Winston Churchill, (b) Mark
   Twain, (c) Lincoln, (d) Ronald Reagan.
   7. ___

8. What is the ideal speech length? (a) ten minutes,
   (b) fifteen minutes, (c) twenty minutes, (d) twenty-
   five minutes.
   8. ___

9. The article discussed (a) question periods, (b) using
   cough drops, (c) having a glass of water handy, (d) how
   to deal with the chairman.
   9. ___

10. The article specifically mentioned (a) Dan Rather,
    (b) David Brinkley, (c) Walter Cronkite,
    (d) Edward R. Murrow.
    10. ___

10 Off for Each Mistake.
Comprehension Score: _____
Answer Key in Appendix.
Enter the Results on the Progress Record Chart.

9 Why 30 Seconds?

WORD POWER WORKOUT

A. Leaning on Context

In each of the blanks provided, place the letter that precedes the best definition of the underlined word in context to the left.

Words in Context	Definitions
1. ___ and <u>compelling</u> reasons	a. kept in mind
2. ___ time <u>constraint</u>	b. required
3. ___ you must be <u>concise</u>	c. necessity
4. ___ swiftly and <u>succinctly</u>	d. idea
5. ___ <u>media</u> research	e. brief
6. ___ the whole <u>concept</u>	f. pressing
7. ___ said and <u>retained</u>	g. briefly
8. ___ that I <u>edit</u>	h. gaining command of
9. ___ shouldn't be a <u>mandatory</u> thing	i. prepare for presentation
10. ___ <u>mastering</u> a few basic principles	j. communication mediums

Check your answers with the Key before going on. Review any that you have missed.

Pronunciation aids: 3. kun sīs´; 4. suk singt´lē.
KEY: add, āce; end, ēven; it, īce; odd, ōpen; pōōl; up.

B. Leaning on Parts

Try to supply the missing word or word part in each of the following sentences. Notice also how prefix meaning relates to word meaning.

1. If you move away from town, you leave or de_____.

2. To climb down a mountain is to de_____.

3. To put money down on a purchase is to make a de_____.

4. To be down in spirits is to be de_____.

5. If you decline an invitation, you turn it _____.

C. Making the Words Yours

In each blank below, enter the most appropriate word from the ten words in context in the first exercise, substituting it for the word(s) in parentheses. Use these words: *compelling, concept, concise, constraint, edit, mandatory, mastering, media, retained, succinctly.*

1. How did the (communication mediums) _____ handle the unexpected invasion?

2. You'll have to plan carefully because of the rigid time (necessity) _____.

3. In preparing for the test, the student fortunately (kept in mind) _____ more than usual.

4. Before you give your speech, you'd better let me (prepare for presentation) _____ it.

5. You'll find (pressing) _____ reasons why you should attend to the matter immediately.

6. When you file a tax return, observance of set procedures is (required) _____.

7. (Gaining command of) _____ certain basic techniques greatly improves your reading ability.

8. You need a workable (idea) _____ to capitalize on the interest.

9. I've often been encouraged to express myself (briefly) _____.

10. To be (brief) _____ is a desirable goal for both writing and speaking.

4 Off for Each Mistake.
Word Power Score: _____
Answer Key in Appendix.

9

Why 30 Seconds?

Milo O. Frank

The following selection comes from a book by "America's foremost business communications consultant," so the book cover proclaims. You'll be reminded that we live in a non-stop, non-wait business world—a world where the "sound bite" reigns supreme. How do you cope? You'll soon find out.

Begin Timing

"If only he'd get to the point!"

"All right, she's got five minutes and out."

"I can't see him today. I haven't got time."

"Don't answer the phone. It might be Ellen. She talks forever."

"This is my first presentation to top management. I'd better be good and fast."

"What kind of memo is this? I haven't got time to read five pages."

"God, he talked for an hour, and I don't know what he said."

"If I get one chance to speak in the meeting, and I have to be brief, can I deliver my whole message?"

"How can I get my point across in a fifteen-minute interview?"

"They're tough businessmen. They won't listen long."

"He wants two or three minutes and that means fifteen or twenty, and it'll be a waste of time anyway."

In this hurry-hurry world, does all this sound familiar?

There are two clear and compelling reasons why 30 seconds is the ideal length of time in which to get your point across. The first is *time constraint*—not only on yourself, but also on those you're trying to convince.

Through my film and TV work, I've seen time and tastes change; fast food, fast cars, and fast deals are commonplace today. Time waits for no man; you have to move faster just to stay even. And to move faster, you must be concise.

Do you ever think about how people judge you and about how you judge others? Your deals, jobs, money, and success can all hang on first impressions. Isn't it true that with just a few words, an image is formed in your mind and in theirs, and you and they act accordingly? Often there's only time for a few words, so they had better be the right ones. The hour of years ago is the 30 seconds of today. To survive and move ahead in business or in any other relationship, you must be able to get your point across swiftly and succinctly in 30 seconds or less.

The second and more important reason why 30 seconds is the ideal length of time to get your point across is that even when a person has time to listen to you, his mind can accept only so much information in one steady flow. How long can you or anyone pay attention to what someone is saying without letting your mind wander off to sex, money, or the other good things in life? When I ask this question, I get answers of anywhere from four hours to four seconds. One businessman in a particularly sour mood from his most recent sales meeting said zero was the attention span of his associates. That happened to be true, but only because he always talked so long and boringly that his audience turned him off before he even opened his mouth. *The attention span of the average individual is 30 seconds.*

Let me give you an example. Look around the room and concentrate on a lamp. You'll find your mind goes to something else within 30 seconds. If the lamp could move or talk, or go on and off by itself, it would recapture your attention for another 30 seconds. But without motion or change, it cannot hold you.

Think of someone's attention span as a quarter slot machine. This machine must take in the first twenty-five cents before you can put in the second twenty-five cents. If you put in fifty cents or a dollar all at once, you'll have wasted your money and maybe even jammed the machine. It can take in only twenty-five cents at a time. Your listener can take in only 30 seconds at a time.

So if you want your listener to give up thoughts of sex and money and pay attention to you, you've got just 30 seconds. That is the attention span of the human race. Nowhere is this better illustrated than in the field of radio and television commercials. Media research has determined 30 seconds to be the attention span of the average viewer. That's why you and I live with the 30-second attention span theory every day of our listening and viewing lives. Almost all commercials on television and radio are 30 seconds long. If those commercials didn't sell the product, whether it's a refrigerator or a politician seeking votes, the whole concept of radio and television advertising would change.

When I discuss the 30-second message with people in my communications workshops, I hear the same thing over and over again: "I can't possibly make my point in such a short time."

My answer is that television and radio do it all the time. Commercials not only grab your attention but also tell you all about the product and where and when to buy it. Here's an example of a 30-second television commercial for Galpin Ford:

Galpin purposely bought a lot of motor homes. But all the rain kept many of our customers away. We've got too many motor homes. Buy them during our three-day sale. Save up to eighteen thousand dollars off our regular list price. The savings can pay for your vacations for years. You can take up to twelve years to pay; many have an 11.9 percent finance plan. Prices start at $16,996. See Friday's *L.A. Times* sports section. Don't wait forever. It's the things you don't do that you regret.

The result was the most successful sale of motor homes in the history of Galpin Ford, one of the largest dealers in the country. The commercial told the potential buyer what he needed to know, and all within his attention span. The important point is that a lot can be said and retained in 30 seconds. And if radio and television can do it, so can you.

Radio and television news also make use of the 30-second attention span. It's called the "sound bite." I asked a television news anchorwoman-reporter friend of mine, Terry Mayo, to explain to some business people just what a sound bite is, and she said:

Because of attention span, the average time of all television news stories is one and a half minutes. The reporter needs 30 seconds to set up the story, another 30 seconds is reserved for the actuality, which means an interview or tape of what's happening, then another 30 seconds for the reporter to summarize and end the story. If I go out to interview someone about a story, I want that person to make his point in 30 seconds or less so I can pull it out and use it. That 30-second portion of the entire interview that I edit at the studio is called a "sound bite." If the subject doesn't make his statement in 30 seconds or less, I can't use it and it doesn't make the air.

Terry had something else to say about the 30-second rule on TV news: "We've discovered that if you can't say it in 30 seconds, you probably can't say it at all. If you know how, you can make any point very well in 30 seconds."

An example is a moving message delivered in this dramatic and emotional television news story: An old man had gone into the water fully clothed to save two seven-year-old children. He was still soaking wet when the television reporter interviewed him. He said, "Sure, I'm sixty-five. So what? Anybody who could swim would have gone in to save those kids, but maybe I did something else important. Maybe people should realize that when you're over sixty, you're not dead. You're productive, and retirement shouldn't be a mandatory thing."

There's a powerful message in less than 30 seconds, and the point certainly gets across. It was made by an average person under stress. It proves conclusively that you or anyone can do the same thing if you know how.

The 30-second message is always applicable, anytime and anywhere. It's a basic tool. When you master it, it'll become second nature to you.

It'll create a whole new mind-set. It'll transform the way you think and deal with others every day. You'll find yourself instinctively prepared and using it all the time.

Anybody can master the art of the 30-second message by mastering a few basic principles.

Reading Time: _____
See Conversion Table.
Enter WPM Rate on the Progress Record Chart.

9 Why 30 Seconds?

COMPREHENSION CHECK

1. The author uses the phrase (a) quick-paced world,   1. __
(b) speed-demon world, (c) hurry-hurry world, (d) stop-
and-go world.

2. How many reasons are given for the 30-second ideal?   2. __
(a) only one, (b) two, (c) three, (d) four.

3. It was said we are gauged by (a) clothes, (b) our ability   3. __
to get results, (c) our sincerity, (d) first impressions.

4. One man spoke of a zero attention span because he   4. __
(a) always talked too long, (b) only thought people were
not paying attention, (c) was just pessimistic, (d) felt
his associates were disagreeable.

5. To prove his point about the 30-second span, the author   5. __
asks you to concentrate on a (a) lamp, (b) chair, (c) book,
(d) table.

6. The article refers to a (a) dollar bill, (b) pay phone,   6. __
(c) slot machine, (d) vending machine.

7. People in the communications workshop said (a) it was   7. __
easy to reach the 30-second limit, (b) they were amazed
at how much could be said in 30 seconds, (c) one minute
was better, (d) they couldn't make a point in 30 seconds.

8. The highly successful Galpin Ford commercial was for   8. __
(a) vans, (b) motor homes, (c) Taurus cars, (d) station
wagons.

9. The average TV news story runs (a) 30 seconds, (b) one   9 __
minute, (c) one and a half minutes, (d) three minutes.

10. How old was the man who saved the children from   10. __
drowning? (a) fifty-five, (b) sixty, (c) sixty-five,
(d) seventy.

10 Off for Each Mistake.
Comprehension Score: _____
Answer Key in Appendix.
Enter the Results on the Progress Record Chart.

10 How Can You Speed Up Your Reading?

WORD POWER WORKOUT

A. Leaning on Context

In each of the blanks provided, place the letter that precedes the best definition of the underlined word in context to the left.

Words in Context	Definitions
1. ___ student <u>plodded</u> along	a. gave in, yielded
2. ___ comprehension suffers <u>temporarily</u>	b. moved slowly
3. ___ <u>reinforce</u> your bad habits	c. strengthen
4. ___ need added <u>impetus</u>	d. stimulus, impulse
5. ___ single <u>key</u> principle	e. beginning
6. ___ I finally <u>relented</u>	f. basic
7. ___ <u>sliver</u> of time	g. small splinter
8. ___ strange <u>phenomenon</u>	h. reduce
9. ___ <u>minimize</u> those brakes	i. fact, happening
10. ___ your <u>initial</u> rate	j. for a time

Check your answers with the Key before going on. Review any that you have missed.

Pronunciation aids: **3.** rē in fors´; **4.** im´pe tus; **8.** fi nom´e non.

KEY: add, āce; end, ēven; it, īce; odd, ōpen; pōol; up.

B. Leaning on Parts

Well over a thousand words contain the prefix *un-*, meaning "not." Supply the missing word or word part in each of the following blanks.

1. If a story or article is not usual, call it un_____.

2. If you are not certain about something, you are un_____.

3. If your actions are not wise, they can be called un_____.

4. If I am not worthy of praise, I am un_____.

5. If you are unconscious, that means you are _____ conscious.

C. Making the Words Yours

In each blank below, enter the most appropriate word from the ten words in context in the first exercise, substituting it for the word(s) in parentheses. Use these words: *impetus, initial, key, minimize, phenomenon, plodded, reinforces, relented, sliver, temporarily.*

1. To lose weight, (reduce) _____ the amount of food you eat.

2. He (moved slowly) _____ through the material.

3. Reading for facts instead of ideas (strengthens) _____ poor reading habits.

4. A (small splinter) _____ of wood caught under my fingernail.

5. The store was (for a time) _____ out of meat.

6. After thinking things over, the father (gave in) _____.

7. Being attacked by a giant bird was an unbelievable (happening) _____.

8. A (basic) _____ element in successful reading is concentration.

9. The teacher's praise was (stimulus) _____ enough to get the boy started.

10. The speaker's (beginning) _____ remarks caught everyone's attention.

4 Off for Each Mistake.
Word Power Score: _____
Answer Key in Appendix.

10

How Can You Speed Up Your Reading?

Begin Timing

At this point you should be progressing nicely. You've checked reading strengths and weaknesses. You've started to build vocabulary and improve factual comprehension. It's time now to speed up your reading.

How do you do that? By taking off the brakes! You wouldn't think of driving your car with the brakes on. Yet, as a reader, you may have as many as three brakes slowing you down. One brake is *regressing*, or looking back as you read. Another is *vocalizing*, or pronouncing words to yourself, and a third is *word-for-word reading* instead of phrase reading.

Faster-than-comfortable Reading

How can you eliminate or minimize those brakes that hold your reading to a snail's pace? Fortunately, one single key principle, properly applied, will do the job. Try faster-than-comfortable reading.

Faster-than-comfortable reading reduces regressions. You just don't have time to look back. Furthermore, you have less time to vocalize, so that bad habit begins to disappear. Finally, that extra speed forces you into dealing with word groups, not single words.

Put a faster-than-comfortable reading plan into effect immediately. Set aside fifteen minutes a day for practice. To be sure, you've practiced reading for years, but probably never the uncomfortable variety. That means you've probably done little more than reinforce your bad habits. You can practice 20 years at 200 wpm and *never* develop skill at double that rate. Push uncomfortable speeds with the selections in this book, as well as with other easy reading. Keep a careful record of changes in rate. If those practice sessions don't tire you, you know you're not pushing hard enough to get maximum results.

Whenever you first push into faster speeds, you will probably feel you are not actually reading. Remember—you need new experience to make those faster speeds comfortable. And don't worry if comprehension suffers temporarily. It will improve as soon as you gain sufficient additional experience.

Pacing

At some point in your development, you're going to find yourself just unable to read any faster. Continual checks of your Progress Chart in the back will help you know when that point is reached. The minute your latest entry is less than 20 wpm faster than the preceding one, you know you need added impetus. That's true especially if you find yourself saying, "I just can't push myself any faster!"

That's when you need the special technique of pacing. Almost without exception, there are hidden potentials in all of us that become available only under crisis or unusual pressure. Pacing provides the key for unlocking such resources. For that reason it is the oldest, most widely used, yet newest approach for speeding your reading.

Why is pacing so common? The answer is simple. It works. This was brought dramatically home to me in one of my adult efficient reading classes at the university. At our first session, one student plodded along at 80 wpm while the rest of the class patiently waited for him to finish.

After class, I told him he'd better cancel. In desperation, he said, "I need this more than anyone." I had to agree, but added that it seemed hardly fair to make all the others wait for him to finish. He begged to stay, saying, "All right. Don't wait for me. Let me get what I can." I finally relented.

As the course progressed, I noted an amazing change. While the class moved up nicely from 254 to 481 wpm, the plodder had shot up from 80 to 460 wpm! "What are you doing?" I asked him. He explained. He told me he had wired his electric clock to the radio. Every time the sweep second hand passed 12, the radio came on briefly to let him know a minute had passed.

Every night, without fail, for only fifteen minutes, he used that device to pace himself in the *Reader's Digest*, which contains about 500 words per full page. At first he tried to read half a column in a minute—125 words. When he could manage that, he tried a full column, then a full page. The results were spectacular.

Why not enjoy similar results yourself? Use a 15-minute sliver of time. Have someone pace you by saying "next" every minute. Pace at speeds at least 75 wpm faster than your last entry on the progress sheet. In this way you will gradually build the ability to read quite effectively at the faster speeds.

Add pacing to faster-than-comfortable reading. It's like firing what might be called a second-stage rocket to blast you into speedier orbit.

Swing Two Bats

As a booster rocket, tap an important psychological principle. If you've never once driven at 100 mph, imagine how that would feel. As you accelerate beyond your usual 65 mph, can't you feel the tension build, your grip on the steering wheel tighten? One slip would be fatal. After a time, when you dropped back to your usual 65 mph, you would notice a strange phenomenon. That 65 mph speed would seem much slower—almost like a leisurely 50 mph. In essence, that's the same psychological principle a baseball player uses when he swings two bats before dropping one and stepping up to the plate. The one remaining bat seems much lighter and easier to swing.

Capitalize on this to develop increased reading speed. When you're reading normally at 250 wpm, practice at 350 to make yourself more comfortable at 300 wpm. Your top reading speed will always be uncomfortable. That's why you should practice at even faster speeds. Suppose you double your initial rate, moving from 250 to 500 wpm. Be sure to make yourself comfortable at 500 wpm by practicing some at a 600 to 700 figure. This insures maximum progress.

Judging from class results here at Minnesota, when you finish this program you should read at least twice as fast, with the same or better comprehension. Of our students, about 72 percent double their rate, 20 percent triple it, and 8 percent quadruple it.

Reading Time: _____
See Conversion Table.
Enter WPM Rate on the Progress Record Chart.

10 How Can You Speed Up Your Reading?

COMPREHENSION CHECK

1. To speed your reading you are told to (a) set a new purpose, (b) think speed, (c) take off the brakes, (d) analyze yourself.   1. ___

2. One slowing-down factor mentioned is (a) fatigue, (b) drowsiness, (c) lack of concentration, (d) regressing.   2. ___

3. Another factor mentioned is (a) vocalizing, (b) background deficiency, (c) eyestrain, (d) inattention.   3. ___

4. You are told to keep a careful record of (a) material read, (b) changes in rate, (c) time spent in reading, (d) special reading difficulties.   4. ___

5. You re cautioned not to (a) lose any comprehension, (b) read too fast, (c) worry over temporary loss of comprehension, (d) read too long at any one time.   5. ___

6. Pacing is commonly used because (a) it works, (b) it is simple, (c) it is convenient, (d) it requires minimal equipment.   6. ___

7. A normal full page of the *Reader's Digest* contains about how many words? (a) 200, (b) 300, (c) 400, (d) 500.   7. ___

8. Pacing is likened to (a) a super-charged engine, (b) a second-stage rocket, (c) a second-wind effort, (d) high gear on a car.   8. ___

9. You are asked to imagine yourself (a) driving at 100 mph, (b) piloting a jet plane, (c) speeding down a mountainside on skis, (d) steering a toboggan.   9. ___

10. You are told that your top speed would (a) eventually become comfortable, (b) be impossible to sustain, (c) always be comfortable, (d) have to be practiced daily.   10. ___

10 Off for Each Mistake.
Comprehension Score: _____
Answer Key in Appendix.
Enter the Results on the Progress Record Chart.

Making the Application

Pacing suggestions: To estimate the number of words per page, take any book or magazine that you plan to use for pacing. Turn to a full page and count up to 100 words. A word is any letter or combination of letters that stands alone, *I* and *a* as well as longer ones. Count the number of lines in that 100-word sample and use that figure to estimate the number of words on a full page. A magazine the size of the *Reader's Digest*, for example, has about 500 words per full page, which gives you an idea of what to expect with other page sizes.

To pace, first select an easy, popular book that you want to read. Pace for about ten minutes a session a day. You can enlist the help of a room-mate or friend—someone who will say "begin reading" and say "next" at the end of every minute for ten minutes. You, the reader, try to cover each page so that at the word "next" you are just reading the last words. If you are a bit slow, skip to the next page and read faster, gradually adjusting rate to the pacing figure settled on. For your first pacing, if you read at about 250 wpm, try a 500 wpm rate. This would mean reading ten 500-word pages in ten minutes or twelve-and-a-half 400-word pages.

Pacing can also be done with your textbooks. Here your first move is to read the text for exactly one minute to see what your usual wpm rate is for that text. Suppose you find it to be 125 wpm. You then pace yourself through an assignment at about 250 wpm. Determine the number of words per page as discussed and figure the number of pages you must read in ten minutes to read at 250 wpm. Divide that number by ten to know where you should be at the command of "next."

Even if you don't have a friend or roommate to help, you can still pace yourself. Do it by placing a marker in at the point of the book where you should be in exactly ten minutes. See if you can make it. If not, go slightly faster for the next ten minutes.

Pacing both with easy reading as well as with more difficult reading will encourage you to develop real flexibility of rate, a flexibility that can be readily modified by purpose to your advantage. The added concentration that comes from pacing should let you handle faster speeds with real effectiveness.

A pacing record similar to the one that follows should point up progress. Under the heading *Subjective Feeling*, enter a descriptive word or phrase to indicate your feeling—such as *impossibly fast, frustrating, manageable*, or *understandable*. It is most satisfying to see a given speed become *manageable*, when at first it was quite *frustrating*.

Title of book used for pacing: _____

	Minutes of Pacing	Pacing Rate	Subjective Feeling
Week 1	_____	_____	_____
Week 2	_____	_____	_____
Week 3	_____	_____	_____
Week 4	_____	_____	_____
Week 5	_____	_____	_____
Week 6	_____	_____	_____
Week 7	_____	_____	_____
Week 8	_____	_____	_____

11 The Happiest Man

WORD POWER WORKOUT

A. Leaning on Context

In each of the blanks provided, place the letter that precedes the best definition of the underlined word in context to the left.

Words in Context	Definitions
1. ___ silk and cotton <u>swatches</u>	a. uneasy
2. ___ long, <u>auburn</u> hair	b. distorted
3. ___ sheer loving <u>exuberance</u>	c. dedicate
4. ___ events were <u>hilarious</u>	d. close friends
5. ___ especially five <u>cronies</u>	e. reddish brown
6. ___ could not be <u>warped</u> by envy	f. unbearable
7. ___ his <u>insupportable</u> sadness	g. sample cloth pieces
8. ___ began to get <u>apprehensive</u>	h. high spirits
9. ___ he can <u>devote</u> his life to	i. funny
10. ___ was an <u>extravaganza</u>	j. spectacular theatrical production

---

Check your answers with the Key before going on. Review any that you have missed.

Pronunciation aids: 1. swot′ches; 3. ig zōō′bur unce; 10. ik strav′uh gan′zuh.

KEY: add, āce; end, ēven; it, īce; odd, ōpen; pōōl; up.

B. Leaning on Parts

The prefix *trans-* means "across" or "beyond." Supply the needed word or word part in each of the following sentences to see that prefix at work.

1. They went across the Atlantic in a trans_____ liner.

2. This ticket allows you to trans_____ across to another bus.

3. If you lose too much blood, you'll need a blood trans_____.

4. If you can't read French, find someone to trans_____ this letter.

5. If it transcends expectations, it goes _____ what you expected.

C. Making the Words Yours

In each blank below, enter the most appropriate word from the ten words in context in the first exercise, substituting it for the word(s) in parentheses. Use these words: *apprehensive, auburn, cronies, devote, extravaganza, exuberance, hilarious, insupportable, swatches, warped.*

1. The detective interviewed the suspect's (close friends) _____ for help with the case.

2. Are you (uneasy) _____ about walking through that district at night?

3. Some of the lumber was badly (distorted) _____.

4. You should get some (sample cloth pieces) _____ to see what looks best with the pictures.

5. The humorist's one-liners were (funny) _____.

6. Did you meet the new girl with the long (reddish brown) _____ hair?

7. After their rescue, the passengers were in a state of rare (high spirits) _____.

8. To (dedicate) _____ your life to the service of others is most worthy.

9. A Hollywood (spectacular theatrical production) _____ should provide top entertainment.

10. The close friend's death brought a feeling of (unbearable) _____ loss.

4 Off for Each Mistake.
Word Power Score: _____
Answer Key in Appendix.

11

The Happiest Man

Danny Kaye

Our Declaration of Independence reminds us that we have certain inalienable rights. Among them is our right to the "pursuit of happiness." Unfortunately, no government can give us happiness—just the right to pursue it. A look at the happiest man may be of invaluable help in our pursuit.

Begin Timing

Jacob Kominiski never achieved fame, never accumulated wealth. He was a simple tailor, and pleased to be one. He walked the streets of our Brooklyn neighborhood with great dignity, but always with a glint of laughter in his eye. He was my father, and the most successful human being I ever knew.

As a child I didn't fully understand his worth. When I saw how hard he worked for so little material reward I felt sorry for him and a little ashamed at his lack of ambition. I was wrong on both counts.

He worked for a Seventh Avenue dress manufacturer, and one summer evening he brought home an enormous sketch pad, a handful of soft pencils, and some wool and silk and cotton swatches. He announced that the boss was giving him a chance to become a dress designer, something he had long hoped for.

Night after night he worked until midnight or later. A slight man with thin blond hair and shoulders rounded by his trade, he stood by the kitchen table, bending over the sketch pad to make quick, swirling lines while Mother sat nearby, mending. She was a beautiful woman with long, auburn hair piled high above a serene face.

Supposedly asleep in the next room, my two brothers and I listened to the nightly routine: the sibilance of pencil on paper for a long time, then Pop calling Mother, "Chaya, come look."

Her dress rustled as she moved to stand beside him. Sometimes she made a suggestion for a change; usually she said, "I think it's just fine." And sometimes Pop would draw an outlandish ornament so they could both laugh. Laughter was a part of everything he did.

When at last the sketches were finished, he took them off to work. Nothing more was said about them. Finally I asked him, "Pop, what happened to the drawings?"

"Oh," he said, "they weren't any good."

Seeing my dismay, he said, "Danny, a man can't do everything in this world, but he can do one job well. I found out I'm not a good designer, but I *am* a good tailor."

And there I found the key to the man, the key that let me understand him better as I grew older. Jacob Kominiski never pretended to be something he wasn't. Free from vanity or unrealizable ambition, he was able to enjoy each day as it came.

The core of Pop's happiness was his family. Almost any event served as an excuse for a reunion with all our uncles and aunts and cousins. Such laughter and jokes and sheer loving exuberance—and all sparked by my mother and father. They were always the first couple on the floor to dance, and the first to start singing the old folk songs while the rest of us clapped hands to the rhythm. Part of Pop's pleasure was showing off his wife, with a shy sort of reverence. He thought no one in the world could match her. He once said of her, "Where she walks there is light."

Every night at dinner he reported the amusing things that happened to him during the day (we never heard of any defeats or frustrations). The most ordinary events were hilarious when Pop told about them.

There were serious days, of course—as when Pop received his naturalization papers. He burst into the house. "Chaya! Come here. Bring the children."

We all came running to find him holding a large and very official-looking certificate. "What does it say, Pop?" I cried.

"It says that Jacob Kominiski is a citizen of the United States of America! What do you think of that?"

We all thought it was wonderful. He framed the certificate and hung it in the living room for all to see. Thereafter he voted in every election, putting on his best suit for the occasion. One election day he was ill, and Mother insisted he stay in bed. "It's raining and very cold. Surely you can miss voting this once."

He saw me standing in the doorway and spoke for my benefit as well as hers. "In Russia I was not allowed to vote, but here I can help select men who will govern this great America. Do you know how many votes the President of the United States can cast? One! The same number as Jacob Kominiski! Isn't that a remarkable situation?"

Then he dressed and went to the polls.

Pop enjoyed all men, but he reserved his friendship for a few—especially five cronies who had emigrated with him at the time of World War I. Once a month they gathered in our kitchen for an evening of talk. All these men had achieved business success. Yet in many matters it was to Jacob Kominiski they turned for advice, knowing that he saw life clearly and his opinions could not be warped by envy.

They came to our rather shabby neighborhood in big automobiles, wearing expensive suits, and smoking 25-cent cigars. I once asked my mother, "Why do they come here instead of meeting in their own big houses?"

She thought a moment, then said, "I think maybe they left the best part of themselves here. They need to come back to it every now and then."

When I was 13 my mother died. Through my own grief I was aware of the great loss this was to Pop. But he made only one reference to his almost insupportable sadness. He said, "To be happy every day is to be not happy at all." He was saying to his sons that happiness is not a state you achieve and keep, but something that must be won over and over, no matter what the defeats and losses.

In my early teens I ran away from home, for the simple reason that I was bursting with curiosity about the world outside of Brooklyn. I talked a pal of mine into going along. Our thumbs got us rides, we sang for food, and at night we appeared at the local police station to announce we were hitchhiking to relatives and asked to be put in a cell until morning. It worked fine until we hit a small town in Delaware.

The chief of police said, "You kids look like a couple of runaways. You say you're from Brooklyn? I'll just telephone and see if there's a 'wanted' on you."

He found that there was indeed a missing-persons alarm for me. He soon had my father on the phone. After hearing I was all right, Pop seemed to relax. "You want me to send him home?" the chief asked. "Oh, no," Father said. "He wants to find out something. He'll come home when he's ready."

I was on the road two weeks and when I finally walked down the familiar street toward our house I began to get apprehensive. I was afraid I had hurt Pop by running away. How could I find the right words to explain to him why I went?

As it turned out, it was Pop who found the right words. When I stepped in the front door he looked up from his newspaper, and a wonderfully warm and relieved smile went over his face. Then he gave me a wink and said, "There's food in the icebox, Danny"—the words he had always greeted me with when I came home from school or play. So nothing had changed between us. He understood me, and my searchings and longings, so unlike his or my brothers'.

His patience with me during my late teens was infinite. Both my brothers had jobs and were hard-working, responsible citizens, but I was moody and restless and couldn't settle down. I wanted to express myself, but I didn't know how. Pop supported me uncomplainingly; once a week I found a $5 bill tucked beneath my pillow, to save me the embarrassment of openly receiving spending money.

My shortcomings did not escape the notice of Pop's cronies. Every time they gathered in our kitchen they would ask, "Danny got a job yet?" Pop would shake his head and change the subject.

One evening I heard a voice say, "Jacob, I speak to you as a friend must speak. Danny is becoming a bum. You should not allow this to happen."

Pop said, "My son is searching for something he can devote his life to. I can't tell him what it is. He'll never be happy unless he finds it for himself. It may take him longer than others, but he'll find it. I do not worry about him."

Later that year I got a job as an entertainer on the borscht circuit, and suddenly I knew this was the career I had been searching for. The world of the theater was far removed from the world of Jacob Kominiski, the tailor, yet I found myself returning to him time and again, for the same reason his cronies did.

When I was 20 I got what every actor dreams of—a permanent job! The A. B. Marcus show, *La Vie Paree*, was an extravaganza that had been touring the world for a quarter of a century, and I joined the cast. We played the Orient for a couple of years and then returned to the States for a series of one-night stands. When we finally hit Newark I went home to see Pop.

I had a problem, and I placed it before him. This was at the depth of the Depression, actors were out of work by the hundreds, yet I wanted to quit the show because I needed new experiences and challenges. But also I was scared.

Pop heard me out, then said, "It's very comfortable to have a steady job. You shouldn't be ashamed of liking it. But there are some people who always have to test themselves, to stretch their wings and try new winds. If you think you can find more happiness and usefulness this way, then you should do it."

This advice came from a man who never left a secure job in his life, who had the European tradition of family conformity and responsibility, but who knew I was different. He understood what I needed to do and he helped me do it.

For the next few years I worked in nightclubs, and then I got my big theatrical break appearing in *Lady in the Dark* with Gertrude Lawrence. After that I went to Hollywood, but even the glamour of the movie capital did not awe Pop.

For some of the time between his retirement and his death at the age of 80, Pop lived with me and my family there. We had a big party one evening, and soon there was a crowd around him listening to his stories about Brooklyn and his Ukrainian legends.

That night I thought Pop might enjoy hearing some of the old folk songs we used to sing at home. When I began to sing, the music and the memories were too much for him to resist, and he came over to join me. I faded away, and he was in the middle of the room singing alone—in a clear, true voice. He sang for 15 minutes before some of the world's highest-paid entertainers. When he finished there was thunderous applause.

This simple, kindly old man singing of our European roots had touched something deep in these sophisticated people. I remembered what my mother had said about Pop's rich cronies: "I think maybe they left the best part of themselves here. They need to come back to it every now and then."

I knew the applause that night was not just for a performance; it was for a man.

Reading Time: _____

See Conversion Table.

Enter WPM Rate on the Progress Record Chart.

11 The Happiest Man

COMPREHENSION CHECK

1. Jacob Kominiski lived in (a) Brooklyn, (b) Queens, (c) Newark, (d) Manhattan.

   1. ___

2. Jacob hoped to be (a) an office supervisor, (b) a foreman, (c) a dress designer, (d) a shop manager.

   2. ___

3. At the core of Pop's happiness was his (a) work, (b) humor, (c) cronies, (d) family.

   3. ___

4. Jacob said of his wife: Where she walks there is (a) beauty, (b) light, (c) charm, (d) fun.

   4. ___

5. Jacob emigrated to America from (a) Poland, (b) Czechoslovakia, (c) Russia, (d) Hungary.

   5. ___

6. Jacob's special five cronies visited him (a) once a month, (b) irregularly, (c) separately, (d) at unspecified times.

   6. ___

7. His cronies were said to (a) smoke 25-cent cigars, (b) drive big automobiles, (c) wear expensive suits, (d) do all the preceding.

   7. ___

8. How old was Danny when his mother died? (a) nine, (b) eleven, (c) thirteen, (d) fifteen.

   8. ___

9. Every week when Danny didn't settle down, his father gave him (a) chores to do at home, (b) $5 under his pillow, (c) $10 for spending money, (d) help in finding work.

   9 ___

10. Danny's big theatrical break was getting to appear with (a) Gertrude Lawrence, (b) Elsa Lanchester, (c) Irene Dunne, (d) A. B. Marcus.

    10. ___

10 Off for Each Mistake.
Comprehension Score: _____
Answer Key in Appendix.
Enter the Results on the Progress Record Chart.

12 Happiness

WORD POWER WORKOUT

A. Leaning on Context

In each of the blanks provided, place the letter that precedes the best definition of the underlined word in context to the left.

Words in Context	Definitions
1. ___ <u>strive</u> toward it	a. use wastefully
2. ___ the <u>gnawing</u> feeling	b. rank, high place
3. ___ the <u>apocryphal</u> story	c. work, struggle
4. ___ have <u>sophisticated</u> our tastes	d. action, motion
5. ___ the <u>dynamic</u> is supposed	e. supposition, belief
6. ___ <u>pampered</u> college people	f. tormenting
7. ___ way to achieve <u>status</u>	g. made-up, fictitious
8. ___ <u>Madisonian</u> man or woman	h. indulged
9. ___ <u>squander</u> our rights	i. made worldly-wise
10. ___ based on the <u>presumption</u>	j. advertising, public relations

Check your answers with the Key before going on. Review any that
you have missed.

Pronunciation aids: 2. naw'ing; 3. uh pok'ruh ful: 8. Mad uh sōn'ian.

KEY: add, āce; end, ēven; it, īce; odd, ōpen; po͞ol; up.

B. Leaning on Parts

The useful and easily identified prefix *over-* means "above." Supply the needed word or word part in each of the following sentences.

1. To price a thing above its proper retail value is to over _____ it.

2. If someone is far above normal weight, the person is over_____.

3. A coat worn above other clothes is called an over_____.

4. If a river rises above its banks, it over_____.

5. When you drive under an overpass, the overpass is _____ you.

C. Making the Words Yours

In each blank below, enter the most appropriate word from the ten words in context in the first exercise, substituting it for the word(s) in parentheses. Use these words: *apocryphal, dynamic, gnawing, Madisonian, pampered, presumption, sophisticated, squander, status, strive.*

1. For most people to achieve (rank, high place) _____ requires above-average effort.

2. One heir had no trouble to (use wastefully) _____ millions.

3. The (action, motion) _____ of change fascinates some people.

4. Stories like that sound (made-up, fictitious) _____ to me.

5. (Advertising, public relations) _____ people seem like a special breed.

6. In the accident, the driver escaped with a (tormenting) _____ pain in one arm only.

7. Always (work, struggle) _____ to enlarge your vocabulary with the help of these exercises.

8. The advanced art course certainly (made worldy-wise) _____ their tastes.

9. The parents (indulged) _____ their one and only child beyond belief.

10. The committee action was based on the (supposition, belief) _____ that all authority was theirs.

4 Off for Each Mistake.
Word Power Score: _____
Answer Key in Appendix.

12

Happiness

David F. Schuman with Bob Waterman

Happiness! Pursuing it is one thing—finding it quite another. Is Mr. Dooley right when he says, "Iverywhere happiness. . . . except in places where there ar-re people." Or is Dostoevski right with his "We are all happy, if we but knew it." More reading will help.

Begin Timing

It seems fairly obvious that if we had our choice, we would choose to be happy rather than unhappy. We want to be happy; we aim at it and plan for it and sometimes even strive toward it. But it seems to me that we have more of a passion for happiness than we have knowledge about it. As with so many seemingly important things, the greatness of our wants is equaled only by the greatness of our ignorance. . . .

Happiness is not *the* goal of humanity, or even of politics, and I do not want to argue that it is. I would simply like to suggest that to begin to think about how we think about happiness may help us to understand not only what we have but possibly what we don't have. By exploring happiness we may be able to see more clearly how to get what we want, and we may also be able to ask ourselves if what we want is worth getting. To begin with, we should try to understand a little of what happiness consists of in ourselves and in our relationship with society.

There is no obvious beginning point to a happiness discussion. No point that is so natural a place to begin that it cannot be ignored. Dictionaries may help; so too may Aristotle or Augustine or Jesus. But a discussion that thorough may serve to confuse as much as to make clear.

For a laugh, we could start at an unlikely place—with the Puritans. They serve as models for many things, but I doubt that they have ever been a model for happiness. H. L. Mencken once wrote that Puritanism was the gnawing feeling that someone somewhere might be happy.

So much for the Puritans.

By the time of the Constitution, we had already decided that happiness—at least the pursuit of it—was something "originally" guaranteed. The apocryphal story goes that when Thomas Jefferson was drafting the Declaration of Independence, he wrote about the right to life, liberty, and property. That is said to be the true phrasing of the thought, but it was not much artistically. So Jefferson rewrote. He changed it. Instead of pursuing property we were to pursue happiness. The point is an obvious one: In many American minds there is no difference. Any subtle distinctions are unclear. They are the same—property is happiness is property is happiness.

But what does that mean now? What does it mean to us? One could easily imagine that it means something like this. Before, to have property was enough. An individual was thought to be more or less happy if he or she owned things. But times have changed. We have changed. We have sophisticated our tastes, modified our styles; now, we consume. Maybe happiness is no longer just the pursuit of property.

Maybe happiness in America means buying things we won't use, using things we don't need, and wasting things we don't want. To consume is to destroy, yet our happiness is in the consumption. Our credit revolves as our purchasing power increases, and the dynamic is supposed to bring smiles to our faces and happiness to our hearts.

Of course, as middle-class, cared-for, mostly pampered college people, we think the consumption formulation vulgar and offensive. "No," you think, "that is for the others. *They* have to buy to be happy. Not me. Not us. No sir. For us to be happy, we just have to have fun."

So that is what you do: run after fun. Have a drink, smoke some dope. Now that is fun. Or you might ski. Or you might play bridge. Or you might go out and kill animals. Now that is really fun. What *more* could we want? Aren't we all happy now?

But is happiness just fun? Fun is cheap. Fun may be little more than a way to fill empty hours, or it may be a way to achieve status and social approval. In the final analysis, fun may have about as much to do with happiness as buying things does. Buying and having fun may simply be methods of display, motion, and instant reward.

If we look around for happiness, or even for fun, it is reasonable to assume that we will continue to be disappointed. The fact seems to be that society gives us few choices. We watch dull television, or the beautiful people in movies, or read *Penthouse* or *Mademoiselle*. And we think that is cool, and so we accept it and think ourselves happy. But that is little more than a sophisticated, societal lie.

The Madisonian man or woman in us will be content with new dresses or pictures of naked men and women, and we shall feel a little guilty and a little good, and go harmlessly on our way.

We somehow squander our right to pursue happiness for the security of mindless, inoffensive fun. We confuse internal pursuits—beauty, nobility, excellence—with the pursuit of happiness understood as the fulfillment of desire. We are too well trained in our own evilness and too used to our own self-interest to accept the task of trying to be happy while living with other people or while seeking values that do not have an obvious, tangible reality.

Maybe there is no such thing as happiness in our society. The harder we look, the more hopeless we become. We grow further apart and pretend somehow that loneliness is happiness. We consume, and we kill, and we read and watch things that only limit our perceptions, dull our imaginations.

To begin to think hard about happiness is to begin to feel cheated. It is to feel that there is an empty space where fullness should be. The more we pursue happiness in a society based on the presumption of our own evilness, the less well off we are as human beings.

But to end "happiness" in great despair does not make much sense, at least not much good sense. If I really agreed with Archbishop Whately that happiness was no laughing matter, I should be forced to believe that happiness was probably not worth the trouble of figuring out. No, what I want to say is the obvious: I have seen people happy, and have even felt it, and have certainly enjoyed it. Not only that, happiness might be important. It was Hawthorne who suggested the likeness of happiness to a butterfly, which flits away when chased but which may come and light on your hand if you will only sit quietly, occupied with something else.

It is wholly possible that we have been searching in the wrong place, pursuing the wrong question. If we take Hawthorne seriously, it may be best to occupy ourselves with that "something else."

Reading Time: _____
See Conversion Table.
Enter WPM Rate on the Progress Record Chart.

12 Happiness

COMPREHENSION CHECK

1. The greatness of our wants was said to be equaled by
   the greatness of our (a) inexperience, (b) neglect,
   (c) ignorance, (d) opportunity.   1. ___

2. There was specific mention of (a) Aristotle, (b) Plato,
   (c) Lincoln, (d) Archimedes.   2. ___

3. There was a reference to the (a) Indians, (b) Pilgrims,
   (c) Puritans, (d) British.   3. ___

4. Originally Jefferson wrote the phrase: right to life,
   liberty and (a) health, (b) property, (c) wealth
   (d) freedom.   4. ___

5. It was said to consume is to (a) make life easy, (b) make
   work, (c) destroy, (d) stimulate economic growth.   5. ___

6. The selection referred specifically to (a) shop clerks,
   (b) politicians, (c) managers, (d) college people.   6. ___

7. To have fun you were said to (a) go out and kill animals,
   (b) attend a football game, (c) bicycle, (d) play poker.   7. ___

8. Mention was made of (a) *House Beautiful*, (b) *Time*,
   (c) *Home and Garden*, (d) *Penthouse*.   8. ___

9. We pretend somehow that (a) loneliness is happiness,
   (b) beauty is happiness, (c) love is happiness, (d) playing
   an instrument is happiness.   9 ___

10. Hawthorne likened happiness to (a) a bluebird, (b) a fire,
    (c) a butterfly, (d) a filled stomach.   10. ___

10 Off for Each Mistake.
Comprehension Score: _____
Answer Key in Appendix.
Enter the Results on the Progress Record Chart.

13 Speeding by Surveying

WORD POWER WORKOUT

A. Leaning on Context

In each of the blanks provided, place the letter that precedes the best definition of the underlined word in context to the left.

Words in Context	**Definitions**
1. ___ surveying into better <u>perspective</u>	a. succeeding
2. ___ a <u>veritable</u> avalanche of print	b. brief
3. ___ a neat manageable <u>capsule</u>	c. relationship
4. ___ <u>compressed</u> the essentials of chapters	d. small case
5. ___ amazingly <u>concise</u> indication	e. condensed, brought together
6. ___ This chapter <u>zeros in</u>	f. focuses
7. ___ <u>apportion</u> to each article	g. procedure, way
8. ___ <u>subsequent</u> reading rate	h. distribute, allot
9. ___ a useful <u>technique</u>	i. actual
10. ___ book <u>jacket</u>	j. cover

Check your answers with the Key before going on. Review any that you have missed.

Pronunciation aids: 2. vair'uh tuh bul; 3. cap'sul; 5. kun sīs'; 9. tek nēk'.

KEY: add, āce; end, ēven; it, īce; odd, ōpen; po͞ol; up.

B. Leaning on Parts

The prefix *mono-* means "one" or "alone." Supply the appropriate word or word part in each of the following sentences.

1. An airplane with only one wing is called a mono_____.

2. A word of only one syllable is a mono_____.

3. If some company has exclusive control, it has a mono_____.

4. Doing one and the same thing day after day soon becomes mono_____.

5. A monochrome is a painting or drawing done in _____ color.

C. Making the Words Yours

In each blank below, enter the most appropriate word from the ten words in context in the first exercise, substituting it for the word(s) in parentheses. Use these words: *apportion, capsule, compressed, concise, jacket, perspective, subsequent, technique, veritable, zeros in.*

1. His father tried to (allot) _____ the money equally.

2. Watch the hunter as he (focuses) _____ on the moving deer.

3. A description of the novel was written on the book (cover) _____.

4. The (brief) _____ summary made the chapter clear.

5. The speaker (condensed) _____ the speech in order to save time.

6. Doing these exercises will help you with the (succeeding) _____ readings.

7. To put things into better (relationship) _____ , include examples of all types.

8. That (actual) _____ wall of water demolished the houses.

9. Six vitamins and four minerals are packed inside this one (small case) _____.

10. Surveying is an excellent (procedure) _____ for getting the essentials of an article.

4 Off for Each Mistake.
Word Power Score: _____
Answer Key in Appendix.

13

Speeding by Surveying

Begin Timing

Rapid reading is good, but not good enough. Of necessity, you should also know and use three superspeeds—*surveying, skimming,* and *scanning.* This chapter zeros in on the first of the three—surveying. Let's see exactly what it is, how it works, and when to use it.

To put surveying into better perspective, ask yourself a question. Who would buy a car—even a racy sports model—if it ran at only one speed? No one! In traveling we obviously demand choices, such as going by jet, by car, by bicycle, or on foot. Each choice has its own speed range, its own advantages and disadvantages, and serves quite different needs.

What about reading speeds? Here a variety of speeds is even more important. You face a veritable avalanche of print. Without a fantastically wide range of speeds, you'll soon feel buried alive. That's why you need superspeeds.

What Is Surveying?

Surveying is a specialized technique for getting a mountaintop view of an article, chapter, or entire book. With it, you catch a broad, overall picture of basic essentials. You speed through material anywhere from ten to over fifty times faster than with ordinary reading. That means you can survey up to fifty articles, chapters, or books in the time it usually takes to read just one. Obviously, a most useful technique!

How Does It Work?

Written communication has, fortunately, certain characteristics that make surveying possible. Usually, for example, the title of an article provides an amazingly concise indication of article content. The first paragraph normally adds substance, suggesting more exactly what is to follow.

From that point on, major divisions are often marked with headings. Other especially important points are apt to appear in italics, graphs, or tables. Finally, more often than not, the last paragraph will summarize or suggest key implications or applications.

Now translate those characteristics into action. You'll soon see exactly how to survey. _**Read the title, the first paragraph, all headings, italicized words, graphs, and tables, and the last paragraph**_. Simple? Yes. And you'll usually end up with the best possible overview with a minimal investment of time.

Stop right here. Survey this entire article before reading on. To guide you, the key words are all underlined. Just read all underlined words, starting with the title. Then come back to this spot and continue with your timing of this chapter.

Now you can see for yourself. You do have the essentials. A survey functions much as an abstract. It compresses the essentials of a full-length chapter into a neat, manageable capsule.

With certain modifications, you can also survey an entire book. To do this, read the title and table of contents. If there is a book jacket, read the material on the front, back, and inside flaps. This provides a broad overview of the entire book. Then go ahead to survey each chapter individually, as described earlier. Read chapter title, first paragraph, headings, italicized words, graphs, tables, and last paragraph. That's how it works.

Surveying as a Reading Expeditor

One important use for surveying is to facilitate your reading. Think back to what happened when you surveyed this chapter. You caught the essentials and the writer's plan.

In planning a car trip, you normally get out maps to see exactly what route to travel. Reading an article without an overview is much like traveling a strange highway. You don't know what towns or cities to expect or what intersections or junctions to note. Surveying serves as a road map. Obviously, when you know the road even slightly, you travel it more confidently and easily. So it is with reading. When you know in general where the writer is going, you can follow more easily.

In short, surveying should actually increase your subsequent reading speed. After all, you're traveling a more familiar road. It should also improve comprehension. You have the advantage of double coverage of key parts. Use surveying, then, as a prereading step, to gain added speed and comprehension.

Surveying as a Decision Expeditor

Still another use for surveying focuses on an age-old problem. Sir Francis Bacon put it this way. "Some books are to be tasted, others to be swallowed, and some few to be chewed and digested." Unfortunately, Bacon left the heart of the problem untouched. How do you decide which books belong where? Well, who knows your own personal background, interests, problems, and specific needs best? You yourself, of course. Yet, how can you tell, before you read a book, exactly what attention it deserves?

Surveying is your answer. A quick survey provides an ideal basis for deciding intelligently whether to taste, swallow, or chew and digest.

Actually, you have four possibilities—to skip, skim, read, or study. Suppose your initial survey reveals no information of interest. Well, you've already given it all the attention it deserves. Put it aside. Remember—that decision was not made blindly. You know what's there.

If the material seems more pertinent, put it into the next category. Skim it. Skimming takes much less time than reading yet brings more information than surveying. The third choice is to read it. Do this with material deserving even more attention. Finally, it may be so important as to deserve careful study. Many make the mistake of trying to read almost everything—an impossible task. Only after reading an entire book do they realize it was a waste of time.

To remember these choices, put them into a formula—the _SD4 Formula_. You _Survey_ in order to _Decide_ which of _4_ things to do—_skip, skim, read,_ or _study_.

To summarize, surveying lets you apportion to each article or book precisely the time it deserves—no more, no less. Furthermore, that decision is solidly based on evidence gained in a minimum of your precious time.

Here's your first superspeed. Let it help you read more rapidly, comprehend better, and decide more intelligently what attention you should give to all the reading material around you. Put it to immediate use.

Reading Time: _____
See Conversion Table.
Enter WPM Rate on the Progress Record Chart.

13 Speeding by Surveying

COMPREHENSION CHECK

1. Surveying is said to be about how many times faster
   than ordinary reading? (a) 5 to 8 times, (b) 20 to 30
   times, (c) 10 to 50 times, (d) not specifically mentioned.

   1. ___

2. Mention is made of a (a) 10-speed bicycle, (b) racing
   car, (c) turtle, (d) one-speed car.

   2. ___

3. To survey, you read (a) every other paragraph, (b) the
   first paragraph, (c) no paragraph completely, (d) all
   paragraphs in part.

   3. ___

4. Specific reference is made to (a) italicized words,
   (b) headings, (c) graphs and tables, (d) all the
   preceding.

   4. ___

5. You are told how to survey a (a) letter, (b) book,
   (c) report, (d) summary.

   5. ___

6. Reference is made to (a) road maps, (b) patterns,
   (c) recipes, (d) guidelines.

   6. ___

7. Specific reference is made to (a) William Shakespeare,
   (b) Francis Bacon, (c) Alexander Pope, (d) the Bible.

   7. ___

8. After the quick survey, how many choices are mentioned? (a) one, (b) two, (c) three, (d) four.

   8. ___

9. What does the *D* in SD4 stand for? (a) determine,
   (b) demand, (c) decide, (d) describe.

   9 ___

10. What is the first choice mentioned? (a) study,
    (b) select, (c) skip, (d) save.

    10. ___

10 Off for Each Mistake.
Comprehension Score: _____
Answer Key in Appendix.
Enter the Results on the Progress Record Chart.

Making the Application

You know in theory, now, exactly how to survey an article. But that is only a beginning. How do you move effectively from theory to practice? How do you make yourself a superb surveyor? Try these three steps.

One: Using a colored felt-tip pen, turn back to the selection you just read—"Speeding by Surveying." Underline in color all the underlined words. This provides a much clearer visualization of what is read in a survey, thus reinforcing the pattern to be used.

Two: Now turn immediately to a chapter in a textbook or to an explanatory article. Again, using your felt-tip colored pen, underline the portions to be read in surveying the material.

Three: This last step is the pay-off and is of most importance, deserving special attention and thought. How well can you read between the paragraphs and headings? How accurately can you arrive at conclusions about the unread portions? Here's where practice and experience will pay off to best advantage.

You will find it helpful to use a heading like this to provide the proper mental set: *Assumptions about the content of the unread portions.* Under that general heading, list from four to six assumptions based on your survey.

Repeat these steps often enough to become a genuinely skilled surveyor. You will soon see that this view down the road ahead makes any subsequent reading that much easier. Use surveying frequently.

Your LDE Formula

Can you get meanings for strange words or word parts without your dictionary? Certainly! It's just a matter of harnessing brain power to word power and applying the LDE Formula. Here's how it works.

Take the strange Latin word *omnis*, which gives us the prefix *omni-*. What does it mean? You don't know? You've never taken Latin? When dealing with words, never say, "I don't know." That shuts the door to important vocabulary growth. You probably do know, but just don't know that you do. Think again. What's an omnidirectional radio receiver? One that receives sound waves from all directions, you say. Now if you know that, you really know what *omni-* means. It means "all."

That kind of reasoning lies behind the LDE Formula. Your first step when meeting a strange prefix, root, or suffix is to LIST several words containing that element. With *omni-*, let's say you listed *omnidirectional* and *omnipotent*. Maybe that's all you thought of. Or perhaps you also listed *omnipresent* and *omniscient*. You don't necessarily need that many. Sometimes one word is enough, although usually the more the better. That's step one of the formula: LIST.

The second step? DEFINE each word you listed. Let's say you define *omnidirectional* as "in all directions," *omnipotent* as "all-powerful," *omnipresent* as "always present," and *omniscient* as "all-knowing." That's step two: DEFINE.

The third and last step is to EXTRACT the common denominator or meaning. What do the *omni-* words have in common? The meaning "all"! The formula made you aware of that meaning. From now on when you see a word beginning *omni-*, look for that meaning. An omnivorous reader has to be a reader of "all" kinds of things.

That's how the three-step LDE Formula works. It's not only three-step, it's also three-way—to be used with all three kinds of word parts: prefixes, roots, and suffixes. Furthermore, if one word part can be a shortcut to the meanings of over a thousand words, this formula deserves the label *super-shortcut*, for it works with all elements. You'll be more than pleased with the way it speeds your vocabulary growth, not one word at a time but up to a thousand.

That doesn't mean you'll always arrive at the right meaning, but you should always be closer. Even if the formula works only 70 percent of the time, that gives you a 70 percent advantage over those who don't apply it—an advantage well worth having.

(To develop added skill with the formula, do the exercise on page 143.)

14 My Greatest Adventure

WORD POWER WORKOUT

A. Leaning on Context

In each of the blanks provided, place the letter that precedes the best definition of the underlined word in context to the left.

Words in Context	Definitions
1. ___ I <u>embarked</u> on	a. support
2. ___ into the wedded <u>abyss</u>	b. tendency
3. ___ trying to <u>sustain</u>	c. trying out
4. ___ no more <u>alluring</u>	d. kind of kale
5. ___ my <u>instinct</u> was	e. started
6. ___ let us now <u>set forth</u>	f. kinds
7. ___ what <u>patronizing</u> nonsense	g. condescending
8. ___ is <u>auditioning</u> for the	h. profound depth
9. ___ only <u>collard</u> greens	i. highly attractive
10. ___ belong to different <u>species</u>	j. state

Check your answers with the Key before going on. Review any that you have missed.

Pronunciation aids: 2. uh bis!

KEY: add, āce; end, ēven; it, īce; odd, ōpen; pōol; up.

B. Leaning on Parts

The Greek prefix *epi-* means "upon." Supply the appropriate word or word part relating to that prefix in each of the following sentences.

1. A commemorative inscription upon a tomb is an epi_____.

2. The outer or upon layer of your skin is called the epi_____.

3. A nervous disorder characterized by convulsions is called epi_____.

4. A rapidly spreading disease is often spoken of as an epi_____.

5. The epilogue contained comments _____ the meaning of the play.

C. Making the Words Yours

In each blank below, enter the most appropriate word from the ten words in context in the first exercise, substituting it for the word(s) in parentheses. Use these words: *abyss, alluring, auditioning, collard, embarked, instinct, patronizing, species, state, sustain.*

1. That actress really deserves to be called (highly attractive) _____.

2. You don't have to take that (condescending) _____ down-the-nose look.

3. Here's news to (support) _____ you in this time of grief.

4. Are you (trying out) _____ for a part in the new play?

5. Some people have a natural (tendency) _____ for doing the right thing.

6. In this climate you need different (kinds) _____ of plants.

7. That was the year I (started) _____ on a totally new career.

8. They stared into the (profound depths) _____ in awe.

9. Let me (set forth) _____ exactly what is required.

10. You can have either a lettuce salad or (kind of kale) _____ greens.

4 Off for Each Mistake.
Word Power Score: _____
Answer Key in Appendix.

14

My Greatest Adventure

Bill Cosby

A wedding ring was first used in Egypt around 2800 B.C. To the Egyptians a circle—a ring—signified eternity for it had no beginning or end. When you think of the ring symbol, how long should a marriage last? For eternity! Look in on one famous adventuresome couple.

Begin Timing

And so, Camille and I embarked on the greatest adventure of all: a man and a woman daring to plunge into the wedded abyss and spend their entire lives together. If the amusement park called Great Adventure had been created by me, it would have no slides or rides: it would simply have one married couple trying to sustain the glow of their love while the wife gave the husband's favorite suits to the Salvation Army. For the last twenty-five years, since a certain wedding in Olney, Maryland, in 1964, the Salvation Army has been fighting Satan not only with the cross of Jesus but the cream of my coats and pants.

When I got married, one of the many things I didn't know was that Camille would grow tired of looking at some of my suits, even two I hadn't worn; but I loved her so much that I didn't mind her secretly recycling my wardrobe. I rejoiced that I now was married to the most beautiful woman I had ever seen, a woman who suddenly made Jane Russell no more alluring to me than Nipsey. My instinct was to break the rules of marriage and be honest with her about everything. I quickly realized, however, that even the deepest love doesn't stop a marriage from being a constant struggle for control. Any husband who says, "My wife and I are completely equal partners" is talking either about a law firm or a hand of bridge.

Yes, let us now set forth one of the fundamental truths about marriage: the wife is in charge. Or, to put it another way, the husband is not. Now I can hear your voices crying out:

What patronizing nonsense.
What a dumb generalization.
What a great jacket for the Salvation Army.

Well, my proof of the point is a simple one. If any man truly believes that he is the boss of his house, then let him do this: pick up the phone, call a wallpaper store, order new wallpaper for one of the rooms in his house, and then put it on. He would have a longer life expectancy sprinkling arsenic on his eggs. Any husband who buys wallpaper, drapes, or even a prayer rug on his own is auditioning for the Bureau of Missing Persons.

Therefore, in spite of what Thomas Jefferson wrote, all men may be created equal, but not to all women, and the loveliest love affair must bear the strain of this inequality once the ceremony is over. When a husband and wife settle down together, there is a natural struggle for power (I wonder why he bothers); and in this struggle, the husband cannot avoid giving up a few things—for example, dinner.

To be fair, I must admit that Camille did wait a few years before allowing me to make this particular sacrifice. I had just sat down at the table one night with her and our three children when I happened to notice that my plate contained only collard greens and brown rice.

"Would you please donate this to the Hare Krishna and bring me my real meal," I said to the gentleman serving the food.

"You have it all," he replied.

"No, what I have is a snack for the North Korean Army. The meat must have slipped off somewhere. Why don't we try to find it together?"

"Mrs. Cosby said we are no longer eating meat."

"She *did*?" I looked down the table at Camille. "Dear, if I got a letter from the Pope, do you think I could—"

"Bill, meat is bad for us and we just have to cut it out. It's full of fat that could kill you. I'm sorry I forgot to tell you."

"So am I. I could've started eating out at a place where they don't mind who they kill."

"Honey, *lots* of people are vegetarians."

"And lots of people like to get hit with whips, but I've managed to be happy not joining them."

Nevertheless, I became a vegetarian. A husband should go with the flow of his marriage, even when that flow leads over a cliff.

About two years later, however, I sat down to dinner one night and a steak suddenly appeared on my plate.

"Look at this," I said to the gentleman serving the food. "Someone has lost a steak. Would you please return it to its owner."

"Mrs. Cosby said we are eating meat again," he told me.

"How nice to see the cows come home," I said.

The unexpected return of the cows that night taught me an important lesson about marriage: just when you think you know all there is to know about your mate, just when you think you have enough to begin the divorce, something new pops up to bewilder you, for men and women belong to different species and communication between them is a science still in its infancy.

Reading Time: _____
See Conversion Table.
Enter WPM Rate on the Progress Record Chart.

14 My Greatest Adventure

COMPREHENSION CHECK

1. Cosby's wife is named (a) Carmen, (b) Camille,   1. ___
   (c) Carol, (d) Carrie.

2. When did the marriage take place? (a) in 1960, (b) in   2. ___
   1962, (c) in 1964, (d) in 1968.

3. Cosby's wife gave away how many suits Bill hadn't even   3. ___
   worn? (a) none (b) one, (c) two, (d) three.

4. There was mention of (a) Jane Russell, (b) Dorothy La-   4. ___
   mour, (c) Betty Grable, (d) Lana Turner.

5. Cosby tries to prove that man isn't boss in his own home   5. ___
   by suggesting he order new (a) furniture, (b) wallpaper,
   (c) wall paint, (d) kitchen cabinets.

6. Cosby quotes (a) Benjamin Franklin, (b) George Wash-   6. ___
   ington, (c) Abraham Lincoln, (d) Thomas Jefferson.

7. How many children do the Cosbys have? (a) none,   7. ___
   (b) only one, (c) two, (d) three.

8. What was on Cosby's plate one night? (a) collard greens   8. ___
   and brown rice, (b) beans and mashed potatoes, (c) peas
   and macaroni, (d) lettuce and chicken breast.

9. How long did the steakless regime last? (a) less than a   9 ___
   year, (b) about a year, (c) about two years, (d) time not
   mentioned.

10. Communication between the sexes was called a science   10. ___
    (a) still in its infancy, (b) never to be mastered,
    (c) always changing, (d) impossible to understand.

10 Off for Each Mistake.
Comprehension Score: _____
Answer Key in Appendix.
Enter the Results on the Progress Record Chart.

15 Are You Different?

WORD POWER WORKOUT

A. Leaning on Context

In each of the blanks provided, place the letter that precedes the best definition of the underlined word in context to the left.

Words in Context	Definitions
1. ___ identical <u>genetic</u> structures	a. cautious, on guard
2. ___ all are <u>unique</u>	b. cruelty
3. ___ follow the <u>fads</u>	c. origin and growth
4. ___ are extroverted, <u>affable</u>	d. one of a kind
5. ___ introverted, <u>wary</u>	e. show clearly
6. ___ some of your <u>aspirations</u>	f. agreeable, pleasant
7. ___ our subjects <u>demonstrate</u>	g. passing fashions
8. ___ with <u>anxiety</u>	h. desires
9. ___ had <u>neurotic</u> symptoms	i. uneasiness
10. ___ withdrawal, coldness, <u>sadism</u>	j. maladjusted personality

---

Check your answers with the Key before going on. Review any that you have missed.

Pronunciation aids: 2. yōo nĕk´;10. sā´ diz um.

KEY: add, āce; end, ēven; it, īce; odd, ōpen; pōol; up.

B. Leaning on Parts

The prefix *mis-* means "wrong" or "wrongly." Supply the missing word or word part in each of the following sentences.

1. Wrong behavior is, of course, mis_____ .

2. To lead you in the wrong direction is to mis_____ you.

3. They laughed when they heard you mis_____ the speaker's name.

4. I can't find my billfold; I must have mis_____ it somewhere.

5. An act of misfeasance is an act of _____ doing.

C. Making the Words Yours

In each blank below, enter the most appropriate word from the ten words in context in the first exercise, substituting it for the word(s) in parentheses. Use these words: *affable, anxiety, aspirations, demonstrate, fads, genetic, neurotic, sadism, unique, wary.*

1. You have to be (cautious, on guard) _____ about some proposals.

2. Without strong (desires) _____ people tend to drift through life aimlessly.

3. The salesman offered me a (one of kind) _____ opportunity to save.

4. The exact (origin and growth) _____ makeup of the creature is yet to be determined.

5. Who can keep up with the current clothing (passing fashions) _____!

6. Some of your friends are probably known for their (agreeable, pleasant) _____ nature.

7. The growing tensions put everyone into a state of great (uneasiness) _____ .

8. Can you (show clearly) _____ exactly what needs to be done?

9. The last act of terrorism showed extreme (cruelty) _____ .

10. Psychiatrists provide the help needed to deal with (maladjusted personality) _____ problems.

4 Off for Each Mistake.
Word Power Score: _____
Answer Key in Appendix.

15

Are You Different?

Morris K. Holland

John Newbern divided people into three groups—"those who make things happen, those who watch things happen, and those who wonder what happened." Mae West said she liked only two kinds of men—"domestic and foreign." Differences do make interesting reading. Are you different?

Begin Timing

No two people are alike. Even twins from the same egg, with identical genetic structures, are different as a consequence of differences in their experiences. In the English language there are more than 1,000 words to describe individual differences in personality. The number of combinations possible of those thousand words, according to one estimate, exceeds by far the total number of atoms in the universe! The possible varieties of personality are equally numerous.

What does being different mean for you? Your body, your needs, your memories, your thoughts, your personality—all are unique. There has never been someone like you, there is no one quite like you now in the world, and there never will be. Your individuality does not make you worse or better than anyone else: everybody is in the same boat.

Try *feeling* your difference. Imagine that your eyes were orange and you had green spots on your nose and you were the tallest person in the world. How would you feel at a party?

Why does being different, or even the thought of being different, cause so much worry? Imagine looking the way you look right now in a world where everybody else was eight feet tall with orange eyes and green spots on their noses. You might feel like painting green spots on your nose to hide your difference. Even now, at this moment, you are trying not to be different. The clothes you wear, to some extent, follow the fads or fashion of the day for your age group. Why, in fact, are you wearing clothes at all? We seem to have a basic desire not to stand out in the crowd, not to be very different. There is security in joining the crowd, but there is something lost, too: the possibility to be truly yourself, to be entirely free. Suppose you did not try to cover up the ways you were different from other people; suppose you did not hide your differences in body, feelings, desires, thoughts, and personality. Would you still be normal?

Have you ever wondered whether certain of your thoughts, feelings, or behaviors were normal or not? Perhaps you have feared that in some ways you are not normal. Deciding whether you or someone else is normal is not at all easy to do. Here is a personality description of an individual written by a psychologist. Would you say that the person described here is normal or abnormal?

> You have a strong need for other people to like you and for them to admire you. You have a tendency to be critical of yourself. . . . Your sexual adjustment has presented some problems for you. Disciplined and controlled on the outside, you tend to be worrisome and insecure inside. At times you have serious doubts as to whether you have made the right decision or done the right thing. . . . You have found it unwise to be too frank in revealing yourself to others. At times you are extroverted, affable, sociable, while at other times you are introverted, wary, and reserved. Some of your aspirations tend to be pretty unrealistic.

What kind of person has just been described? Is it possible for a person who has those kinds of problems to be a *normal person*? The description was invented by a psychologist, then given to college students. Surprisingly, a survey showed that over 90 percent of the college students rated the personality description given as a "good" or "excellent" interpretation of their own individual personalities. Some of the comments made by the students were: "I agree with almost all your statements and think they answer the problems I may have"; "On the nose! True without a doubt"; "This interpretation applies to me individually"; "Unbelievably close to the truth." Almost all of the students accepted the *same* statement as a description of themselves.

"Normal" does not mean "having no problems." Everybody has problems that worry them to some extent. The typical student in high school or college has doubts and worries about physical attractiveness, ability to love and be loved, the control of anger, the sex drive, and sexual behavior. The secret fears we all have are, remarkably enough, very similar; what you fear and what I fear are not that different. Many of the weaknesses you see in yourself are felt by almost everyone else; your feelings of guilt or shame about the things you have done are felt by almost everyone, for almost everyone has done the things you have done.

What is the normal person like? Psychologists who have tried to study the normal person can't agree among themselves. One psychologist, after studying seventy young persons selected because of their normality, concluded: "The vast majority of our subjects exhibit some anxiety about sexual role function. . . . Our subjects demonstrate specific struggles with anxiety, depression, shame, and guilt." Another psychologist selected 50 men from over 1,900 men on the basis of their being "most normal." His testing of them showed that over 50 percent of them had neurotic symptoms, although the disorders were mild. The elected student councils from three colleges were tested in another study. One college president commented, "It is as normal a group as you'll ever get." The psychologist found that some of the "normal" students had alarming problems, such as extreme depression, withdrawal, coldness, sadism, and other symptoms of neurosis. He concluded that 57 percent could benefit from mental health services and 14 percent urgently needed psychiatric care. Obviously, being normal does not mean being without problems.

Reading Time: _____
See Conversion Table.
Enter WPM Rate on the Progress Record Chart.

15 Are You Different?

COMPREHENSION CHECK

1. You are told that (a) no two people are alike,
   (b) only twins are alike, (c) almost all people are
   different, (d) only identical twins are alike.   1. ___

2. About how many words in the English language describe personality differences? (a) 400, (b) 600,
   (c) 800, (d) 1,000.   2. ___

3. A comparison was made with the total number of atoms
   (a) in the moon, (b) in our planet, (c) in our solar
   system, (d) in the universe.   3. ___

4. You were asked to imagine your nose had (a) orange
   spots, (b) yellow spots, (c) green spots, (d) red spots.   4. ___

5. You were asked why you (a) fixed your hair as you
   do, (b) wore clothes, (c) said "hello" as a greeting,
   (d) slept at night.   5. ___

6. The quoted personality description specifically mentioned (a) a tendency to be self-critical, (b) a feel-
   ling of insecurity inside, (c) having unrealistic aspirations, (d) all the preceding.   6. ___

7. About what percentage of the college students thought
   the description fitted their own personality? (a) 100%,
   (b) 90%, (c) 80%, (d) 70%.   7. ___

8. One study of 70 normal young people concluded that
   the sexual role function bothered (a) 40%, (b) 60%,
   (c) 80%, (d) a vast majority.   8. ___

9. Another study was done of (a) honor students, (b) elected
   student councils, (c) students on probation, (d) scholarship students.   9 ___

10. What percentage of the students in that study urgently
    needed psychiatric care? (a) 14%, (b) 33%, (c) 46%,
    (d) 57%.   10. ___

10 Off for Each Mistake.
Comprehension Score: _____
Answer Key in Appendix.
Enter the Results on the Progress Record Chart.

16 Speeding by Skimming

WORD POWER WORKOUT

A. Leaning on Context

In each of the blanks provided, place the letter that precedes the best definition of the underlined word in context to the left.

Words in Context	Definitions
1. ___ to your <u>repertoire</u>	a. take
2. ___ <u>reiterates</u> the topic idea	b. range of skills
3. ___ skip completely <u>intervening</u> paragraphs	c. preference
4. ___ effectively <u>counteract</u> an hour of slow reading	d. surface, limited
5. ___ improve learning <u>productivity</u>	e. repeats
6. ___ develop such <u>exceptional</u> skill	f. offset, change
7. ___ <u>cultivate</u> different skimming patterns	g. abundant or favorable production
8. ___ <u>snatch</u> the key words	h. coming between
9. ___ <u>superficial</u> careless reading	i. outstanding, excellent
10. ___ give this pattern top <u>priority</u>	j. form, refine

---

Check your answers with the Key before going on. Review any that you have missed.

Pronunciation aids: 1. rep'ur twahr; 2. rē it'uh rāts; 3. in tur vēn'ing; 9. soo pur fish'ul; 10. prī or'uh tē.

KEY: add, āce; end, ēven; it, īce; odd, ōpen; pool; up.

B. Leaning on Parts

The prefix *com-* (also written *col-*, *cor-*, *con-* or *co-*) means "together or with." Supply the missing part in each of the following blanks.

1. Pressing leaves together makes a more com_____ pile.

2. A person traveling with you is called a traveling com_____.

3. To com_____ two things more easily, put them side by side.

4. Salt, composed as it is of two elements, is a chemical com_____.

5. A compromise is sometimes necessary to bring two sides _____.

C. Making the Words Yours

In each blank below, enter the most appropriate word from the ten words in context in the first exercise, substituting it for the word(s) in parentheses. Use these words: *counteract, cultivated, exceptional, intervening, priority, productivity, reiterate, repertoire, snatched, superficial.*

1. In a year of wide reading he (formed) _____ many new interests.

2. His top (preference) _____ was college.

3. Both classical and rock music were within his (range of skills) _____.

4. Often a boxer's desire to win will (offset) _____ physical disadvantages.

5. The paragraphs (coming between) _____ need not be read.

6. A (limited) _____ knowledge could be dangerous.

7. High-grade seed and fertile land are important factors for (favorable production) _____.

8. (Repeat) _____ your point if you want people to remember it.

9. The third baseman (took) _____ the ball from the ground and threw it home.

10. He was termed an (excellent) _____ student.

4 Off for Each Mistake.
Word Power Score: _____
Answer Key in Appendix.

16

Speeding by Skimming

It's time now to add a second superspeed to your repertoire. *Skimming*. This technique speeds you through print at three to five times your usual reading speed. The secret? Paragraph structure.

A paragraph is a paragraph because it explains or develops *one* single idea. When you're served a big, juicy T-bone steak, you normally concentrate on the meat—not the bone, fat, or gristle. Similarly, skimming concentrates your attention on the meat of the paragraph—the important part, the essentials.

How Do You Skim?

Let's see how skimming works. Try it on the next paragraph. Instead of reading it as usual, word by word, read *only* the underlined parts. Skip the other two-thirds.

How exactly do you get paragraph meaning without reading the paragraph? You use skimming. Fortunately, 55 to 85 percent of the paragraphs you read are expository. They explain. Most textbooks are, of course, expository in nature. They explain such things as a theory, process, procedure, technique, development, or situation. From 60 to 90 percent of such paragraphs have the topic sentence first. The next most likely spot is the last sentence. And if the last sentence is not the topic sentence, more often than not it summarizes or reiterates the topic idea. In between the first and last sentences you'll normally find key words or phrases that expand, clarify, or further support the main idea. Capitalize on these common paragraph characteristics and get the heart of the paragraph without reading it word by word.

That's how you skim a single, fairly long paragraph. You read the first and last sentences and snatch the key words in between. Done properly, skimming is a far cry from superficial, careless reading. It is a careful reading of selected parts. Based on characteristics common to written communication, it helps you zero in on essentials.

But what about skimming an entire article or chapter? To do that, just add paragraph skimming to the survey technique that you already know. You remember how. You read the title, first paragraph, subheadings, tables, graphs, italicized words, and the last paragraph. You skip completely all the intervening paragraphs.

To skim an *entire article*, you don't skip a single paragraph. That's the difference. You skim all paragraphs except the first and last, which you read.

Two Skimming Patterns

Actually, you should cultivate two somewhat different skimming patterns to match the two common styles of writing—formal and informal.

The formal style, typical of most textbooks, is characterized by such things as long paragraphs, involved sentences, and few personal pronouns. The specially marked paragraph above, containing over 130 words, is closer to the formal style in length. With such paragraphs, read both first and last sentences, plus key words. You're still reading less than a third of the paragraph.

For more informal writing, such as in this text, with its shorter paragraphs, read only the first sentence and, possibly, key words. Even for the longer paragraphs, you may want to give this pattern top priority. It will usually give you the essentials. Furthermore, it is an easier and faster pattern to apply.

Skimming—Your Reading Substitute

Take this situation. You've surveyed an article. You feel it doesn't merit reading but seems too important to discard. That's when you need skimming. That kind of in-between coverage serves ideally as a reading substitute.

Remember also that skimming skills vary widely. You may develop such exceptional skill in skimming that you can actually skim an article at 2,000 wpm and get more out of it than an average or poor reader, plodding along at 200 wpm. So, in deciding when to skim and when to read, keep your own level of skill development in mind.

Skimming—Your Reading Speed Generator

Here you are—working to improve reading ability. Perhaps you practice rapid reading thirty minutes every day, conscientiously. But you may also be reading other things more slowly for two hours daily. You're practicing slow reading more than rapid reading. Progress is bound to suffer. How can this be avoided?

If you want to teeter-totter with a thirty-pound youngster, yet weigh four times more, what do you do? That's easy. You sit closer to the fulcrum, where you can both balance perfectly. Similarly, why not use skimming to balance the slowing pull of normal reading. Ten minutes of skimming should effectively counteract an hour of slower reading.

Let's look at one specific way to insure frequent use of skimming. Suppose you're going to read an important 4,000-word article. Reading it at 200 wpm will take exactly twenty minutes. Here's how to introduce skimming without taking any additional time. Skim the article first at 1,000 wpm, a four-minute task. Then read the article once at 250 wpm, a sixteen-minute task. Four plus sixteen equals twenty minutes.

That skim-read combination takes no more time than one slightly slower reading. But it has two advantages. First, comprehension should be better; second, reading rate should be improved.

Skimming—Your Review Aid

Make skimming serve still a third function. When you open a psych text and spot the Ebbinghaus curve of forgetting, you're bound to feel discouraged. His research indicates that thirty minutes after you've barely learned something, you will have forgotten half of it. In eight hours, two-thirds will be gone.

Take a typical situation—a test over three chapters of chemistry. Last night you studied them and felt rather well prepared. But here it is—fourteen hours later. When you start the test you soon realize how much you have forgotten.

This suggests another important use of skimming. In a free hour just before the test, skim all three chapters. You haven't time to read them, but you have plenty of time to skim them. Now as you take the test, you should notice greatly improved sureness and confidence—and improved grades.

So—begin now. Develop added skimming skill. Be sure to make skimming a daily activity. Use it (1) to reduce your reading load, (2) to generate added speed, and (3) to improve learning productivity.

Reading Time: _____
See Conversion Table.
Enter WPM Rate on the Progress Record Chart.

16 Speeding by Skimming

COMPREHENSION CHECK

1. The secret of skimming lies in (a) paragraph structure, (b) sentence structure, (c) outlining, (d) word usage.

   1. ___

2. Skimming lets you cover print how many times faster than usual? (a) two to three, (b) three to five, (c) four to eight, (d) not specifically mentioned.

   2. ___

3. The most common paragraphs you read are (a) expository, (b) narrative, (c) persuasive, (d) descriptive.

   3. ___

4. In skimming, what part of a paragraph do you read? (a) no sentence in entirety, (b) both first and last sentences, (c) first sentence only, (d) last sentence only.

   4. ___

5. To skim an article, you (a) skip every other paragraph, (b) skim every paragraph, (c) skim all but the first and last paragraphs, (d) skip all but the first and last paragraphs.

   5. ___

6. Skimming is spoken of as a reading (a) refresher, (b) stimulus, (c) supplement, (d) substitute.

   6. ___

7. One illustration involves a (a) pair of scales, (b) teeter-totter, (c) balloon, (d) fishing line.

   7. ___

8. In reading an important 4,000-word article, it is suggested that you (a) read it once at 200 wpm, (b) read it once at 250 wpm, (c) skim it first, then read it, (d) read it first, then skim it.

   8. ___

9. The part about forgetting indicates that we forget how much in the first 30 minutes after learning something? (a) 15%, (b) 30%, (c) 42%, (d) half.

   9. ___

10. Specific mention is made of (a) improving grades, (b) taking tests, (c) taking chemistry, (d) all the preceding.

   10. ___

10 Off for Each Mistake.
Comprehension Score: _____
Answer Key in Appendix.
Enter the Results on the Progress Record Chart.

Making the Application

This is the time to compare surveying, skimming, and reading to sharpen your awareness of the role each technique should play. For example, see what you can get from surveying a selection. Here's what you read:

Surveying

Title	Women in Management
First paragraph	Women managers can expect to confront a number of barriers as they struggle up the corporate ladder. Several surveys of female managers in all types of industries show that the one obstacle standing out above all others is male prejudice.
Headings	Stereotypes Family Demands Age Discrepancies Pay Differential A Look to the Future
Last paragraph	Most female managers plan to continue their climb up the corporate ladder. Younger female managers will find a more favorable environment than their predecessors simply because their presence has been accepted. Surveys conducted to assess the opportunities for female managers in the future reveal that the opportunities are increasing. In one survey, 75% of the respondents stated that they believed the opportunities for women starting out today are better than they have ever been. Even so, the road will be bumpy. Unfortunately, perhaps the best advice that could be offered is that given by a lower-level female bank executive: "Work twice as hard and three times as long as a man in the same position."

What kind of overview do you have? What would you infer is said between the first and last paragraphs, based on the sketchy information you have? That is the mental process you go through to make surveying the effective aid it should be.

Skimming

Now see what you get from skimming the same selection. Use the pattern most useful with informal writing, reading only the first sentence of each paragraph.

Title	Women in Management
First paragraph	(Reread the first paragraph as printed under the *Surveying* heading, then read the following first sentences.)
First sentence of all following paragraphs up to the last paragraph	Actually, such prejudice is manifested in a number of ways.
	But men can prove helpful to women in their careers, too.
	Contrary to popular belief, female managers do not view family responsibilities and a lack of formal education as major stumbling blocks.
	Older female managers are finding that working under the supervision of younger female managers can be particularly frustrating.
	Today, nearly 1.5 million women under the age of thirty-five hold managerial jobs, up from 322,000 in the early 1970s.
	Older women tend to be deferential with coworkers and maternal with supervisors.
	On the average, women earn about two-thirds of what men do for similar work.
	For years, women struggled to achieve "equal pay for equal work."
	Most employers insist that their salary programs are already fair and equitable and that federal law does not apply to "comparable" jobs.
	Fearful that the government will ultimately require equal pay for comparable work, some firms are beginning to devise their own comparable work plans.
	Although female managers will be required to overcome a host of barriers as they pursue their corporate careers, the payoffs appear to justify the effort.

Last **paragraph**	(Now reread the last paragraph as printed under the *Surveying* heading.

Now turn to page 304 and take the usual ten-item comprehension test. Do not check your answers, however. You just want to see exactly how much you get out of surveying and skimming an article. When you have finished the test, then turn to page 301 and read the selection as usual, timing yourself and taking the same test over again. This will let you compare the comprehension you've been getting from one reading with that from surveying and skimming. Also notice your wpm rate for the reading. Most students find that they tend to read material faster after skimming it than when just reading it. In short, the time you invest in skimming may be repaid wholly or in part by the faster reading you do after skimming.

17 Lincoln at Gettysburg

WORD POWER WORKOUT

A. Leaning on Context

In each of the blanks provided, place the letter that precedes the best defini-tion of the underlined word in context to the left.

Words in Context	Definitions
1. ___ the thick <u>pamphlet</u>	a. sang
2. ___ flag hung <u>listlessly</u>	b. equipment
3. ___ on a <u>sorrel</u> horse	c. lifelessly
4. ___ like some huge <u>effigy</u>	d. booklet
5. ___ looked <u>sublimely</u> sloppy	e. countless number
6. ___ <u>premier</u> was blithely indifferent	f. image, likeness
7. ___ <u>myriad</u> of New England points	g. reddish brown
8. ___ Glee Club <u>intoned</u> a hymn	h. chief officer
9. ___ with his <u>paraphernalia</u>	i. unconsciously
10. ___ Seward nodded <u>inadvertently</u>	j. blissfully

Check your answers with the Key before going on. Review any that you have missed.

Pronunciation aids: 4. ef'i jē; 9. par'uh fer nāl'yuh.

KEY: add, āce; end, ēven; it, īce; odd, ōpen; p͞ool; up.

B. Leaning on Parts

Supply the missing part in the following sentences. Note also how the meaning of *in-* (also spelled *il-*, *ir-*, or *im-*) relates to word meanings.

1. One who is not dependent is in_____.

2. One who is not capable of doing something is in_____.

3. A situation that is not formal is in_____.

4. If you do not like the direct route, try the in_____.

5. Someone who is insufferable is _____ sufferable.

C. Making the Words Yours

In each blank below, enter the most appropriate word from the ten words in context in the first exercise, substituting it for the word(s) in parentheses. Use these words: *effigy, inadvertently, intoned, listlessly, myriad, pamphlet, paraphernalia, premier, sorrel, sublimely.*

1. During the demonstration the crowd burned the dictator in (image, likeness) _____.

2. The (countless number) _____ of stars sprinkled the sky.

3. The cowboy's favorite mount was his (reddish brown) _____ horse.

4. It took some time to set up all the recording (equipment) _____ to telecast the ceremony.

5. The promoters got out a special (booklet) _____ to publicize the big event.

6. At the reception both bride and groom looked (blissfully) _____ happy.

7. The big banner hung (lifelessly) _____ above the bleachers.

8. The (chief officer) _____ of the country stepped up to the rostrum.

9. A mixed chorus (sang) _____ before the main event.

10. One student (unconsciously) _____ went to sleep during the important lecture.

4 Off for Each Mistake.
Word Power Score: _____
Answer Key in Appendix.

17

Lincoln at Gettysburg

Gore Vidal

*Perhaps the most famous speech ever made dates back well over
a hundred years. That means no one alive today heard it. But—
let Gore Vidal transport you right to Gettysburg. Listen to the
speech yourself. It's a most important part of our cultural
literacy—"What Every American Needs to Know."*

Begin Timing

The morning of November 19, 1863, was warm and still. Indian summer
had set in. The celebrated old orator Edward Everett had already sent the
President a printed copy of his speech. "My God, John!" Lincoln had said,
as he sat in the special railroad car. "He will speak for two hours." Lincoln
had handed the thick pamphlet to Hay; and taken off his glasses.

"I suppose that is what he's always expected to do." Hay had decided
not to read what he would be obliged to hear.

"A splendid old man." Lincoln had held in one hand a single sheet of
White House notepaper on which he had written half of what would be, he
said, "a short, short, short speech," dedicating the cemetery. "You know, I
have heard of Everett all my life, and he has always been famous, and yet I
never could find out why."

"Our greatest orator?"

"Greater than Clay or Webster?" Lincoln had smiled. "No, he is just
famous, that's all. There are people like that in public life. They are there,
and no one ever really knows why."

They were all there the next morning on Cemetery Hill. There were
seven governors, among them Seymour and Curtin; many diplomats and
members of Congress. A platform had been erected, with a tall flagpole
next to it. In the warm stillness, the flag hung listlessly. A military band
played. A crowd of some thirty thousand people had already gathered
when, finally, at ten o'clock, the presidential procession came into view,
and the military band struck up "Hail to the Chief."

Lincoln rode at the head of the ragged column of notables. He sat
very straight on a sorrel horse too small for him. He was like some huge

effigy, thought Hay, who rode with Nico behind him. It was odd that the biggest man in the country should also be among the very biggest—or at least tallest—of men. Seward looked sublimely sloppy at the Tycoon's side. Trousers pulled up to reveal thick, wrinkled gray stockings, the premier was blithely indifferent to how he or anyone else looked.

Earlier that morning, Nico had gone to the house where the President had spent the night; and he had stayed alone with the Tycoon for an hour. "What news?" asked Hay. The procession was now stopped by crowds singing, "We are coming, Father Abraham." Hay could see Lamon furiously shouting orders; but no one listened. The people wanted to see and touch the President.

"Tad is improved," said Nico.

"That is earth-shaking. What else?"

"A battle has begun at Chattanooga. Grant is attacking. Burnside is safe at Knoxville; he does not attack."

"How is the Tycoon?"

"He just finished rewording the speech an hour ago. He complains of dizziness."

Alarmed, Hay turned to Nico. "Oh God! You know, in the train, he told me that he felt weak."

Nico nodded. "There's something wrong. I don't know what."

But if there was something wrong with the Ancient, there was nothing wrong with the Tycoon, who sat dutifully through Edward Everett's extended version of Pericles's commemoration of the Athenian dead. But where Pericles had been very much to the Attic point, Everett was to a myriad of New England points.

As the beautiful voice of Everett went on and on, Hay looked out over the battlefield. Trees had been smashed into matchwood by crossfire, while artillery shells had plowed up the muddy ground. Here and there, dead horses lay unburied; as they were not yet turned to neat bone, the smell of decomposing flesh intermingled with the odor of the crowd was mildly sickening. Now, in the noonday sun of an airless sort of day, Hay began to sweat.

When Everett sat down, Lincoln pulled out his sheet of paper; and put on his glasses. But there was a musical interval to be endured; and so he put away the paper. The Baltimore Glee Club intoned a hymn especially written for the occasion. A warm breeze started up, and the American flag began to snap like a whip cracking. Opposite the speaker's platform, a photographer had built a small platform so that his camera would be trained straight on the President when he spoke. He was constantly fiddling with his paraphernalia; raising and lowering the cloth hood at the back, and dusting his glass plates.

Finally, there was silence. Then Lamon stood up and bellowed, "The President of the United States!"

Lincoln rose, paper in hand; glasses perched on his nose. He was, Hay noted, a ghastly color, but the hand that held the paper did not tremble, always the orator's fear. There was a moment of warm—if slightly exhausted by Everett—applause.

Then the trumpet-voice sounded across the field of Gettysburg, and thirty thousand people fell silent. While Everett's voice had been like some deep rich cello, Lincoln's voice was like the sound that accompanies a sudden crack of summer lightning. "Fourscore and seven years ago," he plunged straight into his subject, "our fathers brought forth upon this continent a new nation, conceived in liberty and dedicated to the proposition that all men are created equal."

That will please the radicals, thought Hay. Then he noticed two odd things. First, the Tycoon did not consult the paper in his hand. He seemed, impossibly, to have memorized the text that had been put into final form only an hour or so earlier. Second, the Tycoon was speaking with unusual slowness. He seemed to be firing each word across the battlefield—a rifle salute to the dead?

"Now we are engaged in a great civil war, testing whether that nation—or any nation, so conceived and so dedicated—can long endure."

Seated just to the right of Lincoln, Seward began actually to listen. He had heard so many thousands of speeches in his life and he had himself given so many thousands that he could seldom actually listen to any speech, including his own. He, too, noted Lincoln's unusual deliberateness. It was as if the President was now trying to justify to the nation and to history and, thought Seward, to God, what he had done.

"We are met on a great battle-field of that war. We are met to dedicate a portion of it as the final resting place of those who have given their lives that that nation might live." Seward nodded, inadvertently. Yes, that was the issue, the only issue. The preservation of this unique nation of states. Meanwhile, the photographer was trying to get the President in camera-frame.

"It is altogether fitting and proper that we should do this." Lincoln was now staring out over the heads of the crowd to a hill on which a row of wooden crosses had been newly set. For an instant, the hand that held the speech had dropped to his side. Then he recalled himself, and glanced at the text. "But, in a larger sense, we cannot dedicate, we cannot consecrate, we cannot hallow, this ground. The brave men, living and dead, who struggled here, have consecrated it, far above our power to add or to detract." Lincoln paused. There was a patter of applause; and then, to Seward's amazement, a shushing sound. The audience did not want to break into the music until it was done.

Seward studied the President with new—if entirely technical—interest. How had he accomplished this bit of magic with his singularly unmellifluous voice and harsh midwestern accent?

Lincoln was now staring off again, dreamily; this time at the sky. The photographer was under his hood, ready to take the picture.

"The world will very little note nor long remember what we say here; but it can never forget what they did here." The hand with the text again fell to his side. Hay knew that the Tycoon's eyes had turned inward. He was reading now from that marble tablet in his head; and he was reading a text written in nothing less than blood. "It is for us, the living, rather, to be dedicated, here, to the unfinished work that they have thus far so nobly carried on. It is rather for us to be here dedicated to the great task remaining before us; that from these honored dead we take increased devotion to that cause for which they here gave. . ." Hay was aware that the trumpet-voice had choked; and the gray eyes were suddenly aswim with uncharacteristic tears. But the Tycoon quickly recovered himself. ". . . the last full measure of devotion; that we here highly resolve," the voice was now that of a cavalry bugle calling for a charge, "that these dead shall not have died in vain; that the nation shall," he paused a moment then said, "under God . . ." Seward nodded—his advice had been taken.

Nico whispered to Hay, "He just added that. It's not in the text."

". . . have a new birth of freedom, and that government of the people, by the people, for the people, shall not perish from the earth."

Lincoln stood a moment, looking thoughtfully at the crowd, which stared back at him. Then he sat down. There was some applause. There was also laughter at the photographer, who was loudly cursing: he had failed to get any picture at all.

Lincoln turned to Seward and murmured, "Well, that fell on them like a wet blanket."

Reading Time: _____

See Conversion Table.

Enter WPM Rate on the Progress Record Chart.

17 Lincoln at Gettysburg

COMPREHENSION CHECK

1. The Gettysburg address was given in (a) 1861, (b) 1863,   1. ___
   (c) 1865, (d) 1867.

2. Lincoln thought Everett would speak for (a) one hour,   2. ___
   (b) one and a half hours, (c) two hours, (d) two and a
   half hours.

3. How many had gathered for the occasion? (a) ten   3. ___
   thousand, (b) twenty thousand, (c) thirty thousand,
   (d) forty thousand.

4. In the presidential procession, (a) Lincoln was first,   4. ___
   (b) Lincoln followed the color guard, (c) Lincoln
   followed the band, (d) Lincoln followed the flag bearers.

5. There was specific mention of (a) Lincoln's wife,   5. ___
   (b) General Lee, (c) Tad, (d) the White House.

6. Lincoln was said to complain of (a) tiredness,   6. ___
   (b) nausea, (c) dizziness, (d) faintness.

7. Everett's speech dealt with the (a) Athenian dead,   7. ___
   (b) Gallic Wars, (c) Roman dead, (d) Alexander the Great.

8. Lincoln's voice was likened to a (a) rush of wind,   8. ___
   (b) sweet-toned violin, (c) deep rich cello, (d) trumpet-
   voice.

9. At one time Lincoln stared at (a) the busy photographer, 9 ___
   (b) the row of wooden crosses, (c) Edward Everett, (d) the
   fluttering flag.

10. The phrase "under God" was used at (a) Hay's advice,   10. ___
    (b) Everett's advice, (c) Seymour's advice, (d) Seward's
    advice.

10 Off for Each Mistake.
Comprehension Score: _____
Answer Key in Appendix.
Enter the Results on the Progress Record Chart.

18 Biographies Bring New Companions

WORD POWER WORKOUT

A. Leaning on Context

In each of the blanks provided, place the letter that precedes the best definition of the underlined word in context to the left.

Words in Context	Definitions
1. ___ able to <u>encounter</u>	a. origins
2. ___ has to be <u>reconstructed</u>	b. loose outer garment
3. ___ from <u>documents</u>	c. makes clear
4. ___ figure in a <u>toga</u>	d. three-cornered
5. ___ wore a <u>cocked</u> hat	e. meet
6. ___ a starched <u>ruff</u>	f. unlikely
7. ___ in <u>improbable</u> costumes	g. re-created
8. ___ <u>pasteurizing</u> of milk	h. pleated collar
9. ___ a good biography <u>illuminates</u>	i. anything printed or written
10. ___ the <u>springs</u> of their heroism	j. method of heating to kill bacteria

---

Check your answers with the Key before going on. Review any that you have missed.

Pronunciation aids: 4. tō'guh.

KEY: add, āce; end, ēven; it, īce; odd, ōpen; pōol; up.

B. Leaning on Parts

The prefix *ex-* (also spelled *ec-*, *ef-*, *es-* or *e-*) means "out" or "out of." Supply the missing word or word part in each of the following.

1. When you breathe out, do you inhale or ex_____?

2. The way out of the building is marked with an ex_____ sign.

3. If you're completely worn out after work, you're ex_____.

4. The dynamite caused a tremendous ex_____.

5. If you exclude them from the meeting, you keep them

   _____.

C. Making the Words Yours

In each blank below, enter the most appropriate word from the ten words in context in the first exercise, substituting it for the word(s) in parentheses. Use these words: *cocked, documents, encounter, illuminates, improbable, pasteurizing, reconstructed, ruff, springs, toga.*

1. Napoleon is usually pictured in a (three-cornered) _____ hat.

2. The detective (re-created) _____ the crime with meticulous care.

3. A good speaker (makes clear) _____ even complex subjects.

4. Such an (unlikely) _____ story was hard to believe.

5. The painting of Queen Elizabeth showed her in a large (pleated collar)

   _____.

6. The research involved a careful examination of many old (anything printed or written) _____.

7. Did you see the statue of Cicero in his flowing (loose outer garment)

   _____?

8. The general expected to (meet) _____ stiff opposition as his troops advanced.

9. The (heating to kill bacteria) _____ was done right after the milk was collected.

10. Soon the discussion revealed the (origins) _____ of their sharp disagreement.

4 Off for Each Mistake.
Word Power Score: _____
Answer Key in Appendix.

18

Biographies Bring New Companions

Marchette Chute

People! How fascinating they are! Take a close look at some you know. Just how well do you know them? For that matter, how well do you know your best friend? And how detailed a biography could you write about anyone you know? The selection which follows suggests how to make reading add life to your living!

Begin Timing

There are many ways of enjoying ourselves, and one of the pleasantest is to meet interesting people.

The world is full of remarkable men and women, but even if we had time to go all over the earth to visit them and carried a suitcase stuffed with letters of introduction, we should still not be able to encounter more than a small fraction of the people we admire. Soldiers, statesmen, writers, scientists, inventors, actors, painters—most of them we shall never meet. But there is one easy way to get to know them all, and that is in the biographies that are written about them.

A biography is the life story of a real person. If it is a good biography it brings its hero as vividly to life as if he were standing in the same room. If you met him in person you would probably not get more than a polite handshake and a "How do you do?"; but in a biography you can find out all about him—what he did when he was a small boy, the way he went about his work, the friends he made, even his taste in neckties. It is not surprising that so many people like to read biographies, for they are a kind of window into a man's life; the better the biography the larger and clearer the window.

Moreover, anyone who reads biographies meets not only the people who are alive today but those who lived in all the past centuries. The men and women whose lives are worth remembering stretch over the whole of history, like a great, lighted procession, and we could never make their acquaintance if it were not for biographies.

It is true that a biographer has an easier time of it if the man he is writing about is still alive. James Boswell, for instance, could sit in the same room with Dr. Johnson, with his eyes and ears open like a good reporter's, listening delightedly and remembering what he heard, so that when he came to write his book he could transfer Johnson's bossy, magnificent self to paper and catch the very sound of his voice. If the hero is no longer living and his life has to be reconstructed from documents, the biographer has a more difficult time of it. But everyone leaves records of himself, and it is the biographer's task to put them together and bring back a living man.

This sense of reality, of showing great people as they really were, is one of the best things about biography. A non-reader, for instance, might think of George Washington as being the way he is shown on dollar bills. He looks strong-minded and dignified in a stuffed kind of way, what with his unyielding mouth and glassy eyes, but he does not look as if he had ever really been alive. But a good biography shows the real man, the Washington who took such enormous risks and who knew that he would be hanged for treason if he failed in what he was trying to do. Washington was not a great man because he somehow soared above the troubles of ordinary people—confusion and discouragement and a sense of defeat; he was a great man because he never gave in to them.

A good portrait can sometimes bring a man back to life, but even then it fixes him at just one moment of time. The pictures of Longfellow, for instance, show him with a beard, and it is hard to remember that he was once a small boy going to school, or a young man trying to work out his first rhymes. Cicero is a marble figure in a toga, and no one would guess what a complex, sensitive, brilliant, and irritating man he was in real life. A biography of Cicero brings him back as his friends in politics knew him, and a schoolroom bust turns into an interesting person to know.

A good biography takes away the sense of "costume" that often blocks our imagination when we think about the past. Because Napoleon wore a cocked hat and Queen Elizabeth a starched ruff and Richard the Lion-Hearted armor instead of khaki, we forget that these were just their ordinary clothes, and we think of them as being remote, unfamiliar, and just a little odd. This is hardly fair, because if you look at old photographs of your friends, the clothes of ten or twenty years ago will look just as odd. It is time that turns clothes into costume, and a good biography can destroy time. What happened to Abraham Lincoln or Joan of Arc becomes "now" as long as you are reading about them, and no one who reads a good biography of Leonardo da Vinci could ever again think that Renaissance Italy was peopled by remote figures in improbable costumes. Biography brings the times to life again, just as it brings the people; and it makes the world a more spacious and interesting place to live in.

Another advantage of reading biography is that it widens your sense of enjoyment over things that have nothing to do with books. Even the pasteurizing of milk is more interesting if you know something about that stubborn man, Louis Pasteur. Brooklyn Bridge is twice as impressive if you know about the father and son who gave their lives to bring it into being, and traveling in the Far West becomes a special adventure to anyone who has read about Lewis and Clark. Radium becomes an even more awe-inspiring discovery if you know how a small woman in black named Madame Curie struggled with fierce patience to find it; and even a new type of wheat becomes more important if you know about the man who brought it into being.

So many things that now seem like fixed stars were born of fierce struggle and apparent defeat. Lincoln believed that he had done a poor job after he delivered the Gettysburg Address, and Keats died believing that his name would not be remembered. Beethoven wrote his greatest music after he became deaf, and Milton his greatest poetry after he became blind. The people who are worth knowing are the people who never gave up, and a good biography illuminates the springs of their heroism. From the outside, to their own friends, many of them seemed ordinary enough people; but each of them held a kind of special light inside himself, and a good biography shows why.

Even in the case of Shakespeare, whose life has nothing to do with the delight that any reader can get from his plays, it gives an added interest to know something about him as a man. It is interesting to know he worked in the theater all his adult life; he himself was an actor. Other playwrights of the time usually entered the theater only for conferences. He helped build the finest theater in London and owned part of it, and a little of the greatness of his plays comes from his thorough understanding of stagecraft and the needs of an audience. Many people in his own day did not think Shakespeare's plays were very good, since they pleased ordinary people and it was felt that really good work ought to please only a chosen few; but everyone liked him as a man and two of his fellow actors loved him so much that they saved all his plays in the special collection that is now known as the First Folio.

Good biography brings the past near and makes it real. It gives us a more spacious world to live in and heroes for our companions, and it pushes back the horizon so that we can make friends not only with the people around us but with all the people in history who have made the world a place worth living in.

Reading Time: _____
See Conversion Table.
Enter WPM Rate on the Progress Record Chart.

18 Biographies Bring New Companions

COMPREHENSION CHECK

1. Mention was made of (a) letters of introduction, (b) traveling by magic carpet, (c) speaking several foreign languages, (d) conducting interviews.

   1. ___

2. Meeting someone was said to mean no more than (a) a polite nod, (b) a hurried "hello" and "goodbye," (c) a polite handshake, (d) a "glad-to-meet-you."

   2. ___

3. Biographies are likened to (a) dreams, (b) doors, (c) imaginings, (d) windows.

   3. ___

4. The writer mentioned (a) Leo Tolstoy, (b) James Boswell, (c) Henry the Eighth, (d) Socrates.

   4. ___

5. A non-reader was said to think of Washington as he appeared (a) on famous paintings, (b) in well-known statues, (c) on dollar bills, (d) in history books.

   5. ___

6. Most people remember Longfellow (a) going to school, (b) with a beard, (c) first writing poetry, (d) getting married.

   6. ___

7. Richard the Lion-Hearted was said to wear (a) armor, (b) a gold breast-plate, (c) an embroidered vest, (d) a plumed hat.

   7. ___

8. The selection mentioned (a) Aristotle, (b) Plato, (c) Mary Queen of Scots, (d) Joan of Arc.

   8. ___

9. You're told about (a) Custer, (b) Jim Bridger, (c) Lewis and Clark, (d) Pocahontas.

   9 ___

10. In addition to writing plays, Shakespeare also was (a) a theater manager, (b) a director, (c) an actor, (d) a stage designer.

    10. ___

10 Off for Each Mistake.
Comprehension Score: _____
Answer Key in Appendix.
Enter the Results on the Progress Record Chart.

Applying the LDE Formula

Work through this exercise so you can use the LDE Formula (page 106) to better advantage.

What does the prefix *syn-* mean? First, list some *syn* words. Suppose you list *synchronize*, *synonym*, and *synthesize*. Now define each. To synchronize two watches is to bring them together in time. Synonyms are words that belong together in meaning. And to synthesize is to bring separate parts together into a whole. Finally, extract the common meaning. You see that *syn-* probably means "together."

Now try the formula with another prefix: *hyper-*. What does it mean? Again, make a list—perhaps *hyperactive*, *hypertension*, and *hypersensitive*. Define each. *Hyperactive* means "more active than normal." *Hypertension* means "abnormally high tension"; and *hypersensitive*, "excessively sensitive." Extract the common meaning and you have "more" or "above normal" as meanings of *hyper-*.

Now try the formula with some roots. What does *gress* (from Latin *gradi*) mean? First, make a list. Since you may not think of any words beginning with *gress*, try adding some prefixes. Let's say you list *progress*, *regress*, and *digress*. If you progress, you "move forward." If you regress, you "move back"; and if you digress, you "move away" from the subject or point you're making. Extract the common denominator and you get "move" as the meaning of *gress*. Actually *gress* means "step," but if you got "move" or "go," that's close enough.

Try another: the Latin root *tractus*. What does it mean? Take off the ending to get closer to the English form, in this case *tract*. Suppose you list *tractor*, *attract*, and *contract*. Define them, filling in the blanks below.

A tractor is a vehicle for _____ loads.
To attract is to _____ attention to.
A contract is an agreement _____ up between two or more parties.

The Latin word *tractus* apparently means "to draw."

Finally, try the formula on a suffix. What does *-ic* mean? Let's say you list *metallic* and *angelic*. You define them: *metallic* is "like metal" and *angelic* is "like an angel." Extracting the common meaning, *-ic* apparently means "like."

Never say that you don't know what any and all such elements mean. Just put the LDE Formula to work and discover the meanings.

19 Speeding by Scanning

WORD POWER WORKOUT

A. Leaning on Context

In each of the blanks provided, place the letter that precedes the best definition of the underlined word in context to the left.

Words in Context	Definitions
1. ___ the <u>proverbial</u> needle-in-a-haystack	a. adequate
2. ___ an accelerator <u>surpasses</u> that	b. desirable
3. ___ goals are <u>feasible</u>	c. not understood
4. ___ <u>jog</u> your memory	d. many-sided
5. ___ a <u>versatile</u> reader	e. typical
6. ___ uncover <u>relevant</u> information	f. exceeds
7. ___ most <u>enviable</u> position	g. refresh
8. ___ develop <u>sufficient</u> scanning skill	h. pertinent
9. ___ such <u>elusive</u> things	i. workable
10. ___ mass of <u>undigested</u> material	j. evasive

Check your answers with the Key before going on. Review any that you have missed.

Pronunciation aids: 1. pruh vur′bē ul; 3. fē′zuh bul; 5. vur′suh til; 6. rel′uh vunt; 7. en′vē uh bul; 9. i lōō′siv.

KEY: add, āce; end, ēven; it, īce; odd, ōpen; pōōl; up.

B. Leaning on Parts

The prefix *dis-* (also spelled *dif-*, or *di-*) means "apart" or "away." Supply the needed word or word part in each of the following blanks.

1. If the two sides are far away from agreement, they dis_____.

2. If you send a message away, you can be said to dis_____ it.

3. To scatter or drive away a crowd is to dis_____ it.

4. The students were dis_____ early from school.

5. If attention is distracted, it's drawn _____ in another direction.

C. Making the Words Yours

In each blank below, enter the most appropriate word from the ten words in context in the first exercise, substituting it for the word(s) in parentheses. Use these words: *elusive, enviable, feasible, jog, proverbial, relevant, sufficient, surpasses, undigested, versatile.*

1. Try a mnemonic device to (refresh) _____ your memory.

2. My ability as a skier (exceeds) _____ that of my brother.

3. Their answers were (evasive) _____.

4. I make a quite (adequate) _____ salary.

5. A doctor has a very (desirable) _____ position.

6. A (workable) _____ plan is needed for success.

7. A novel that is (not understood) _____ may be criticized by the reader.

8. The one who hid his money under the bed was a (typical) _____ miser.

9. A (many-sided) _____ athlete will be successful.

10. Are these statistics (pertinent) _____ to your question?

4 Off for Each Mistake.
Word Power Score: _____
Answer Key in Appendix.

19
Speeding by Scanning

Now for the third and last superspeed technique. It's called *scanning*. To function effectively, a mechanic needs many tools. So does a reader. The different techniques are the tools. After all, you don't tighten bolts with a file or loosen screws with a wrench. And you don't *read* an entire article just for *one single fact*.

What Is Scanning?

Scanning is the special technique you use to find one specific bit of information within a relatively large body of printed matter. It's the proverbial needle-in-a-haystack situation. Of all the superspeeds, this is the highest gear of all.

Notice how it fits into place with the other techniques. The survey is like a quick, high-altitude glimpse of a large city from a plane. Skimming is a lower-altitude view, with more details observable. And scanning is a supersonic zooming in for a close glance at only one specific house.

Your Scanning Speed Potential

How fast should you scan? To answer that question, let's look at students in efficient reading classes at the University of Minnesota. Without special training, classes will, on the average, scan initially at about 1,800 wpm. Of course, they vary. Since 1972 class averages have ranged from 1,569 to 2,924 wpm. Accuracy has hovered around 75 percent, with a range from 65 to 89.

Later in the quarter, we spend an entire class period in practice. Students try one scanning problem after another, with instructional tips in between to hasten progress. That single practice session is sufficient to push scanning speeds from 1,800 wpm to 15,000 wpm. Some students even reach speeds of 24,000 wpm with 100 percent accuracy.

At the end of the quarter we asked this question: "What do you feel is your probable upper rate limit for scanning, if you were to develop your full potential?" The answer was 18,959. Individual figures ranged from 1,700 to 75,000 wpm. These figures suggest three things: (1) how quickly scanning speeds can be improved, (2) how much individuals differ, and (3) what goals are feasible.

How Do You Scan?

You have certainly noticed how, in looking over a new telephone directory, your own name tends to jump out at you. It's almost like magic. This psychological fact suggests the first of four tips for insuring accuracy in scanning.

1. *Visualize the thing to be spotted*. If you are scanning for the date 1970, for example, visualize exactly how those four numbers will look in print. That clear mental picture will make the date stand out, just as your own name.

2. *Use all available clues*. If, for example, you are scanning for a proper name, use the inevitable capital letter as an aid. With other problems, use quotation marks, hyphens, or italics. And for more complex scanning, resort to computerlike search techniques. Think of possible synonyms or key words that will lead you to the desired information.

3. *Use paragraph topical clues*. To locate average rainfall figures, find the paragraph dealing with weather.

4. *Use systematic scanning patterns*. To scan material printed in columns, as newspapers and some magazines, run your eyes rapidly down the middle of each column, using a slight zigzag motion. For solid pages of print, use a wider side-to-side movement.

Judging from class results, you should scan at about ten times your present rate. To develop that facility, however, you must practice. It's not automatic. One or two scanning problems every day will do wonders. Let it grow naturally out of your usual reading. Whenever you finish reading something, ask yourself a question. Was there mention of a name, date, formula, or statement that you're not sure about? A quick scan will bring that bit of information into sharp focus. Even more important, that daily scanning will gradually make you enviably proficient.

Functions of Scanning

Generally speaking, scanning serves two functions. It uncovers relevant information. It also accelerates your reading speed and flexibility.

Since scanning is the fastest coverage of all, its role as an accelerator surpasses that of skimming. In breezing through an article at 18,000 wpm, you are definitely breaking out of the usual reading straightjacket. You'll find it much easier to slip from reading into skimming and into scanning, as purpose dictates. And that's one true mark of a versatile reader.

Common Situations

Actually, two fairly common situations demand scanning. They're alike—yet different. In one situation you deal with the *known*, in the other with the *unknown*.

One has already been mentioned. Remember? That's where you're after such elusive things as a date, formula, name, statement, or list. For example, you *know* that this chapter contains four scanning tips. But do you remember *exactly* what they are? If not, scan to jog your memory. In situations of this kind, scanning serves an important review function.

In the other situation, you're looking for something—but a yet unknown something. Here, you won't *know* exactly until you find it. The dilemma faced by a sales manager for a large firm is typical. Every month, salesmen would mail in lengthy reports, piling up over two feet high on his desk. Ninety-nine percent of that information was purely routine. But every month somewhere in that mass of undigested material there would be three or four bits of important information. Read them? Impossible! But he could and did develop sufficient scanning skill to get what he wanted. Similarly, in school use scanning to get you through a mountain of material to uncover details for a term paper or speech.

There it is. Your third superspeed. Most readers never take time to become skilled in a variety of different techniques. With practice, you can soon develop outstanding ability to apply the right technique at the right time. If the situation demands reading, you read. If it demands scanning, you use your highly developed scanning skills to bring success with a minimum of time and effort. That puts you into a most enviable position. Make the most of it!

Reading Time: _____
See Conversion Table.
Enter WPM Rate on the Progress Record Chart.

19 Speeding by Scanning

COMPREHENSION CHECK

1. Reading techniques are likened to (a) tools, (b) medicines, (c) foods, (d) exercises.

   1. ___

2. Which is like a quick, high-altitude glimpse of a city from a plane? (a) reading, (b) scanning, (c) skimming, (d) surveying.

   2. ___

3. One in-class practice session is enough to push scanning speeds up to about what figure? (a) 2,800 wpm, (b) 5,000 wpm, (c) 9,000 wpm, (d) 15,000 wpm.

   3. ___

4. Mention is made of looking into (a) an encyclopedia, (b) a dictionary, (c) a telephone directory, (d) an index.

   4. ___

5. You are told to (a) squint your eyes, (b) hold material at a distance, (c) visualize appearance, (d) blink often.

   5. ___

6. You are told to use what as clues? (a) quotation marks, (b) hyphens, (c) italics, (d) all of the preceding.

   6. ___

7. In scanning, you are directed to (a) come straight down the middle of the page, (b) run the eyes along each line, (c) use systematic patterns, (d) use no set eye pattern.

   7. ___

8. Scanning is said to serve how many functions? (a) one, (b) two, (c) three, (d) four.

   8. ___

9. One illustration involves (a) an accountant, (b) a sales manager, (c) a personnel director, (d) a vice-president.

   9 ___

10. You are told to scan to get material for (a) a speech, (b) a lab report, (c) a take-home final, (d) a book review.

    10. ___

10 Off for Each Mistake.
Comprehension Score: _____
Answer Key in Appendix.
Enter the Results on the Progress Record Chart.

Making the Application

You should discover your present scanning speed, now that you have completed the instructional selection on scanning. For this, you will probably need help from your teacher or friend. A stop watch is almost a necessity.

Here are two problems, either of which will serve to check both scanning speed and accuracy. Both require you to scan the 1,000-word Selection 19, *Speeding by Scanning*.

Problem 1: In this entire selection how many dates are given—year dates, that is, such as 1972 or 1888? Visualize your problem, then at a given signal, scan the article for the answer. Divide 1,000 (the number of words) by your scanning time in seconds; multiply the resulting figure by 60 to get a wpm scanning figure.

Problem 2: How many times in this entire selection is there a specific reference to *superspeed* or *superspeeds*? Count them as you scan. Again, wait for the given signal. Keep track of the time and figure your scanning rate.

To develop more accuracy or added speed, try one or both of the following problems based on Selection 1, *Reading Power—Key to Personal Growth*, 1,000 words in length.

Problem 1: How many times in that selection is the proper name *Anderson* repeated? Divide 1,000 by your scanning time; multiply the result by 60 to get your scanning rate. Check accuracy.

Problem 2: How many times in that selection is the word *And* repeated, with the *A* capitalized? Follow the same procedure.

As soon as possible, start using this technique as a review device in your regular textbook reading to spot names, dates, formulas, or other facts that you want to fix in mind after finishing the assignment. Soon you will find this an indispensable review tool.

20 How to Become Educated

WORD POWER WORKOUT

A. Leaning on Context

In each of the blanks provided, place the letter that precedes the best definition of the underlined word in context to the left.

Words in Context	Definitions
1. ___ are not very <u>discrepant</u>	a. mental powers
2. ___ <u>disapprobation</u> amounting to scorn	b. portrayed
3. ___ played for <u>untold</u> ages	c. glaring
4. ___ who plays ill is <u>checkmated</u>	d. different
5. ___ my <u>metaphor</u>	e. influenced by
6. ___ has <u>depicted</u> Satan	f. disapproval
7. ___ vigor of his <u>faculties</u>	g. endless, innumerable
8. ___ before we were <u>susceptible</u>	h. completely defeated
9. ___ by the <u>gross</u> disobedience	i. implied comparison
10. ___ pluck means <u>extermination</u>	j. complete destruction

---

Check your answers with the Key before going on. Review any that you have missed.

Pronunciation aids: 1. di skrep'unt; 2. dis'ap ruh bā'shun; 5. met'uh for.

KEY: add, āce; end, ēven; it, īce; odd, ōpen; pōōl; up.

B. Leaning on Parts

The prefix *ad-* (also spelled *ac-*, *af-*, *ag-*, *al-*, *an-*, *ap-*, *ar-*, *as-*, *at-*, or *a-*) means "to" or "toward." Supply the proper entries in the following.

1. When one surface sticks to another, it ad_____ to it.
2. This ticket will ad_____ you to the next performance.
3. Two buildings next to each other can be said to be ad_____ent.
4. The army ad_____ very slowly toward enemy positions.
5. An adjunct is an unessential thing added _____ something else.

C. Making the Words Yours

In each blank below, enter the most appropriate word from the ten words in context in the first exercise, substituting it for the word(s) in parentheses. Use these words: *checkmated, depicted, disapprobation, discrepant, extermination, faculties, gross, metaphor, susceptible, untold.*

1. The writer's interesting (implied comparison) _____ likened life to a flowing river.
2. Despite her advanced years and physical frailties, her (mental powers) _____ were as sharp as ever.
3. The environmentalists worried about the possible (complete destruction) _____ of some rain forest species.
4. The painting (portrayed) _____ Washington crossing the Delaware.
5. The crowd reaction to the announcement was strong (disapproval) _____.
6. The mayor was found guilty of (glaring) _____ mismanagement.
7. The two (different) _____ versions need to be rechecked.
8. The attempts of the opposition were finally (completely defeated) _____.
9. Is anyone on the committee (influenced by) _____ to bribery?
10. Those same problems are prevalent in (endless, innumerable) _____ parts of the world.

4 Off for Each Mistake.
Word Power Score: _____
Answer Key in Appendix.

20

How to Become Educated

Thomas Henry Huxley

Everyone needs an education. The problem? How do you get it?
It depends on who's talking. Sam Lavisky says, "Education is
what you get from reading the small print. Experience is what
you get from not reading it." Another puts it this way: "Never let
your studies interfere with your education." Read on to see how
Huxley puts it.

Begin Timing

What is education? Above all things, what is our ideal of a thoroughly liberal education?—of that education which, if we could begin life again, we
would give ourselves?—of that education which, if we could mold the fates
to our own will, we would give our children? Well, I know not what may be
your conceptions upon this matter but I will tell you mine, and I hope I
shall find that our views are not very discrepant.

Suppose it were perfectly certain that the life and fortune of every one
of us would, one day or other, depend upon his winning or losing a game at
chess. Don't you think we should all consider it to be a primary duty to
learn at least the names and the moves of the pieces; to have a notion of a
gambit, and a keen eye for all the means of giving and getting out of check?
Do you not think that we should look with a disapprobation amounting to
scorn upon the father who allowed his son, or the state which allowed its
members, to grow up without knowing a pawn from a knight?

Yet, it is a very plain and elementary truth that the life, the fortune,
and the happiness of every one of us, and, more or less, of those who are
connected with us, do depend upon our knowing something of the rules of
a game infinitely more difficult and complicated than chess. It is a game
which has been played for untold ages, every man and woman of us being
one of the two players in a game of his or her own. The chessboard is the
world, the pieces are the phenomena of the universe, the rules of the game
are what we call the laws of nature. The player on the other side is hidden
from us. We know that his play is always fair, just, and patient. But also we
know, to our cost, that he never overlooks a mistake or makes the smallest
allowance for ignorance. To the man who plays well, the highest stakes are

paid, with that sort of overflowing generosity with which the strong shows delight in strength. And one who plays ill is checkmated—without haste, but without remorse.

My metaphor will remind some of you of the famous picture in which Retzsch has depicted Satan playing at chess with man for his soul. Substitute for the mocking fiend in that picture a calm, strong angel who is playing for love, as we say, and would rather lose than win—and I should accept it as an image of human life.

Well, what I mean by Education is learning the rules of this mighty game. In other words, education is the instruction of the intellect in the laws of nature, under which name I include not merely things and their forces, but men and their ways; and the fashioning of the affections and of the will into an earnest and loving desire to move in harmony with those laws. For me, education means neither more nor less than this. Anything which professes to call itself education must be tried by this standard, and if it fails to stand the test, I will not call it education, whatever may be the force of authority or of numbers upon the other side.

It is important to remember that, in strictness, there is no such thing as an uneducated man. Take an extreme case. Suppose that an adult man, in the full vigor of his faculties, could be suddenly placed in the world, as Adam is said to have been, and then left to do as he best might. How long would he be left uneducated? Not five minutes. Nature would begin to teach him, through the eye, the ear, the touch, the properties of objects. Pain and pleasure would be at his elbow telling him to do this and avoid that; and by slow degrees the man would receive an education which, if narrow, would be thorough, real, and adequate to his circumstances, though there would be no extras and very few accomplishments.

And if to this solitary man entered a second Adam, or, better still, an Eve, a new and greater world, that of social and moral phenomena, would be revealed. Joys and woes, compared with which all others might seem but faint shadows, would spring from the new relations. Happiness and sorrow would take the place of the coarse monitors, pleasure and pain; but conduct would still be shaped by the observation of the natural consequences of actions; or, in other words, by the laws of the nature of man.

To every one of us the world was once as fresh and new as to Adam. And then, long before we were susceptible of any other mode of instruction, Nature took us in hand, and every minute of waking life brought its educational influence, shaping our actions into rough accordance with Nature's laws, so that we might not be ended untimely by too gross disobedience. Nor should I speak of this process of education as past, for anyone, be he as old as he may. For every man the world is as fresh as it was the first day, and as full of untold novelties for him who has the eyes to see them. And Nature is still continuing her patient education of us in that great university, the universe, of which we are all members.

Those who take honors in Nature's university, who learn the laws which govern men and things and obey them, are really great and successful men in this world. The great mass of mankind are the "Poll," who pick up just enough to get through without much discredit. Those who won't learn at all are plucked; and then you can't come up again. Nature's pluck means extermination.

Reading Time: _____
See Conversion Table.
Enter WPM Rate on the Progress Record Chart.

20 How to Become Educated

COMPREHENSION CHECK

1. Huxley says he is writing about (a) a general education, (b) a universal education, (c) a liberal education, (d) an advanced education.

   1. ___

2. Huxley specifically mentions (a) a rook and a castle, (b) a pawn and a knight, (c) the queen, (d) the king.

   2. ___

3. In Huxley's metaphor, the chessboard is (a) the nation, (b) our work, (c) our surroundings, (d) the world.

   3. ___

4. The rules of the chess game refer to the (a) laws of nature, (b) laws of the country, (c) common customs, (d) the legal code.

   4. ___

5. In a famous picture, Satan is depicted as playing chess for a person's (a) life, (b) soul, (c) love, (d) freedom.

   5. ___

6. In Huxley's version you are asked to substitute what for Satan? (a) Moses, (b) Christ, (c) God, (d) an angel.

   6. ___

7. For Huxley, education is (a) mastering the laws of nature, (b) developing the right values for living, (c) choosing between good and evil, (d) mastering scientific truths.

   7. ___

8. Mention was made of (a) the Garden of Eden, (b) the forbidden tree (c) Eve, (d) the snake.

   8. ___

9. Huxley said that an adult newly placed in the world would become educated in (a) one minute, (b) five minutes, (c) ten minutes, (d) an hour.

   9 ___

10. The university Huxley wrote about is (a) one's intellect, (b) our body of knowledge, (c) the universe, (d) one's instinct.

    10. ___

10 Off for Each Mistake.
Comprehension Score: _____
Answer Key in Appendix.
Enter the Results on the Progress Record Chart.

21 Scientist at Work

WORD POWER WORKOUT

A. Leaning on Context

In each of the blanks provided, place the letter that precedes the best definition of the underlined word in context to the left.

Words in Context	Definitions
1. ___ a <u>variegated</u> iris	a. cold, dry north wind
2. ___ I <u>incarcerate</u> her	b. sudden visit
3. ___ <u>hyperbolical</u> exclamations	c. compelling
4. ___ as yet <u>unprecedented</u>	d. many-colored
5. ___ cause of the <u>incursion</u>	e. informed
6. ___ <u>apprised</u> I know not how	f. extraordinary
7. ___ protected against the <u>mistral</u>	g. imprison
8. ___ directs his <u>tortuous</u> flight	h. exaggerated
9. ___ with his long wings <u>intact</u>	i. undamaged
10. ___ that <u>irresistible</u> lure	j. full of twists, curving

---

Check your answers with the Key before going on. Review any that
you have missed.

Pronunciation aids: 1. văr′i gā′tid; 3. hī′pur bol′ik′l; 4. un pres′i den′tid;
6. uh prīz′d; 8. tor′choo͞ us.

KEY: add, āce; end, ēven; it, īce; odd, ōpen; pool͞; up.

B. Leaning on Parts

The prefix *ob-* (also spelled *oc-*, *of-*, *op-*, or *o-*) means "against" or "to." Supply the missing word or word part in each of the following.

1. If you're against some plan, you ob_____ to it.

2. A barrier that stands against your progress is an ob_____.

3. If you're against a candidate, you can always voice your ob_____.

4. Don't let the darkness ob_____ your vision of the road.

5. To obfuscate someone is to work _____ his or her understanding.

C. Making the Words Yours

In each blank below, enter the most appropriate word from the ten words in context in the first exercise, substituting it for the word(s) in parentheses. Use these words: *apprised, hyperbolical, incarcerate, incursion, intact, irresistible, mistral, tortuous, unprecedented, variegated.*

1. Some humorists make frequent use of (exaggerated) _____ one-liners.

2. The officers will (imprison) _____ the culprit immediately.

3. The old trail up the mountains was (full of twists, curving) _____ and steep.

4. Do you know who (informed) _____ the guide of the changed plans?

5. The flower bed seemed a (many-colored) _____ mass of blooms.

6. In France this is the time of the (cold, dry north wind) _____.

7. The news was of an (extraordinary) _____ storm.

8. The plane skidded off the runway but the wings were still (undamaged) _____.

9. The heavy downpour provided the (compelling) _____ urge to seek shelter.

10. The change of weather explains the (sudden visit) _____ of mosquitoes.

4 Off for Each Mistake.
Word Power Score: _____
Answer Key in Appendix.

21

Scientist at Work

Edwin Way Teale

J. Henri Fabre of France enjoyed adventure and fame from observing the insect dramas and mysteries close about him. His ten-volume entomological contribution, written by hand on a desk no larger than a pocket handkerchief, contains some of the most interesting scientific writing known. The cure for boredom is curiosity. There is no cure for curiosity. Fabre could have told you that. Join him at work!

Begin Timing

It was a memorable evening. I shall call it the Great Peacock evening. Who does not know the magnificent Moth, the largest in Europe, clad in maroon velvet with a necktie of white fur? The wings, with their sprinkling of grey and brown, crossed by a faint zig-zag and edged with smoky white, have in the centre a round patch, a great eye with a black pupil and a variegated iris containing successive black, white, chestnut and purple arcs.

Well, on the morning of the 6th day of May, a female emerges from her cocoon in my presence, on the table of my insect-laboratory. I forthwith cloister her, still damp with the humours of the hatching, under a wire-gauze bell-jar. For the rest, I cherish no particular plans. I incarcerate her from mere habit, the habit of the observer always on the look-out for what may happen.

It was a lucky thought. At nine o'clock in the evening, just as the household is going to bed, there is a great stir in the room next to mine. Little Paul, half-undressed, is rushing about, jumping and stamping, knocking the chairs over like a mad thing. I hear him call me:

"Come quick!" he screams. "Come and see these Moths, big as birds! The room is full of them!"

I hurry in. There is enough to justify the child's enthusiastic and hyperbolical exclamations, an invasion as yet unprecedented in our house, a raid of giant Moths. Four are already caught and lodged in a bird-cage. Others, more numerous, are fluttering on the ceiling.

At this sight, the prisoner of the morning is recalled to my mind. "Put on your things, laddie," I say to my son. "Leave your cage and come with me. We shall see something interesting."

We run downstairs to go to my study, which occupies the right wing of the house. In the kitchen I find the servant, who is also bewildered by what is happening and stands flicking her apron at great Moths whom she took at first for Bats.

The Great Peacock, it would seem, has taken possession of pretty well every part of the house. What will it be around my prisoner, the cause of this incursion? Luckily, one of the two windows of the study had been left open. The approach is not blocked.

We enter the room, candle in hand. What we see is unforgettable. With a soft flick-flack the great Moths fly around the bell-jar, alight, set off again, come back, fly up to the ceiling and down. They rush at the candle, putting it out with a stroke of their wings; they descend on our shoulders, clinging to our clothes, grazing our faces. The scene suggests a wizard's cave, with its whirl of Bats. Little Paul holds my hand tighter than usual, to keep up his courage.

How many of them are there? About a score. Add to these the number that have strayed into the kitchen, the nursery and the other rooms of the house; and the total of those who have arrived from the outside cannot fall far short of forty. As I said, it was a memorable evening, this Great Peacock evening. Coming from every direction and apprised I know not how, here are forty lovers eager to pay their respects to the marriageable bride born that morning amid the mysteries of my study.

For the moment let us disturb the swarm of wooers no further. The flame of the candle is a danger to the visitors, who fling themselves into it madly and singe their wings. We will resume the observation tomorrow with an experimental interrogatory thought out beforehand.

But first let us clear the ground and speak of what happens every night during the week that my observation lasts. Each time it is pitch dark, between eight and ten o'clock, when the Moths arrive one by one. It is stormy weather, the sky is very much overcast and the darkness is so profound that even in the open air, in the garden, far from the shadow of the trees, it is hardly possible to see one's hand before one's face.

In addition to this darkness there is the difficulty of access. The house is hidden by tall plane-trees; it is approached by a walk thickly bordered with lilac- and rose-trees, forming a sort of outer vestibule; it is protected against the mistral by clumps of pines and screens of cypresses. Clusters of bushy shrubs make a rampart a few steps away from the door. It is through this tangle of branches, in complete darkness, that the Great Peacock has to tack about to reach the object of his pilgrimage.

Under such conditions, the Brown Owl would not dare leave the hole in his olive-tree. The Moth, better-endowed with his faceted optical organs than the night-bird with its great eyes, goes forward without hesitating and passes through without knocking against things. He directs his tortuous flight so skilfully that, despite the obstacles overcome, he arrives in a state of perfect freshness, with his big wings intact, with not a scratch upon him. The darkness is light enough for him.

Even if we grant that it perceives certain rays unknown to common retinae, this extraordinary power of sight cannot be what warns the Moth from afar and brings him hurrying to the spot. The distance and the screens interposed make this quite impossible.

Besides, apart from deceptive refractions, of which there is no question in this case, the indications provided by light are so precise that we go straight to the thing seen. Now the Moth sometimes blunders, not as to the general direction which he is to take, but as to the exact spot where the interesting events are happening. I have said that the children's nursery, which is at the side of the house opposite my study, the real goal of my visitors at the present moment, was occupied by the Moths before I went there with a light in my hand. These certainly were ill-informed. There was the same throng of hesitating visitors in the kitchen; but here the light of a lamp, that irresistible lure to nocturnal insects, may have beguiled the eager ones.

Let us consider only the places that were in the dark. In these there are several stray Moths. I find them more or less everywhere around the actual spot aimed at. For instance, when the captive is in my study, the visitors do not all enter by the open window, the safe and direct road, only two or three yards away from the caged prisoner. Several of them come in downstairs, wander about the hall and at most reach the staircase, a blind alley barred at the top by a closed door.

These data tell us that the guests at this nuptial feast do not make straight for their object, as they would if they derived their information from some kind of luminous radiation, whether known or unknown to our physical science. It is something else that apprises them from afar, leads them to the proximity of the exact spot and then leaves the final discovery to the airy uncertainty of random searching. It is very much like the way in which we ourselves are informed by hearing and smell, guides which are far from accurate when we want to decide the precise point of origin of the sound or the smell.

Reading Time: _____
See Conversion Table.
Enter WPM Rate on the Progress Record Chart.

21 Scientist at Work

COMPREHENSION CHECK

1. Fabre describes the Great Peacock Moth as having a (a) fur cap, (b) white necktie, (c) green vest, (d) two long antennae.

1. ___

2. The incident described happened in (a) May, (b) June, (c) July, (d) August.

2. ___

3. Who first saw the moths? (a) the servant, (b) Fabre's wife, (c) Little Paul, (d) Fabre himself.

3. ___

4. The moths were found (a) only by the bell-jar, (b) in the kitchen, (c) in a bedroom, (d) in all the preceding places.

4. ___

5. In all, about how many moths appeared that night? (a) forty, (b) thirty, (c) twenty-five, (d) twenty.

5. ___

6. There was mention of (a) lamps, (b) candles, (c) flashlights, (d) electric lights.

6. ___

7. During the nights of observation, the moths arrived at about what time? (a) between 8 and 10 o'clock, (b) between 9 and 11 o'clock, (c) between 10 and 12 o'clock, (d) time was not specified.

7. ___

8. Fabre's house was protected by (a) pines, (b) cypresses, (c) clusters of bushy shrubs, (d) all the preceding.

8. ___

9. There was specific reference to the (a) Swallow, (b) Thrush, (c) Brown Owl, (d) Raven.

9 ___

10. The captive female moth was in the (a) workshop, (b) study, (c) storage shed, (d) spare bedroom.

10. ___

10 Off for Each Mistake.
Comprehension Score: _____
Answer Key in Appendix.
Enter the Results on the Progress Record Chart.

22 Reading for Meaning

WORD POWER WORKOUT

A. Leaning on Context

In each of the blanks provided, place the letter that precedes the best definition of the underlined word in context to the left.

Words in Context	Definitions
1. ___ fascinating new <u>in-depth</u> side	a. elusive, difficult to detect
2. ___ reading and thinking became <u>inseparable</u>	b. overly proud
3. ___ sensitive to context and <u>ambiguity</u>	c. stress
4. ___ to <u>insinuation</u> and implication	d. charge
5. ___ same words could be an <u>accusation</u>	e. joined together
6. ___ special <u>emphasis</u> on meaning	f. thorough
7. ___ a <u>mature</u> reader	g. sly hint
8. ___ usually they're more <u>subtle</u>	h. uncertainty
9. ___ men are always <u>conceited</u>	i. fully developed
10. ___ a <u>variety of</u> meanings	j. number of different

Check your answers with the Key before going on. Review any that you have missed.

Pronunciation aids: 2. in sep'ur uh bul; 3. am buh gyōō'uh tē; 8. sut'l.

KEY: add, āce; end, ĕven; it, īce; odd, ōpen; pōōl; up.

B. Leaning on Parts

The prefix *in-* (also spelled *il-*, *ir-* or *im-*) means "in" or "into." Fill in each of the following blanks with the needed word or word part.

1. Don't stay outside in the cold; come in _____ by the fire.

2. Have you tried to in_____ the key in the lock the other way?

3. For the best possible return, you must in_____ your money well.

4. Does this typed list in_____ the names of all members?

5. To indoctrinate is to instruct _____ some theory or belief.

C. Making the Words Yours

In each blank below, enter the most appropriate word from the ten words in context in the first exercise, substituting it for the word(s) in parentheses. Use these words: *accusation, ambiguity, conceited, emphasis, in-depth, inseparable, insinuations, mature, subtle, variety.*

1. When I next saw her, there was a very (elusive) _____ difference in her attitude.

2. A star athlete may be (overly proud) _____.

3. The (stress) _____ was placed on reading comprehension.

4. (Uncertainty) _____ in writing can cause the reader to lose interest.

5. An authority should have (a thorough) _____ knowledge of his subject.

6. Certain (sly hints) _____ led me to think he was guilty.

7. There are a (number) _____ of ways to stay physically fit.

8. The (charge) _____ was unfounded.

9. Picnics and ants are (joined together) _____.

10. (Fully developed) _____ judgment is not found in children.

4 Off for Each Mistake.
Word Power Score: _____
Answer Key in Appendix.

22

Reading for Meaning

Begin Timing

Comprehension, when you think of it, has a top side and an under side, just as an ocean. The view from above, sun sparkling on the waves, is totally different from the view from below, with schools of fish darting about the weeds and rocks. Yet—it's the same ocean. So it is with comprehension.

Reading for details or facts focuses on the top side of comprehension—what's on the surface. That's already been discussed. *Reading for meaning* opens up a fascinating new in-depth side of comprehension. Here you plunge into a whole world of previously hidden or partially hidden meaning.

The Detail-Meaning Relationship

One side is not enough. You need both. After all, you build meaning by fitting details together. At this point, reading and thinking become inseparable. Adler, in his book *How to Read a Book*, writes that complete comprehension is always present in one situation. When people "are in love and are reading a love letter, they read for all they are worth . . . they read between the lines and in the margins; they read the whole in terms of the parts, and each part in terms of the whole; they grow sensitive to context and ambiguity, to insinuation and implication. . . . Then, if never before or after, they read." Neither side of comprehension is neglected.

Let's examine more closely the detail-meaning relationship. Two are speaking. One says, "It's ten o'clock." What does he mean? Well, that's easy, you say. He means it's ten o'clock. It's just a pure statement of fact—a detail.

Let's dive in for a below-surface look at some possibilities. You know exactly what he *said*. But what did he *mean?*

Well, he could mean, "Let's go for our usual ten o'clock coffee break." To be sure, that's not what he said; it's what he meant, though. His friend understood perfectly and replied, "Right! Let's go. What are we waiting for?"

Again, those same words could be an accusation. He might mean, "You said you'd be here at nine. You're a whole hour late!" Or he might be expressing surprise. "How come you're so early? You weren't supposed to arrive until ten-thirty." Again, he might mean, "Your watch is slow." Obviously, what's *said* and what's *meant* can be quite different. Beneath the world of surface detail, you can glimpse a truly fascinating new world opening up.

Getting Main Ideas

In the world of meaning, what's most important? It's getting the main or central idea of a book, chapter, paragraph, or example. Some readers can't see the forest for the trees. They get all the details accurately, but don't see how they add up. When they hear a story, they're likely to miss the point. Yes, getting the main idea deserves top priority.

How do you manage that? Just ask the right question. Ask yourself— "What's the point?" That question will start you along the road to the answer. For example, think back to the bit about "It's ten o'clock." Now raise the question: What's the point of that discussion? A variety of different meanings were advanced. But they all pointed up the need to consider both sides of comprehension—detail *and* underlying meaning, with special emphasis on meaning.

Drawing Inferences

Such words as *infer* and *imply* suggest still other areas in the world of meaning. To infer means to reason something out from given evidence. If someone *says* he's pleased, you *know* it. If he smiles, you have to *infer* it. That's the difference.

Try your hand at inferring with this story. A foreman hustled over to the construction site. "How long have you been working here?" he asked one man. The worker replied, "Ever since you arrived."

What inferential leap can you make? Well, you could infer that the worker was both lazy and stupid. True he didn't actually say so. You'd have to infer it. An inference is that kind of thing—a leap from the known into the unknown.

Reaching Conclusions

As a mature reader, you'll also want to become proficient in building a chain of reasoning, the last step of which brings you to a logical finish—a conclusion. Someone yawns, his head nods, and his eyes close. Conclusion? He's sleepy.

Take another illustration. A Texan built three swimming pools in his spacious back yard. One he filled with warm water, another with cool. The third was empty. When asked about that, he explained. "The empty one is for two of my friends who can't swim." Conclusion? The Texan was *more* than rich. He was "filthy rich."

Here, as with the main idea, just ask the right question: What conclusion can I make? With that question in mind, read on. She: "Handsome men are always conceited." He: "Not always. I'm not." What's your conclusion about him? And why?

Determining Importance

Can you think of still another important area of meaning? Well, a really good reader should certainly know what points are most or least important.

How can you tell? Fortunately, writers rely heavily on three devices. First, they come right out and tell you what's most or least important. Usually, however, they're more subtle. You're likely to remember best the first or last point in a series. Writers know that and tend to put their most important points in those positions. Again, if you talk more about one thing than another, you suggest which you consider most important. Again, writers do the same. Lean on those three clues: (1) statement, (2) position, and (3) amount. They really help.

Fortunately, you've already taken the two best steps to improve reading for meaning. You know some specifics. You know what questions to raise. After all, a problem well identified is a problem half solved. You're aware of getting the main ideas, drawing inferences, reaching conclusions, and evaluating importance. Other areas, such as making generalities, classifying, or determining purpose, will gradually be included. It all adds up to more enjoyment with that fascinating in-depth side of comprehension.

Reading Time: _____
See Conversion Table.
Enter WPM Rate on the Progress Record Chart.

22 Reading for Meaning

COMPREHENSION CHECK

Getting the Facts

1. Comprehension is likened to (a) a coin, (b) an ocean, (c) a sheet of paper, (d) a face.

    1. ___

2. What specific time is mentioned? (a) 8 o'clock, (b) 9 o'clock, (c) 10 o'clock, (d) 11 o'clock.

    2. ___

3. Details are likened to (a) the forest, (b) raindrops, (c) the trees, (d) particles of sand.

    3. ___

4. A leap from the known into the unknown is said to be (a) an inference, (b) a suggestion, (c) a guess, (d) a hope.

    4. ___

5. Writers tend to put important points (a) first, (b) last, (c) first or last, (d) in the middle.

    5. ___

Getting the Meaning

6. This selection is mainly about (a) determining what things are important, (b) understanding what complete comprehension means, (c) making the detail-meaning relationship clear, (d) getting the main idea.

    6. ___

7. The quoted bit about reading a love letter is to show (a) the importance of getting the essentials, (b) the importance of noting word meanings, (c) how inferences are made, (d) when complete comprehension occurs.

    7. ___

8. The discussion of "it's . . . o'clock" is intended to point up (a) the confusion of communication, (b) the difficulty of getting meaning, (c) the two aspects of comprehension, (d) the importance of getting what's said.

    8. ___

9. Apparently the most important thing is to (a) read between the lines, (b) draw proper inferences, (c) draw logical conclusions, (d) get the main idea.

    9. ___

10. Judging from the number of questions in this test dealing with facts and meaning, (a) getting details is more important, (b) getting meaning is more important, (c) both are important, (d) both are equally important.

    10. ___

10 Off for Each Mistake.
Comprehension Score: _____
Answer Key in Appendix.
Enter the Results on the Progress Record Chart.

Making the Application

At this point in your development of reading skills, notice what changes, if any, occur in your comprehension scores. Up to this time all ten questions have covered how well you were getting the facts. From now on, five of the ten questions will check your ability to get meaning, for most readers a much more difficult task.

This presents such an important change in your reading development that you should look closely and carefully at what is happening in the first selections with this new and different emphasis. Use the following chart for entering the results on Selections 22 through 31. Total your findings to see exactly how well you are managing both kinds of questions.

Selection	22	23	24	25	26	27	28	29	30	31	Total errors
Number of errors in items 1 through 5											=
Number of errors in items 6 through 10											=

In these same ten readings, how many times did you miss test item 6, always a main idea item? _____

What conclusions can you draw about your present reading habits?

Think over the various kinds of questions that require more than just noting facts. Here are some *general* questions to consider. Space is left under each for you to move into a *specific* example relating to a specific reading. The general questions should apply to all selections, either in entirety or in part.

1. What's the main idea? (Specific example: How would you phrase the main idea for Selection 11, "The Happiest Man"?)

   _____

   _____

2. What do you conclude? (Specific example—again from Selection 11: What specific evidence leads to the conclusion that he was particularly happy?)

_____

_____

3. What inference can you draw?

_____

_____

4. What bias did you note?

_____

_____

5. What purpose does the author have?

_____

_____

6. What generalization can you make?

_____

_____

7. What plan of organization do you see?

_____

_____

8. What words mark structural elements?

_____

_____

9. What are facts and what are opinions?

_____

_____

10. Is there a cause-effect relationship apparent?

_____

_____

23 How to Read a Difficult Book

WORD POWER WORKOUT

A. Leaning on Context

In each of the blanks provided, place the letter that precedes the best definition of the underlined word in context to the left.

Words in Context	Definitions
1. ___ great books <u>seminars</u>	a. ground
2. ___ <u>undeterred</u> by the paragraphs	b. support, uphold
3. ___ let yourself get <u>stalled</u>	c. idly, inactively
4. ___ to terms with the <u>structure</u>	d. study groups
5. ___ all the <u>scholarly</u> footnotes	e. evidence
6. ___ over the <u>terrain</u>	f. learned (not verb)
7. ___ from <u>vantage</u> points	g. stopped
8. ___ lets yourself drift <u>passively</u>	h. organization
9. ___ looking for <u>clues</u>	i. unstopped, undiscouraged
10. ___ helps to <u>sustain</u>	j. lookout, position of advantage

---

Check your answers with the Key before going on. Review any that you have missed.

Pronunciation aids: 2. un di tur'd'.

KEY: add, āce; end, ēven; it, īce; odd, ōpen; po͞ol; up.

B. Leaning on Parts

The prefix *sub-* (also spelled *suc-*, *suf-*, *sum-*, *sup-*, *sur-*, or *sus-*) means "under." Supply the missing parts in each of the following blanks.

1. The basement under the main basement is the sub_____.

2. Any school under the required scholastic standards is sub_____.

3. Traveling under the speed of sound? Not supersonic but sub_____!

4. A secondary or explanatory book title is called a sub_____.

5. To subjugate a country is to bring it _____ control or sub-due it.

C. Making the Words Yours

In each blank below, enter the most appropriate word from the ten words in context in the first exercise, substituting it for the word(s) in parentheses. Use these words: *clues, passively, seminars, scholarly, stalled, structure, sustain, terrain, undeterred, vantage.*

1. The detective discovered (evidence) _____ as to the where-abouts of the suspect.

2. Joining a (learned) _____ society should bring added prestige.

3. My car (stopped) _____ right in the middle of heavy traffic.

4. Sometimes it is difficult to (support) _____ a high level of achievement.

5. (Unstopped, undiscouraged) _____ by the heavy rain, they began their long trip.

6. How many great books (study groups) _____ have you attended?

7. The drive was through very rough (ground) _____.

8. Be sure to find the proper (lookout, point of advantage) _____ point for viewing the Grand Canyon.

9. The five-part (organization) _____ of this book is marked by full-page divisions.

10. Reading should be done actively, not (idly, inactively) _____.

4 Off for Each Mistake.
Word Power Score: _____
Answer Key in Appendix.

23

How to Read a Difficult Book

Mortimer J. Adler

Adler has been a prime mover of a new way to become educated—an education no one gets in an educational institution today. His concern is not with credits, degrees, and diplomas; it's with reading the finest written creations of the human mind—fifty-seven volumes in all—the Great Books. Now you know why he's helping us read difficult books.

Begin Timing

The most important rule about reading is one I have told my great books seminars again and again: In reading a difficult book for the first time, read the book through without stopping. Pay attention to what you can understand, and don't be stopped by what you can't immediately grasp. Keep on this way. Read the book through undeterred by the paragraphs, footnotes, arguments, and references that escape you. If you stop at any of these stumbling blocks, if you let yourself get stalled, you are lost. In most cases you won't be able to puzzle the thing out by sticking to it. You have a much better chance of understanding it on a second reading, but that requires you to read the book *through* for the first time.

This is the most practical method I know to break the crust of a book, to get the feel and general sense of it, and to come to terms with its structure as quickly and as easily as possible. The longer you delay in getting some sense of the over-all plan of a book, the longer you are in understanding it. You simply must have some grasp of the whole before you can see the parts in their true perspective—or often in any perspective at all.

Shakespeare was spoiled for generations of high-school students who were forced to go through *Julius Caesar, Hamlet* or *Macbeth* scene by scene, to look up all the words that were new to them, and to study all the scholarly footnotes. As a result, they never actually read the play. Instead, they were dragged through it, bit by bit, over a period of many weeks. By the time they got to the end of the play, they had surely forgotten the beginning. They should have been encouraged to read the play in one sitting. Only then would they have understood enough of it to make it possible for them to understand more.

What you understand by reading a book through to the end—even if it is only fifty per cent or less—will help you later in making the additional effort to go back to places you passed by on your first reading. Actually you will be proceeding like any traveler in unknown parts. Having been over the terrain once, you will be able to explore it again from vantage points you could not have known about before. You will be less likely to mistake the side roads for the main highway. You won't be deceived by the shadows at high noon, because you will remember how they looked at sunset. And the mental map you have fashioned will show better how the valleys and mountains are all part of one landscape.

There is nothing magical about a first quick reading. It cannot work wonders and should certainly never be thought of as a substitute for the careful reading that a good book deserves. But a first quick reading makes the careful study much easier.

This practice helps you to keep alert in going at a book. How many times have you daydreamed your way through pages and pages only to wake up with no idea of the ground you have been over? That can't help happening if you let yourself drift passively through a book. No one ever understands much that way. You must have a way of getting a general thread to hold onto.

A good reader is active in his efforts to understand. Any book is a problem, a puzzle. The reader's attitude is that of a detective looking for clues to its basic ideas and alert for anything that will make them clearer. The rule about a first quick reading helps to sustain this attitude. If you follow it, you will be surprised how much time you will save, how much more you will grasp, and how much easier it will be.

Reading Time: _____
See Conversion Table.
Enter WPM Rate on the Progress Record Chart.

23 How to Read a Difficult Book

COMPREHENSION CHECK

Getting the Facts

1. Adler mentioned his (a) honor students, (b) college teaching, (c) graduate students, (d) seminars.   1. ___

2. Adler referred to (a) *Merchant of Venice*, (b) *King Lear*, (c) *Julius Caesar*, (d) *Romeo and Juliet*.   2. ___

3. Adler said to read a book through even if you understood (a) only fifty per cent or less, (b) only a third or less, (c) little or nothing, (d) most of it.   3. ___

4. Specific mention was made of (a) trails, (b) side roads, (c) freeways, (d) gravel roads.   4. ___

5. He likened a book specifically to (a) a riddle, (b) a paradox, (c) a puzzle, (d) a mystery.   5. ___

Getting the Meaning

6. The main idea was to show what about reading a difficult book? (a) how to avoid daydreaming, (b) how to get needed perspective, (c) how to read it, (d) what general rule to follow.   6. ___

7. How many rules did Adler discuss? (a) only one, (b) two, (c) three, (d) four.   7. ___

8. His discussion of reading Shakespeare was (a) to criticize teachers, (b) to provide reasons for accepting his method, (c) to suggest the need for more background, (d) to criticize the choice of plays.   8. ___

9. His analogy of reading to traveling was intended to (a) dramatize, (b) clarify his point, (c) add interest, (d) summarize.   9 ___

10. You would infer that Adler's purpose was (a) to explain, (b) to persuade, (c) to entertain, (d) to describe.   10. ___

10 Off for Each Mistake.
Comprehension Score: _____
Answer Key in Appendix.
Enter the Results on the Progress Record Chart.

24 J. T.'s Story

WORD POWER WORKOUT

A. Leaning on Context

In each of the blanks provided, place the letter that precedes the best definition of the underlined word in context to the left.

Words in Context	Definitions
1. ___ <u>leitmotiv</u> has been	a. skilled
2. ___ <u>converge</u> on him	b. distinguished
3. ___ by <u>tacit</u> agreement	c. unspoken
4. ___ that goal <u>garnered</u>	d. dominant theme
5. ___ to <u>confront</u> his big problem	e. come together
6. ___ is <u>adept</u> in explaining	f. collected
7. ___ acts as a <u>liaison</u> between	g. connection
8. ___ won local <u>acclaim</u>	h. praise
9. ___ <u>prestigious</u> National Jefferson Award	i. tangible, concrete
10. ___ almost <u>palpable</u> feeling	j. face boldly

Check your answers with the Key before going on. Review any that you have missed.

Pronunciation aids: 1. līt′mō tēf′; 3. tas′it; 7. lē′ā zon′; 9. pres tij′us; 10. pal′puh bul.
KEY: add, āce; end, ēven; it, īce; odd, ōpen; pool; up.

B. Leaning on Parts

With a few prefixes the final letter often changes in spelling to blend with the letter that follows. To understand such changes, spell the following combinations of *com-*, noting what happens and asking why.

1. com + nect = _____ (fasten together)

2. com + lect = _____ (bring together)

3. com + respond = _____ (write together)

4. com + flict = _____ (fight together)

5. com + operate = _____ (work together)

C. Making the Words Yours

In each blank below, enter the most appropriate word from the ten words in context in the first exercise, substituting it for the word(s) in parentheses. Use these words: *acclaim, adept, confront, converge, garnered, leitmotiv, liaison, palpable, prestigious, tacit*.

1. You need an intriguing (dominant theme) _____ for the big affair.

2. The committee gave (unspoken) _____ approval for the change.

3. Who will act as the (connection) _____ between the two groups?

4. Special (praise) _____ went to the swimmer who won the gold medal.

5. Our school paper (collected) _____ more awards than ever before.

6. Do you have the nerve to (face boldly) _____ the administration about your discoveries?

7. The worker is particularly (skilled) _____ at avoiding work.

8. Don't believe a word of it—it's a (tangible, concrete) _____ lie.

9. What a (distinguished) _____ address the new business had!

10. In that beautiful pen and ink drawing, notice how the lines all (come together) _____ in one spot.

4 Off for Each Mistake.
Word Power Score: _____
Answer Key in Appendix.

24

J. T.'s Story

Hilary Richardson Bagnato

How many illiterates have we in America? Some say six million, some say sixty. Pick one of those millions—one well-documented case—and see just what it's like. Go ahead. Fit yourself into J. T.'s shoes and find out exactly what problems he has to cope with.

Begin Timing

His life story reads like fiction. It weaves a tale of poverty, truancy, war, racism—and throws in a plot twist with a surprise ending. But throughout J. T. Pace's 68 years, the leitmotiv has been his education: his lack of it, his yearning for it, and his eventual achievement of it; he began learning to read and write at age 61.

One of eight siblings born to poor African American sharecroppers on a farm in South Carolina, U.S.A., J. T. has come a long way from his roots, even though he returned to his home county after spending most of his adult life away. Now retired and living comfortably, J. T. not only learned to read late in life; he also admitted his illiteracy through Project Literacy U.S. (PLUS), a national television public awareness campaign sponsored jointly by Capitol Cities/ABC network and PBS television. Through his appearances in several television commercials, J. T.'s story has reached many of the nation's 60 million people who have trouble reading and writing. Others have been impressed with J. T.; he has appeared all over the United States with such respected literacy advocates as First Lady Barbara Bush.

A distinguished-looking man, J. T. is also an eloquent speaker. Listening to him, it is hard to believe he does not have even a high-school diploma. He is passionate in his belief about the benefits of literacy, something most people in the United States take for granted. He says his former illiteracy bound him to a fate he shared with his ancestors: that of slavery. "As someone who could not read or write, I was enslaved," he says. "But becoming literate truly has made me free."

J. T. says his life was full and, for the most part, happy, but that, even this late, learning to read has changed it all. That courageous confession is a big step for a man whose children didn't know he was an illiterate until they saw his first ad on television.

Bessie Lee, executive director of the Greenville (South Carolina) Literacy Association, where J. T. learned to read, praises his commitment to spreading the word. "He has charm and intelligence," she says, "but his genuine warmth stems from his desire to help other people. You feel it immediately."

Actually, J. T. did attend school at one time—for six months in kindergarten. He recalls it now matter-of-factly: "The teacher asked me to stand up and say the alphabet, and I stuttered so badly I couldn't get the letters out. So the teacher picked up a switch and hit me across the back with it. That did it for me. I ran out of that schoolhouse and went home and told my daddy I was never going back."

J. T.'s parents didn't make a fuss; because of the farm, they needed all the help they could get from the children. Besides, education wasn't a top priority for the Pace family. Mr. Pace couldn't read at all or sign his name. Mrs. Pace could read a little; she had a third- or fourth-grade education. And as for J. T.'s five brothers and two sisters, "not a one of us ever finished high school," he says. "We all worked in factories, plants, construction, bakeries—jobs where you didn't need an education."

Tired of life on the farm, J. T. ran away from home when he was 15, into the nearest big city, Greenville. He washed cars in a service station and dishes in a five-and-dime store, all the while staying with one of his sisters and dreaming of a better life.

J. T. was 21 when World War II began, and he enlisted immediately. He recalls, "I signed an 'X' for my signature on the papers, because I couldn't sign my name." He landed in Normandy two days after the D-Day invasion and traveled all through Europe. His life was never the same afterwards.

Most important, it was the first time he felt frustrated because of his illiteracy. He realized he couldn't communicate with his family. He received from home letters he couldn't read, so he occasionally asked someone from the Red Cross to read them to him. "Where I came from, you never thought you were going to need an education," J. T. says, "and now I was so ashamed. I kept it quiet. That's when I knew I would have to get an education; that's when the fire started burning in me."

But the fire didn't become a blaze until almost four decades later. J. T. felt more pressing issues converge on him when he returned home in 1946. When he got back to Greenville, he noticed as he never had before how tight the tension wire of racism was drawn. It hurt and puzzled him. "In the army I had lots of white friends. We fought together, worked together, lived together." That was not reality in his hometown. After hearing about a lynching of another black, J. T. left home, telling his mother he would return to Greenville only to visit—never to live.

He traveled north to Philadelphia, where he met his future wife, Ruth, but didn't marry her until he had first gone up to Niagara Falls, New York, and worked at a plant for about a year. Then he came down to Philadelphia, married Ruth, and the two returned to Niagara Falls, where they spent the better part of three decades. The question of J. T.'s illiteracy never once came up for discussion between the couple. (In fact, J. T. says, the first time they ever talked about it was when he decided to enroll in classes at the Greenville Literacy Association.) By tacit agreement, Ruth, who has a fifth-grade education, simply signed J. T.'s name on the marriage license for him.

The years spent in Niagara Falls were happy ones for the Paces, despite the burden of illiteracy that was getting harder and harder for J. T. to bear. For almost 30 years, he drove a tractor-trailer truck for a construction company, and during that time, he says, his boss never knew he couldn't read. When driving, he would match up written directions with road signs.

Fooling his children—daughter Brenda and son Clarence—was a little harder. "The kids would ask me for help on their homework, but I avoided giving it to them by saying things like, 'Don't bother me now. I worked a full day, and I'm tired. Wait until your mother comes home and ask her.'"

But even those brushes with exposure weren't enough to force J. T. to learn to read. He still had other goals that were more important to him. "My mother used to work for white folks, and occasionally, as a child, I would go up to the big house to be with Mama, and I would lie down for a minute on a big bed and push my fingers into the feather mattress, and I could not believe how soft it was," he explains. "I would think of the straw mattresses my brothers and I slept on at home, and I couldn't understand why we lived so differently. I told myself as I grew up that before I left this earth, I would be able to provide nice things for my family. So I worked hard to build a good life for them. Learning to read came second."

Because his lawyer was a friend who handled his accounts and gave him good investment advice, J. T. was able to provide a comfortable life for his family. And then, that goal garnered, he gathered courage to confront his big problem.

In 1977, J. T. had a heart attack and retired early. His doctor thought he should move out of the windiest part of the country into a warmer climate. And so he found himself back in the state he never dreamed he would live in again. But, to his pleasant surprise, he discovered that things had changed much in Greenville since his days there: attitudes were different; the cloud of racism had lifted; people were friendlier.

J. T. says now: "It seemed like I had just about everything, but there was one huge thing lacking in my life. I said to myself, 'I have just *got* to read the Bible.'"

With a chuckle, he describes how he went one day to nearby Bob Jones University, a religious institution, and asked a woman in the admissions office if they could teach him to read the Bible there. She smiled and said yes, and handed him an admissions form to fill out. Recalls J. T.: "I said, 'You've got it all wrong. I'm here because I literally cannot read the

Bible. I don't want to read Shakespeare. Please, can't you just teach me to read this one book?' "

The woman sadly said no, and J. T. recalls how he went home and cried as he mowed his lawn. Then, one day three weeks later, the same woman from Bob Jones called and told him about the Greenville Literacy Association.

And so his link with the Association began. Since that day in 1981, he has come far in what truly can be described as a battle against illiteracy. After two years of two hours of classes a week, he finally was able to read a simplified version of the Bible.

Whether he is traveling within his home county from school to school, urging kids not to drop out, or visiting Rotary clubs throughout South Carolina, or speaking on the "Oprah Winfrey Show" on national television, the cause of literacy has become J. T.'s life.

He knows both sides of the story, and is adept in explaining how an illiterate feels. "See, a person who can't read is not stupid," he explains. "He just can't read. If you can't read or write, you have to be a quick thinker and have a great memory. I know that's how I got by."

He is a South Carolina Department of Corrections volunteer and, as a member of the Greenville Literacy Association's board of directors, acts as a liaison between new students and the administration. He won local acclaim in 1985 when he volunteered to be featured in a United Way public service spot on television. This led to the national ad with PLUS. Since then he has won many local, state, and national awards for outstanding public service. More recently, he was one of nine people chosen from a pool of 8,000 nominees as a winner of the prestigious National Jefferson Award for Outstanding Service.

Bessie Lee traveled to Washington, D.C., with J. T. to accept that award, and recalls her almost palpable feeling of excitement and pride for her star student: "I remember standing on the steps of the U. S. Supreme Court building and looking at the Capitol in the distance and thinking, 'Miracles *do* happen.' "

J. T. will never earn a degree, but he is a role model for older illiterates, who see in him a bit of themselves, and—perhaps, most important—for young people, who learn from him the importance of an education. For J. T., getting this message across is the ultimate happy ending.

Reading Time: _____
See Conversion Table.
Enter WPM Rate on the Progress Record Chart.

24 J. T.'s Story

COMPREHENSION CHECK

Getting the Facts

1. J. T. was born in (a) Alabama, (b) Georgia, (c) North Carolina, (d) South Carolina.

1. ___

2. In kindergarten he was switched because he couldn't (a) say the alphabet, (b) form letters, (c) keep quiet, (d) get along with other students.

2. ___

3. He worked in a plant in (a) Pittsburgh, (b) Niagara Falls, (c) Washington, D. C., (d) Syracuse.

3. ___

4. He paid a visit to (a) Beria College, (b) Grace Bible Institute, (c) Bob Jones University, (d) Greenshore College.

4. ___

5. J. T. was featured in a TV public service spot for the (a) Red Cross, (b) Salvation Army, (c) United Way, (d) Chamber of Commerce.

5. ___

Getting the Meaning

6. The main idea was to help people (a) to read better, (b) to understand problems arising from illiteracy, (c) to recognize the importance of conquering illiteracy, (d) to know the importance of reading the Bible.

6. ___

7. Developing the main idea was largely through use of (a) narration, (b) explanation, (c) reasoning, (d) repetition.

7. ___

8. The chief purpose was to (a) amuse, (b) inform, (c) inspire, (d) persuade.

8. ___

9. The author's attitude toward J. T. is best described as (a) impressed, (b) understanding, (c) concerned, (d) friendly.

9 ___

10. You would infer the most important motivation for J. T. was his (a) dream of reading the Bible, (b) feelings of shame, (c) yearning for education, (d) desire for nice things.

10. ___

10 Off for Each Mistake.
Comprehension Score: _____
Answer Key in Appendix.
Enter the Results on the Progress Record Chart.

25 Reading Words More Effectively

WORD POWER WORKOUT

A. Leaning on Context

In each of the blanks provided, place the letter that precedes the best definition of the underlined word in context to the left.

Words in Context	Definitions
1. ___ an <u>allied</u> plane	a. concealed, hidden
2. ___ figures are <u>conservative</u>	b. difference
3. ___ a <u>convenient</u> substitute	c. visual
4. ___ that <u>latent</u> potential	d. moderate
5. ___ more <u>complicated</u> than usual	e. removing
6. ___ play <u>havoc</u> with reading	f. further, encourage to flourish
7. ___ in dramatic <u>contrast</u>	g. involved
8. ___ improved <u>perceptual</u> skill	h. associated
9. ___ in <u>eliminating</u> regression	i. easy
10. ___ <u>promote</u> effective word grouping	j. confusion

Check your answers with the Key before going on. Review any that you have missed.

Pronunciation aids: 4. lā′tunt; 6. hav′uk; 8. pur sep′choo ul.

KEY: add, āce; end, ēven; it, īce; odd, ōpen; pool; up.

B. Leaning on Parts

The prefix *sub-* also has different spellings, the *b* changing to blend with the next letter. Spell the following combinations, observing the changes.

1. sub + port = _____

2. sub + fix = _____

3. sub + ceed = _____

4. sub + gest = _____

5. sub + pect = _____

C. Making the Words Yours

In each blank below, enter the most appropriate word from the ten words in context in the first exercise, substituting it for the word(s) in parentheses. Use these words: *allied, complicated, conservative, contrast, convenient, eliminated, havoc, latent, perceptual, promote.*

1. The (moderate) _____ politician was liked by the older citizens.

2. Students with (visual) _____ problems tend to read more slowly.

3. The troublemaker was (removed) _____ from the game.

4. He joined an organization to (further) _____ world peace.

5. His (hidden) _____ interest in acting began to develop in college.

6. In a story, a more (involved) _____ plot demands more careful reading.

7. Making a cake from a cake mix is quite (easy) _____ .

8. There is a marked (difference) _____ between the two brothers.

9. The cry of "Fire" created (confusion) _____ in the crowded theater.

10. During wartime (associated) _____ forces teamed up to defeat a common enemy.

4 Off for Each Mistake.
Word Power Score: _____
Answer Key in Appendix.

25

Reading Words More Effectively

Begin Timing

We're back to words again. But not to vocabulary building. That's already been covered. This chapter focuses on mastering other special problems with words.

WORDS! If you can't see 'em, you can't read 'em. That's a reminder that in dealing with words you need *two* sets of skills. One set brings words from the printed page into your mind. The other set attaches meaning to them, when they arrive. Context, word parts, and dictionary are used here.

What can you do to speed the accurate flow of words from page to brain? That's a whole new area of concern. Fortunately, research has some answers.

Developing Perceptual Skill

As early as World War II, Dr. Samuel Renshaw, psychologist, was able to set up a perceptual training program of amazing effectiveness. With it, over 385,000 men were trained in aircraft recognition. One officer, so trained, paid it the highest tribute. After a year and a half in the thick of the Pacific fighting his crew never once fired on an allied plane and never failed to fire on an enemy one. That's the visual wizardry you want for reading words.

How much improvement can you expect? According to Renshaw, proper perceiving is a learned skill, just like playing the piano or learning French. If you're average, Renshaw's research indicates that you're using your eyes at only about 20 percent efficiency. In short, you should perceive five times better than you do.

Such training is ordinarily given with a tachistoscope. That's a projector with a cameralike shutter. It flashes numbers, words, or phrases on a screen at split-second speeds. Such training helps you (1) see more, (2) see more accurately, and (3) see more quickly.

Actually, classroom results suggest that Renshaw's figures are conservative. You should be able to increase the flow of words from page to brain to ten times your present efficiency, not five.

In our reading classes, we include about twenty ten-minute practice periods. Initial training is at 1/10th of a second. By the end of the course, students perceive as much as 58 percent more accurately *and* ten times faster—1/100th of a second.

To be sure, you probably don't have a tachistoscope handy. You do, however, have a convenient substitute—your hand and something to read. To practice, cover part of a line of print with your hand. Quickly pull your hand down and back to get a split-second look at the words revealed. Repeat that in a readinglike pattern, phrase after phrase. Two minutes a day of such practice will do wonders. In two minutes, you should soon manage from 20 to 40 split-second looks. Twenty days of that regimen and you'll have more practice than our usual students. That's the way you develop that latent potential of yours.

Minimizing Regressions

In reading words, you should know what's meant by regressing. That's looking back at a word or words you have already read. It's like stepping backwards every few yards as you walk—hardly the way to move ahead in a hurry. Notice what regressing does to a complex complex sentence like this, like this, making it seem even more complicated than complicated than usual with its regressive rereading of rereading of words. Confusing, isn't it? Regressing does indeed play havoc with both reading speed and comprehension.

Eye movement photographs of some 12,000 readers show that college students regress an average of 15 times in reading only 100 words. That would work out to 150 regressions in reading this one article. No wonder you should get rid of them. They slow you down tremendously.

Faster-than-comfortable reading is the best way to eliminate them. You can soon reduce the number of regressions by as much as 80 percent, judging from class results. And you're still reading every word. You just aren't reading them twice!

Developing Word Grouping Habits

As he reads, the average college or adult reader takes in only 1.1 words at a glance. Make that 2.2, and he's *doubled* his reading rate. Try it. Superior readers, with speeds of 900 to 1,000 wpm, can manage four words per eye-stop. Out of 30,000 cases photographed, however, with an eye-movement camera, only three have read at rates above 1,000 wpm, a relatively rare achievement.

The eye-movement motion-picture camera reveals the possibilities. It records one reader making nine stops or fixations in reading nine words—an exact word-by-word pattern. In dramatic contrast, it records a highly skilled reader making only three stops in reading those same words.

As in eliminating regressions, practice faster-than-comfortable reading. It's your best move. It forces you to take in more words at a glance.

Noting Key Words

Another special word-reading skill is that of identifying key words. This is part of the skimming technique. But it should also be part of your normal reading. Research shows rather wide variations. Some readers, for example, when asked to list key words in a paragraph with over fifty nouns denoting place, selected only prepositions—*beyond, in, at.* Others were determined by personal concerns. One student, worried about getting a ticket during the experiment, listed *car* and *parking lot.*

The best readers selected nouns almost 90 percent of the time. It makes sense. Take this sentence: "The big _____ from the _____ to the _____." Not very clear, is it? Yet it's 70 percent complete. Let's try the nouns: *book . . . shelf . . . floor.* That's better. Yet that's only 30 percent of the sentence, not 70 percent. Now add the verb—*fell: book fell . . . shelf . . . floor.* That's the best 40 percent. Right?

Other things being equal, then, look for the nouns—the names of persons, places, things, qualities, actions, or ideas. Next, note verbs. By so doing, you'll make sure of focusing your attention on the important things.

Now you know how to read words with enviable skill. Develop improved perceptual skill, minimize regression, promote effective word grouping habits, and zero in on key words—when you do, you'll fine added pleasure, ease, and interest in reading.

Reading Time: _____
See Conversion Table.
Enter WPM Rate on the Progress Record Chart.

25 Reading Words More Effectively

COMPREHENSION CHECK

Getting the Facts

1. What is specifically mentioned? (a) World War II,
   (b) Hitler, (c) the Luftwaffe, (d) Eisenhower.   1. ___

2. A tachistoscope has a (a) stroboscopic shutter, (b) reflective device (c) cameralike shutter, (d) filmstrip
   attachment.   2. ___

3. College students regress on an average of how many
   times in reading 100 words? (a) four, (b) seven,
   (c) eleven, (d) fifteen.   3. ___

4. Eye-movement camera findings show that reading speeds
   above 1,000 wpm (a) have never been recorded, (b) are
   frequent, (c) are relatively rare, (d) are quite common.   4. ___

5. The ability to identify key words is said to (a) be easier
   for girls, (b) show wide variations, (c) come automatically with age, (d) improve in college.   5. ___

Getting the Meaning

6. The main idea of the article is how to (a) speed the flow
   of words, (b) build a vocabulary, (c) spot key words,
   (d) minimize regressions.   6. ___

7. You would infer that the chief reason for regressing is
   (a) lack of training, (b) lack of interest, (c) poor study
   habits, (d) vocabulary weakness.   7. ___

8. The average reader, you would infer, is (a) quite inefficient, (b) quite efficient, (c) tireless,, (d) casual.   8. ___

9. Figures on eye-movement camera cases are cited to show
   (a) how rapidly gains are made, (b) how common the
   1,000 wpm rate is, (c) how improvement varies, (d) how
   inefficient adults are.   9 ___

10. The illustrative sentence beginning, "The big . . . from
    . . ." is to point up the importance of (a) connectives,
    (b) verbs, (c) nouns, (d) skipping.   10. ___

10 Off for Each Mistake.
Comprehension Score: _____
Answer Key in Appendix.
Enter the Results on the Progress Record Chart.

Making the Application

As a warming-up exercise, every now and then run through these three columns, using a 3 x 5 card. Cover the phrase with the card but leave the dot above it uncovered, to keep your eyes on target. Quickly pull the card down and back, uncovering the phrase below the dot for a fraction of a second. See if you perceived the entire phrase accurately in that split second. Go from dot to dot, through all three columns.

2-word phrase	*3-word phrase*	*4-word phrase*
•	•	•
You should	Did you know	But that is only
•	•	•
try to	that Abraham Lincoln	when we can choose
•	•	•
read by	got most of	the exact right word.
•	•	•
the grouping	his fine education	When you say that
•	•	•
of words.	from the reading	words win friends and
•	•	•
Your skill	he did when	influence people, can you
•	•	•
in reading	he was a boy?	think of an example?
•	•	•
is a very	It is said	Can you think of
•	•	•
valuable one.	that the pen	some jobs where people
•	•	•
Practice it	is far mightier	make a living by
•	•	•
every day.	than the sword.	the words they use?

For additional practice, draw two light pencil lines down one of the full pages in this or another textbook. Space the lines evenly so as to divide the line into three equal parts. Then, by using your hand or a 3 x 5 card, see if you can take in the first third at one glance, then the second, then the third. Two minutes of such practice should be an excellent warm-up exercise.

Now select a paragraph and underline all the key words in the entire paragraph. Underline as few as possible, however, making certain you do select only the most important. What kinds of words did you select? How many nouns? Verbs? Other parts of speech?

26 The ABC's of Saving Time

WORD POWER WORKOUT

A. Leaning on Context

In each of the blanks provided, place the letter that precedes the best definition of the underlined word in context to the left.

Words in Context	Definitions
1. ___ <u>delving</u> into the matter	a. ordinary
2. ___ in a dozen other <u>enterprises</u>	b. time between, interval
3. ___ <u>fundamental</u> time-planning tool	c. digging
4. ___ <u>clutter</u> your mind	d. delayed, put off
5. ___ do not list <u>routine</u> items	e. undertakings
6. ___ <u>poke</u> through routine matters	f. withstand
7. ___ if it is <u>inconsequential</u>	g. essential
8. ___ be <u>deferred</u> indefinitely	h. litter
9. ___ in the <u>interim</u>	i. unimportant
10. ___ <u>resist</u> the temptation	j. hunt

Check your answers with the Key before going on. Review any that you have missed.

Pronunciation aids: 7. in'kon suh kwen'shul; 9. in'tur im.

KEY: add, āce; end; ēven; it, īce; odd, ōpen; pōol; up.

B. Leaning on Parts

The identical prefixes *in-* and *in-*, meaning "not" and "in," change their spelling to blend with whatever letter follows. Spell each combination.

1. in + radiate = _____

2. in + luminate = _____

3. in + migrant = _____

4. in + lustrious = _____

5. in + rigation = _____

C. Making the Words Yours

In each blank below, enter the most appropriate word from the ten words in context in the first exercise, substituting it for the word(s) in parentheses. Use these words: *clutter, delving, deferred, enterprises, fundamental, inconsequential, interim, poke, resist, routine.*

1. This (essential) _____ principle must be followed.

2. The freshman (delayed, put off) _____ taking chemistry for another term.

3. How can you (withstand) _____ the temptation to leave?

4. The writer started (digging) _____ into all the research on the subject.

5. The committee got bogged down with (ordinary) _____ matters.

6. Don't get into too many involved (undertakings) _____; time is short.

7. Be sure to focus on major problems, not (unimportant) _____ details.

8. Why (litter) _____ your desk with all those old papers?

9. You'll have to (hunt) _____ around in your text to find the answer.

10. I know where you were in the morning and in the evening, but where were you in the (time between) _____?

4 Off for Each Mistake.
Word Power Score: _____
Answer Key in Appendix.

26

The ABC's of Saving Time

Alan Lakein

One commodity belongs to everyone equally—to the young, the old, the rich, the poor, to women, to men—to everyone alike! Time! Twenty-four hours a day. It's what you do with it that's important. Control your time and you control your life—so says the author of the following selection. Now use some of that "time on your hands." Read on.

Begin Timing

When I first started delving into the matter of getting more done every day, I asked successful people what the secret of their success was. I recall an early discussion with a vice president of a large oil company. "Oh, I just keep a To Do List," he said. I passed over that quickly, little suspecting the importance of what he said.

I was in another city the next day and I had lunch with a businessman who practically owned the town. He was chairman of the gas and light company, president of five manufacturing companies, and had his hand in a dozen other enterprises. I asked him how he managed to get everything done. "Oh, that's easy," he said. "I keep a To Do List."

The first thing in the morning, he told me, he would come in and list what he wanted to accomplish that day. He would arrange the items in priority. During the day he would cross off items as they were completed and add others as they occurred to him. In the evening he would check to see how many of the items he had written down still remained undone and then give himself a score. His goal was to cross off every single item.

Again and again in the years since, when I have talked to successful people, the To Do List has come up. I have found that one difference between people at the top of the ladder and people at the bottom is that those at the top use a To Do List every day to make better use of their time; those at the bottom don't.

Because the To Do List is such a fundamental time-planning tool, let's take a closer look at it.

Some people try to keep To Do Lists in their head, but this is rarely effective. Why clutter your mind? It's much better to leave it free from creative pursuits.

What do you write down? I recommend that you not list routine items but do list everything that has high priority today and might not get done without special attention. Don't forget to put down the activities related to your long-term goals. Although it may appear strange to see "begin learning French" or "find new friends" in the same list with "bring home a quart of milk," you want to do them in the same day. Since you'll use your To Do List as a guide when deciding what to work on next, you need the long-term projects represented, too.

You must *set priorities*. Some people do as many items as possible on their lists. They get a very high percentage of tasks done, but their effectiveness is low because the tasks they've done are mostly of C priority (lowest). Others like to start at the top of the list and go right down it, again with little regard to what's important. The best way is to label each item according to ABC priority and then polish off the list accordingly.

For people who have trouble living with priorities, I have found that it's helpful to use one piece of paper for the A's and B's and another page for the more numerous C's. The A and B paper is kept on top of the C list, and every time you raise it to do a C, you're aware that you're not making the best use of your time. Remember, it's not so much completing the list that counts, but making the best use of your time.

One reason many people poke through routine matters is that they like the feeling of doing something efficiently, even if it is inconsequential. Desk-neatening, for example, is hardly an A activity, but results show immediately. The homemaker who collects another delicious-sounding recipe when she has 500 untried clippings may kid herself into thinking that she is becoming a better cook, but the truth is that she is clipping rather than cooking.

Many activities of top value, on the other hand, cannot, by their very nature, be performed well. The problems associated with them are new, untried and uncertain. Doing them means taking risks, which, whether calculated or not, will sometimes bring an unsuccessful outcome. Is there any wonder that you look around for something you can do well? One of the things you can do well is clear up all the easy C's. And you justify it by saying you are clearing them away so that you will then be free to do the A items later.

There's a rule to help people like that—the 80/20 rule. It says, "If all items are arranged in order of value, 80 percent of the value would come from only 20 percent of the items, while the remaining 20 percent of the value would come from 80 percent of the items." The 80/20 rule suggests that in a list of ten items, doing two of them will yield most (80 percent) of the value. Find these two, label them A, get them done.

Many C items can be turned into what I call "CZ's." CZ's are C's that can be deferred indefinitely without harm. Definite CZ's include watering the lawn when it looks like rain, inventorying the freezer (when you just did it last month and nothing has changed significantly in the interim), mopping the kitchen floor just before the children come home on a rainy day. You can probably think of many other items that are too trivial to do, or will settle themselves by the passage of time.

If you can let the dusting, washing, filing or checking go one more day, then let it. You will have spent less of your life dusting, filing and washing. If you continually resist the temptation to do the C's, you can significantly increase the number that become CZ's. Always keep in mind the question, "How terrible would it be if I didn't do this C?" If your answer is, "Not too terrible," then don't do it.

Do your A's instead. Make the most of your time.

Reading Time: _____
See Conversion Table.
Enter WPM Rate on the Progress Record Chart.

26 The ABC's of Saving Time

COMPREHENSION CHECK

Getting the Facts

1. One talk was with (a) a businessman who practically owned the town, (b) the president of Standard Oil, (c) the mayor of New York, (d) a Fortune 500 magnate.   1. ___

2. With the To Do list, one man's goal was to (a) do all the C items, (b) cross off every item, (c) do all but the C items, (d) do all A items.   2. ___

3. One entry specifically suggested was to begin learning (a) Russian, (b) Spanish, (c) German, (d) French.   3. ___

4. Mention was made of (a) watering plants, (b) desk-neatening, (c) taking bridge lessons, (d) learning to type.   4. ___

5. A CZ item (a) is easily done, (b) can be dropped without harm, (c) should be done first, (d) takes little time.   5. ___

Getting the Meaning

6. This is mainly about (a) making To Do lists, (b) saving time, (c) using ABC priorities, (d) doing your A's.   6. ___

7. The two introductory episodes were primarily to (a) prove the value of To Do lists, (b) get reader attention, (c) establish links with business, (d) show the author's qualifications.   7. ___

8. By implication use your time better primarily to (a) make socializing time, (b) be happier, (c) enjoy more leisure, (d) be more successful.   8. ___

9. By influence the author has learned most from his (a) wide reading, (b) university work, (c) business contacts, (d) management seminars.   9 ___

10. The 80/20 rule is intended to emphasize most strongly (a) a broad approach, (b) doing A items, (c) doing all items, (d) balancing attention.   10. ___

10 Off for Each Mistake.
Comprehension Score: _____
Answer Key in Appendix.
Enter the Results on the Progress Record Chart.

27 Guiding Light

WORD POWER WORKOUT

A. Leaning on Context

In each of the blanks provided, place the letter that precedes the best definition of the underlined word in context to the left.

Words in Context	Definitions
1. ___ <u>diurnal</u> and seasonal cycles	a. developed
2. ___ are indeed <u>affected</u>	b. in phase with
3. ___ are often <u>synchronized</u>	c. healing
4. ___ which <u>secretes</u> the hormone	d. daily
5. ___ and <u>vice versa</u>	e. exciting
6. ___ some of it <u>seeps</u> into	f. influenced
7. ___ humans had <u>evolved</u>	g. forms and releases
8. ___ help <u>alleviate</u> the problems	h. trickles, oozes
9. ___ all very <u>intriguing</u>	i. relieve
10. ___ on its <u>therapeutic</u> effectiveness	j. conversely, in reverse order

---

Check your answers with the Key before going on. Review any that you have missed.

Pronunciation aids: 1. dī ur'nul; 3. sing'kruh nīz'd; 5. vī'sē vur'suh; 8. uh lē'vē āt; 9. in trēg'ing; 10. ther'uh pyoo'tik.

KEY: add, āce; end, ēven; it, īce; odd, ōpen; pool; up.

B. Leaning on Parts

Here are two more quite changeable prefixes: *ad-* and *ob-*. Get better acquainted with them by combining them with the roots given below.

1. ad + cept = _____

2. ad + low = _____

3. ob + press = _____

4. ob + fend = _____

5. ob + cur = _____

C. Making the Words Yours

In each blank below, enter the most appropriate word from the ten words in context in the first exercise, substituting it for the word(s) in parentheses. Use these words: *affected, alleviate, diurnal, evolved, intriguing, secretes, seeps, synchronized, therapeutic, vice versa.*

1. Their watches were now (in phase with) _____ with each other.

2. Those pills have a strong (healing) _____ effect.

3. Will you be (influenced) _____ by the change of regulation?

4. Some rain water often (trickles, oozes) _____ through my coat.

5. My friends said the movie was especially (exciting) _____.

6. The biologist seemed interested in how the animal had (developed) _____.

7. Take this pain-killer to (relieve) _____ your pain.

8. That's the gland which (forms and releases) _____ a hormone.

9. A long overseas flight tends to upset one's (daily) _____ cycle.

10. Am I supposed to register before you or (conversely, in reverse order) _____?

4 Off for Each Mistake.
Word Power Score: _____
Answer Key in Appendix.

27

Guiding Light

Hal Hellman

*So—you're not feeling up to par? It may be the light—its inten-
sity, duration, and color—that's affecting you. Don't make light
of that possibility. The following selection will throw added light
on that very subject. To enlighten yourself, read on!*

Begin Timing

Psychiatrist Alfred J. Lewy tells of a patient whose severe winter depressions
would ease each year only with the coming of spring. "It made sense to try
giving him spring days in the winter," Lewy recalls. "We extended his day
by three hours in the morning and three in the afternoon—using the high
light levels we had been experimenting with—and after only a few days he
came out of his depression as if it really were spring."

Lewy's patient was the first of several who have been treated at the
National Institute of Mental Health for what psychiatrists believe may be a
unique form of depression. It is caused, they suspect, by lack of exposure
to sunlight in winter, due to shorter daylight hours and people's habit of
spending more time indoors. While the results have been encouraging,
NIMH investigators are understandably cautious about drawing conclusions
from such a small sample. Nonetheless, these studies, along with a growing
number of others, suggest the powerful influence that diurnal and seasonal
cycles—and certain kinds of light—have on our moods and mental well-
being.

In recent years, researchers in photobiology (the study of how light
affects animals and plants) and in related fields have discovered a number of
new and unexpected connections between light and health. They are
becoming increasingly convinced that all aspects of our health—mental and
emotional as well as physical—are indeed affected by the intensity of light
to which we are exposed, by the length of the exposure, and by the color
(spectral makeup) of the light.

According to the latest research, light has profound effects on our
immune system and may one day be used to prevent immune reactions that
we don't want (graft rejection, for example, or the body's response to poi-

son ivy). Light is already being used to treat various diseases of the blood, skin, and other parts of the body. In areas closer to psychology, light may be used not only in curing certain kinds of depression, but in treating jet lag and sleep disorders.

Scientists have long known that the daily rhythms of animals are often synchronized with the time of day, and that the amount of sunlight cues various seasonal activities—everything from spring growth in plants to the mating season in animals. The control of seasonal behavior by light cycles, called photoperiodism, has been put to good use by farmers. By using artificial light to lengthen the day, they are able to fool chicken's hormonal systems into thinking it is spring, thereby increasing egg production.

A major part of the control system for light-mediation of biorhythms in animals lies in a tiny gland in the brain, the pineal, which secretes the hormone melatonin. In reptiles and some birds, the gland is a third "eye" on top of the head, which can distinguish between light and dark. In these animals, there is a clear connection between light and hormonal activity: As the sun rises, melatonin secretion goes down, and vice versa. Given experimentally to animals, melatonin induces sleep and inhibits ovulation.

Richard J. Wurtman, director of the endocrine laboratory at the Massachusetts Institute of Technology, and several of his colleagues have worked out a melatonin cycle for humans, but have found that the connection between light and the amount of melatonin produced is far less obvious in humans than it is in animals. For instance, though humans are basically a diurnal species (active during the day), few of us go to sleep at sunset; and women are receptive all year, rather than only at rutting seasons, as is the case with most animals.

In humans, the pineal gland is at the base of the brain, far from the eyes. How does it know the light level outside? Although most light that enters the eye is used for vision, some of it seeps into a different neural pathway entirely, one that passes through the hypothalamus and ends up telling the pineal gland whether it is light or dark in the outside world.

The hypothalamus is the location of a highly important regulatory center. It controls body temperature, blood pressure, pulse rate, perspiration, and other bodily functions by regulating the production and release of hormones. Scientists aren't yet sure how, or even if, the hypothalamus is affected by light, but its location along the route between the eye and the pineal gland suggests strongly that it is.

In 1980, Alfred Lewy and his NIMH co-workers showed that earlier attempts to find a clear connection between light and melatonin secretion in humans had failed because researchers assumed that people would respond to the same low levels of light that animals do. "When this did not happen," Lewy says, "the typical explanation was that humans had evolved, due to their superior intelligence, the discovery of fire, and so on, to the point that they were no longer affected by the light/dark cycle. Our research shows that the human hormonal system does respond to light; we just need brighter light than animals do."

Lewy, now director of the Sleep and Mood Disorders Laboratory at the University of Oregon Health Sciences Center, adds, "This is a very new field and so it's a little early to come to any conclusions. But certainly it is an important area of study because there are many reports of seasonal patterns in humans, including ones that involve depression, suicide, and rate of conception. In northern Finland women conceive more children during the summer than in the winter, which is consistent with the fact that melatonin inhibits ovulation and is produced when it is dark outside."

As for the supposition that light can help alleviate the problems of certain depressives, Lewy warns against making too much of the preliminary studies at NIMH. "We'll need more patients, as well as more seasons, to prove anything. Note, too, that this is not a case of saying, 'Here's brighter light; I hope it makes you feel better.' Instead, we changed the length of the day. It's all very intriguing, but the whole thing is very preliminary at this point."

The man who was treated by Lewy and his colleagues at NIMH stayed at the laboratory for several days, during which he was encouraged to go outdoors as much as possible during daylight hours. In the early morning and late afternoon, he was exposed to high-intensity, broad-spectrum light. In his laboratory at the University of Oregon, Lewy plans to use similar treatments with other patients who become depressed in winter and recover in the spring, as well as with people who have other problems that are seasonal or sometimes seasonal—such as ulcers.

Another NIMH psychiatrist, Thomas Wehr, expects that in the next five to 10 years we will learn more about which aspects of light—intensity, color, or the time of day it is applied—have the greatest influence on its therapeutic effectiveness. NIMH is also studying how light (natural and artificial) affects human sleep. Earlier research with rats has uncovered wide variations in sleep patterns, depending on the light to which the animals were exposed.

Reading Time: _____
See Conversion Table.
Enter WPM Rate on the Progress Record Chart.

27 Guiding Light

COMPREHENSION CHECK

Getting the Facts

1. The patient described in the opening paragraph was troubled with (a) an anxiety state, (b) allergies, (c) depression (d) arthritis.

   1. ___

2. Light was said to have a profound effect on our (a) virus antibodies, (b) immune systems, (c) blood pressure, (d) defense mechanisms.

   2. ___

3. Specific mention was made of the (a) lymph nodes, (b) insomnia, (c) kidney stones, (d) pineal gland.

   3. ___

4. The director of the Sleep and Mood Disorders Laboratory was (a) Lewy, (b) Wehr, (c) Wurtman, (d) Levin.

   4. ___

5. In northern Finland women conceived more children during the (a) winter, (b) fall, (c) summer, (d) spring.

   5. ___

Getting the Meaning

6. This is mainly about light and (a) psychiatry, (b) health, (c) sleep, (d) current research.

   6. ___

7. The opening case history paragraph was primarily to (a) arouse interest, (b) raise questions, (c) present evidence, (d) provide perspective.

   7. ___

8. The thesis idea was developed largely by (a) logical reasoning, (b) citing figures, (c) research findings, (d) contrast and comparison.

   8. ___

9. The author's attitude toward the subject is best described as (a) positive, (b) questioning, (c) critical, (d) pessimistic.

   9 ___

10. In general this is best called (a) practical, (b) theoretical, (c) visionary, (d) vague.

    10. ___

10 Off for Each Mistake.
Comprehension Score: _____
Answer Key in Appendix.
Enter the Results on the Progress Record Chart.

28 Reading Paragraphs More Effectively

WORD POWER WORKOUT

A. Leaning on Context

In each of the blanks provided, place the letter that precedes the best definition of the underlined word in context to the left.

Words in Context	**Definitions**
1. ___ the <u>remotest</u> idea	a. permanent
2. ___ their <u>specialized</u> function	b. center, most important part
3. ___ a <u>transitional</u> paragraph	c. benefit
4. ___ a <u>fixed</u> location	d. deliberate
5. ___ full <u>advantage</u> of all such cues	e. enjoy
6. ___ a directional <u>nudge</u>	f. are plentiful
7. ___ the <u>core</u> of narration	g. most distant
8. ___ pictures to <u>relish</u>	h. change-marking
9. ___ the <u>conscious</u> effort	i. push
10. ___ devices for explaining <u>abound</u>	j. precise, exact

Check your answers with the Key before going on. Review any that
you have missed.

B. Leaning on Parts

The prefixes *ex-* and *dis-* are also changeable. It's easier to say *emerge* then *exmerge*, a help in understanding something about English spelling.

1. ex + fect = _____ (grow out of a cause)

2. ex + centric = _____ (out of the center)

3. ex + mit = _____ (to send out)

4. dis + ficult = _____ (not easy)

5. dis + lapidated = _____ (not in good shape)

C. Making the Words Yours

In each blank below, enter the most appropriate word from the ten words in context in the first exercise, substituting it for the word(s) in parentheses. Use these words: *abound, advantage, conscious, core, fixed, nudge, relish, remotest, specialized, transitional.*

1. You will (enjoy) _____ being chairman of the committee.

2. Hunters know that in the woods up north deer (are plentiful) _____.

3. To write clearly, one must use proper (change-marking) _____ words.

4. A reader should try to find the (most important part) _____ of the article.

5. A (deliberate) _____ understanding of one's abilities is particularly important.

6. Medicine is a very (exact) _____ field.

7. There are few hiking trails in the (most distant) _____ forest areas.

8. Persons with (permanent) _____ opinions about politics seem narrow-minded.

9. A lazy person needs an occasional (push) _____.

10. Knowing how to read is a real (benefit) _____.

4 Off for Each Mistake.
Word Power Score: _____
Answer Key in Appendix.

28

Reading Paragraphs More Effectively

Begin Timing

How do you get more out of a paragraph? It's like getting food out of a container. With some you need a can opener. With others you just unscrew a lid. Sometimes you use a key to remove a metal strip or pull on a tab. It depends on the container. There's no point trying to unscrew a pry-off lid. So it is in reading paragraphs. How you do it depends on the paragraph.

Special Paragraph Functions

And so, to summarize, be sure to remember those three structurally oriented kinds of paragraphs just discussed.

Are you confused? You're supposed to be. That paragraph lets you see for yourself how important it is to fit a paragraph into a proper frame of reference.

Imagine a big league baseball game. Suppose the catcher never had the remotest idea what kind of pitch he was about to catch. Curve? Sinker? Slider? Spitball? What problems he'd have! Think of the ones he'd miss. That's one very good reason for signals. The catcher *has* to know, if he's to play his position well.

And so does the reader of paragraphs. He has to know what kind of paragraphs he's dealing with. Otherwise, he can't read them effectively.

Let's look at one important way to classify paragraphs. According to their specialized function, they're either introductory, transitional, or concluding. And you read each in a very special way.

Take introductory paragraphs. They usually have two special functions: they arouse interest; they suggest direction and content. It's as if the author shone a flashlight in your face to attract attention, then turned the beam down a path to indicate where he's going. As a reader, you must take full advantage of all such cues. If you don't, you may lose your way before you're well started in the article.

The second kind of paragraph is called transitional. The writer has your attention and has pointed the way; you start along the path indicated. When he wants to make an important change of direction, he must let you know. Otherwise he may lose you. That calls for a transitional paragraph. Its sole function is to shine a flashlight off on a different path.

Transitional paragraphs are usually short—sometimes only one sentence. After all, they're like a one-word traffic sign—TURN or STOP. You don't need details—just a directional nudge. "Turning now to . . ." or "Still another aspect . . ." are typical signposts.

Finally, alert yourself to concluding paragraphs. Introductory and concluding paragraphs have a fixed location—an expected place. Always read the concluding paragraph slowly and carefully. It probably summarizes the most important points or reexpresses the main idea. It flashes the beam back in the path just traveled. Phrases such as "In conclusion . . . ," "Finally . . . ," or "In closing . . ." label this type of paragraph.

So much for the special paragraphs. What about all the others? Let's try another vantage point and classification.

Types of Paragraphs

You can fit any paragraphs into one of four categories—*expository*, *narrative*, *descriptive*, and *persuasive*. Each demands somewhat different treatment from you, the reader.

Take expository paragraphs. About 55 to 85 percent of those you read fit that category. They explain—explain how to read paragraphs, how an electric motor works, or how clouds can be classified.

Devices for explaining abound. The phrase *for example* reminds you of one good way. An example is like a picture—"worth more than ten thousand words," so the proverb goes. The phrase *in detail* suggests another way. Don't overlook *repeat* or *restate*, other ways to insure clear exposition. The phrases *by comparison* or *by contrast* open up still other ways to explain. Black seems even blacker when contrasted with white.

An analogy is a special kind of comparison—one between two quite unlike things that still have similarities. By analogy, for example, life is like a river. It really isn't. But a river begins, runs its course, and ends, sometimes flowing quietly and slowly, sometimes tumbling over rocks with difficulty. Just like life!

Once you become aware of such road signs, following the author's train of thought is simplified. Often one word or phrase fits a whole paragraph into a clear frame of meaning. You comprehend almost without reading further.

In addition to expository paragraphs, you'll find narrative ones. Here the emphasis is not on explaining, but on telling a story. Explaining how to drive is not the same as telling about getting a traffic ticket for speeding! Action is the core of narration. Focus centers on what happened next. Such words as *then*, *later*, *soon* suggest an unfolding of events in time.

The descriptive paragraphs—not nearly so common—give you a picture of something, with emphasis on the five senses. As a reader, savor each detail of taste, smell, sound, sight, and touch. These are word-pictures to relish, not skip.

Finally, persuasive paragraphs are designed to get you to *do* something or believe something—a step beyond pure explanation. Someone may explain the issues. Or he may explain with the intention of getting you to vote a certain way or believe a certain thing.

An awareness of both of those paragraph classifications will help. You do anything better when you know what you're dealing with.

The Main Idea

One last tip. No matter what kind of paragraph, remember it's about one thing. Discover what that one thing is. If you get the main idea, you can make some amazing inferences about details you never even read.

Now you should be able to read paragraphs more easily. You recognize the functions of introductory, transitional, and concluding paragraphs. You know the four types, plus some subvarieties of expository paragraphs. You are reminded to lean on main ideas.

To be sure, you can say these things are commonly known. They may be. *But*—how many readers actually take the next step—*apply* what they know? That's the payoff step. Why not make the conscious effort required?

Reading Time: _____

See Conversion Table.

Enter WPM Rate on the Progress Record Chart.

28 Reading Paragraphs More Effectively

COMPREHENSION CHECK

Getting the Facts

1. Getting meaning from a paragraph is likened to getting (a) food from a container, (b) meat off a bone, (c) water from a sponge, (d) fruit from a tree.

   1. ___

2. Normally, introductory paragraphs are said to have how many functions? (a) one, (b) two, (c) three, (d) four.

   2. ___

3. Expository paragraphs are said to (a) expose, (b) suggest, (c) explain, (d) summarize.

   3. ___

4. Life is likened to a (a) tree, (b) storm, (c) river, (d) planted seed.

   4. ___

5. Such words as *then, later, soon* are typical of what kind of paragraph? (a) expository, (b) narrative, (c) persuasive, (d) descriptive.

   5. ___

Getting the Meaning

6. The article's main focus is on (a) how to get main paragraph ideas, (b) how to deal with paragraphs more effectively, (c) how paragraphs develop ideas, (d) how to classify paragraphs.

   6. ___

7. The sensation of falling suggests what kind of paragraph? (a) expository, (b) persuasive, (c) narrative, (d) descriptive.

   7. ___

8. Which kind of special paragraph is probably most difficult to spot? (a) introductory, (b) concluding, (c) transitional, (d) all equally so.

   8. ___

9. Most emphasis is placed on what kind of paragraph? (a) persuasive, (b) expository, (c) descriptive, (d) narrative.

   9 ___

10. Mention of analogy is to show one way of (a) describing, (b) telling, (c) explaining, (d) persuading.

    10. ___

Making the Application

As a means of getting a clearer picture of the four types of paragraphs, reread carefully the characteristics of each. With that fourfold classification in mind, turn to the paragraphs indicated below. Read each one and then label each properly, as *expository*, *narrative*, *descriptive*, or *persuasive*. No two paragraphs should have the same label. Each is a different type.

Turn to the following paragraphs in Selection 2, "Instrument of Evil," beginning on page 17.

1. The paragraph beginning, "The fourth . . . " is primarily of what type?
   _____

2. The paragraph beginning, "In the presence . . . " is primarily of what type? _____

3. The paragraph beginning, "It's also . . . " is primarily of what type?
   _____

4. The paragraph beginning, "These things come . . . " is primarily of what type? _____

To get additional practice in discovering the essence or main idea of a paragraph, turn to Selection 9, page 69. Try to state the idea of each of the six paragraphs indicated below using fewer than ten words. Start with the paragraph beginning, "Do you . . . ," calling that paragraph 1. Take that one and the next four to analyze below.

1. _____

   _____

2. _____

   _____

3. _____

   _____

4. _____

   _____

5. _____

   _____

29 The Urge to Create

WORD POWER WORKOUT

A. Leaning on Context

In each of the blanks provided, place the letter that precedes the best definition of the underlined word in context to the left.

Words in Context	Definitions
1. ___ is <u>innately</u> creative	a. future
2. ___ that private <u>reservoir</u>	b. smothering
3. ___ the <u>exalted</u> heights	c. fix, plight
4. ___ <u>coping</u> with challenges	d. naturally
5. ___ how to <u>unleash</u>	e. lofty
6. ___ <u>imprints</u> from ancestors	f. release
7. ___ can become <u>stultifying</u>	g. struggling
8. ___ is in the <u>offing</u>	h. storehouse
9. ___ recognized the <u>fallacy</u>	i. impressions
10. ___ to the <u>predicament</u>	j. falseness, error

Check your answers with the Key before going on. Review any that you have missed.

Pronunciation aids: 1. i nāt'lē; 2. rez'ur vwar; 7. stul'tuh fī ing; 9. fal'uh sē.
KEY: add, āce; end, ēven; it, īce; odd, ōpen; pōōl; up.

B. Leaning on Parts

The Latin root *ducere* means "to lead." Whenever you see a *duc(e)*, *duct*, or *duit*, look for the meaning "lead." Now complete the following.

1. The passage through which air is led is called a _____.

2. An article usually leads into the main part with an intro_____.

3. To lead yourself back to your slender self, you have to re_____.

4. To lead finished goods out of a factory, you must pro_____ them.

5. A tube leading electric wires around a house is called a con_____.

C. Making the Words Yours

In each blank below, enter the most appropriate word from the ten words in context in the first exercise, substituting it for the word(s) in parentheses. Use these words: *coping, exalted, fallacy, imprints, innately, offing, predicament, reservoir, stultifying, unleash.*

1. The change of schedule poses a real (fix, plight) _____.

2. When do you (release) _____ your dogs?

3. Don't worry now. That problem is still in the (future) _____.

4. Did you note the (falseness, error) _____ in the reasoning?

5. Some people are just (naturally) _____ optimistic.

6. Over the years the Red Cross has built a tremendous (storehouse) _____ of good will.

7. Will you have any trouble (struggling) _____ with the crowd?

8. Such close and continuous supervision is most (smothering) _____.

9. The natives showed obvious (impressions) _____ from their long-forgotten ancestors.

10. The (lofty) _____ heights of genius are indeed dazzling to behold.

29

The Urge to Create

Bill Moyers

James Russell Lowell once wrote that "in creating, the only hard thing's to begin." But isn't that assuming we're all creative? What if that isn't so? Just how creative are you? And can you do anything to make yourself more so? Bill Moyers thinks so. Let him help you.

Begin Timing

Are you a creative person? I think you might be—and not know it.

Not for a minute am I suggesting that you may be the next Picasso, Bach, Shakespeare or Einstein (although I am willing to be surprised). But after completing a television series about creativity in America, I am convinced that each of us is innately creative and, with effort and discipline, can open that private reservoir of creativity to improve our daily lives.

But first: What is creativity? Perhaps the simplest definition comes from scholar Herbert Fox, who wrote that "the creative process is any thinking process which solves a problem in an original and useful way." I like that because it brings creativity down—from the exalted heights where only the genius can work—to my level and yours. It means that we do not have to be a Michelangelo or a Mozart to exercise our creative powers. Who among us is not constantly coping with challenges that require us to think in original ways? Scientists have only begun to explore those steps that occur in the brain in the highest realms of creative activity, but there's no need to wait for an explanation of genius for us to become more aware of our own creativity and to use it every day.

But how to unleash our creativity? Begin by "letting down your shield." Stop being self-conscious—afraid of playing the fool—and be open to experience. All of us live behind a shield. It's an important part of our equipment, for it protects us against personal, social and political information that might shatter our relationships with family, colleagues and institutions. But sometimes the shield shuts out experiences that could stimulate our creative powers. We conform to things as they are instead of taking risks to change them. We settle for less when there is more.

Next, "erase your blackboard." We all have blackboards, too—scribbled upon by other people. No one comes into the world a blank slate; there are messages in the unconscious from far back in time, imprints from ancestors lost in the misty past and from our own parents. In such a way are we programmed by our culture to provide continuity for the race. But, again, what is good up to a point can become stultifying. To be creative, we have to "erase" some of what others have written upon us and "reinvent" ourselves.

It is not easy. You have to pay attention—to your unconscious, which slips messages to you much as a note is slipped under the door; to your own intuition and intelligence, and to the world around you.

Creativity, then, is first about paying attention to the unexpected. One artist told me, "If you know what you are looking for, you will never see what you do not expect to find." To pay attention means to expect without knowing what to expect. Writers say this experience happens to them all the time. "I have no idea whence this tide comes, or where it goes," author Dorothy Canfield once explained, "but when it begins to rise in my heart, I know that a story is in the offing."

It also happens to scientists. Physicist Charles Townes has told of the time he was frustrated in solving a huge problem on which he and others had worked long and hard. One Sunday morning he went to the park to sit on a bench among the azaleas, "and there in the early spring morning enjoyed the freshness and beauty of these gay flowers, musing over why we had so far failed. Suddenly I recognized the fallacy in my previous thinking and that of others."

Famed Hollywood director John Huston told me that when he encountered a mental block while on location, he was careful not to "spook," not to panic. Instead, he relaxed and waited. "When the right idea comes along," he said, "you'll recognize it."

No one, of course, can pay attention to everything. All of us are bombarded daily with stimuli pouring in from society around us. Creativity requires that we stop paying general attention to everything in order to pay particular attention to something. Then we can see what previously we missed. We can look at the commonplace in a brand-new way and discover the surprising in the familiar. In the words of one student of creativity, "If most of us tend to keep on going through the same old familiar motion, that is not because we are short on creativity but because we stifle it. Creativity demands certain leaps that we consider too daring."

How do we break the mold, climb out of the rut and overcome the routine? Well, there are as many creative processes as there are creative personalities; no universal ingredient will produce creativity on demand. However, I have a suggestion, though you will have to apply it in your own way to your own life. Aristotle said that philosophy begins in wonder. Jesus of Nazareth said that to see the Kingdom of Heaven we must become as little children. To approach life with the perpetual curiosity of a child is to open our creative energies to the happy circumstance of discovery.

There is no exact formula, but you might try this: First, focus—if by changing or solving one dilemma in your life you could most likely climb out of the rut, which dilemma would that be? How are you looking at that dilemma now? Consider the complete opposite way of looking at it. Go back to the predicament as if for the first time and ask the simplest questions about it—as a child's poem asks of a rose: "Where did you get that red?" Approach a dilemma humbly, as the child looks at the world in wonder, and it may suddenly be amenable.

Samson Raphaelson, the 85-year-old playwright who taught at Columbia University, summed it up as we were filming one of his classes: "Imagination," he told his students, "is the ability to see what's there."

But sometimes you have to look twice.

Reading Time: _____
See Conversion Table.
Enter WPM Rate on the Progress Record Chart.

29 The Urge to Create

COMPREHENSION CHECK

Getting the Facts

1. Moyers mentioned (a) Bach, (b) Picasso, (c) Shakespeare, (d) all the preceding.

   1. ___

2. Creativity was defined as the thinking process which solved a problem in an original and (a) useful way, (b) clever way, (c) amazing way, (d) new way.

   2. ___

3. Reference was made to (a) posters, (b) signposts, (c) blackboards, (d) billboards.

   3. ___

4. Moyers mentioned (a) Woody Allen, (b) John Huston, (c) Howard Hawks, (d) Clint Eastwood.

   4. ___

5. Moyers quoted (a) Caesar, (b) Plato, (c) Aristotle, (d) Copernicus.

   5. ___

Getting the Meaning

6. This is mainly to (a) define creativity, (b) suggest where it occurs, (c) suggest how to develop it, (d) indicate who has it.

   6. ___

7. The chief emphasis is on (a) how, (b) what, (c) when, (d) why.

   7. ___

8. This was organized (a) from the known to the unknown, (b) from the ordinary to the unusual, (c) chronologically, (d) from the less to the more important.

   8. ___

9. The story about sitting in the park was used primarily to get you to (a) change your thinking place, (b) stop trying, (c) get close to nature, (d) avoid people.

   9 ___

10. You would infer that formal education tends to (a) stimulate creativity, (b) diminish creativity, (c) have no effect on creativity, (d) affect people differently.

    10. ___

10 Off for Each Mistake.
Comprehension Score: _____
Answer Key in Appendix.
Enter the Results on the Progress Record Chart.

30 Creativity in the Advertising Mix

WORD POWER WORKOUT

A. Leaning on Context

In each of the blanks provided, place the letter that precedes the best definition of the underlined word in context to the left.

Words in Context	Definitions
1. ___ the least <u>quantifiable</u>	a. call forth
2. ___ the greatest <u>leverage</u>	b. equality
3. ___ in the product <u>category</u>	c. all-out
4. ___ through <u>sheer</u> media weight	d. measurable
5. ___ <u>virtually</u> force	e. effectiveness
6. ___ <u>parity</u> upon products	f. influence
7. ___ communicate <u>efficacy</u>	g. division
8. ___ more <u>salient</u>	h. apt, appropriate
9. ___ intended to <u>evoke</u>	i. essentially
10. ___ a <u>felicitous</u> phrase	j. notable, striking

Check your answers with the Key before going on. Review any that you have missed.

Pronunciation aids: 1. kwon tuh fi′uh bl; 6. pair′uh tē; 7. ef′uh kuh sē; 8. sa′le unt; 10. fuh lis′uh tus.

KEY: add, āce; end, ēven; it, īce; odd, ōpen; po͞ol; up.

B. Leaning on Parts

Scribere means "to write." Whenever you see a *scrib(e)* or *scrip(t)* in a word, look for the meaning "write." Fill in the following blanks.

1. You fill a doctor's pre_____ at a drug store.

2. A handwritten paper is rightly called a manu_____.

3. The radio announcer read the statement from a typed _____.

4. I have sub_____ to that magazine for three years.

5. To write down details about someone's appearance is to de_____ her.

C. Making the Words Yours

In each blank below, enter the most appropriate word from the ten words in context in the first exercise, substituting it for the word(s) in parentheses. Use these words: *category, efficacy, evoke, felicitous, leverage, parity, quantifiable, salient, sheer, virtually.*

1. Which (division) _____ do you put these entries into?

2. The new taxes will (call forth) _____ sharp criticism.

3. The farmers pushed for (equality) _____ in the new regulations.

4. What's the (striking, notable) _____ feature of the luxury model?

5. You should have a more (apt, appropriate) _____ phrasing for your first sentence.

6. To swing the deal you should have added (influence) _____.

7. (All-out) _____ persistence usually leads to success.

8. To make your point well, get some solid (measurable) _____ evidence.

9. Yes, everything I said is (essentially) _____ true.

10. (Effectiveness) _____ is of the utmost importance.

4 Off for Each Mistake.
Word Power Score: _____
Answer Key in Appendix.

30

Creativity in the Advertising Mix

Burt Manning

*What are your chances of interviewing a top executive of a pres-
tigious New York advertising agency—of interviewing the man
responsible for such creative ads as Ford's "The closer you look,
the better we look"? Very slim! But—here he is in front of you
ready to talk about creativity. Books and reading! What wonders they provide.*

Begin Timing

Of all the elements in the advertising mix, creativity is the least quantifiable.
Yet it has potentially the greatest leverage on the media dollars spent. The
best way to understand the importance of creativity in advertising is to
understand what it does for the advertiser.

Creativity first separates the individual advertisement from all the
advertisements surrounding it. In the process of doing that, creativity
achieves its real goal: to separate the brand in a positive and motivating way
from all other brands in the product category.

It may be possible to do something like this through sheer media
weight, by simply outspending your competitors. But creativity is usually
the least expensive way to make both ad and brand stand out in the crowd.
This is not to say it is necessarily the best way. The best way to make a
brand stand out is to put a significantly superior or unique product behind
it. In the real world, however, competition and technology virtually force
parity upon products in the same category—close similarity in function,
quality, price, and often appearance.

Can you give a branded parity product distinction through unique
advertising strategy? Sometimes. Still, that is a very limited opportunity.
Brands of parity products all marketed to the same group of consumers
most likely will have the same advertising strategy, because it is the only one
that makes sense. Dishwashing liquids will need to communicate efficacy
and mildness, fluoride toothpaste cavity-prevention and taste, sports cars
performance and status, and so on.

When brands all have the same essential advertising strategies, what is it that makes one brand's advertising more salient and more effective? It is the creativity with which the strategy has been executed.

When advertising works, it works because it makes something happen inside the consumer. An advertisement is, after all, no more than a set of stimuli intended to evoke a set of desired responses among a specific group of consumers. The effect of a "creative" advertisement is to generate a more intense positive response to the brand than a "noncreative" advertisement. Whether it achieves its ends through the use of words, images, sounds, or music, whether it evokes laughter, fear, shock, or feelings of warmth and tenderness, the creative advertisement stands out in the consumer's mind and makes the brand stand out too.

How do creative people create? Nobody really knows. Nobody really knows where ideas are born; where an unforgettable bar of music comes from; why a felicitous phrase pops into someone's head. No one really knows how some people can put words and pictures and sounds and ideas together in ways that can move millions of other people to think and feel and act.

But we do know the most effective advertising (which I contend is the most creative) always has at least two or three elements and often has all three.

Relevance Surprise Emotion

Relevance, of course, is strategically, not creatively, driven. But advertising cannot be creative without it. It is based on knowledge; knowledge of what the consumer wants and what the product has to offer. It is present in all but the most dismally poor advertising.

It is the other two characteristics in combination with relevance that distinguish the best advertising. Relevant surprise. Relevant emotion. Arthur Koestler said that "surprise is at the heart of every creative act." But why does the element of surprise help to make advertising more effective? Consider one dictionary definition: "surprise: to capture unexpectedly."

Advertising that captures the consumer unexpectedly not only gets attention, not only stands out in the mind, it stays in the mind. It is remembered long after the immediate experience has passed. The usual and the expected are barely noticed and quickly forgotten.

Emotion—relevant emotion—is the other element common to the most effective advertising. Advertising that warms or charms or amuses or otherwise stirs up real and positive feelings about a brand is advertising that separates that brand from its competitors. And because purchase decisions are rarely made on a purely rational basis, advertising that adds emotional value to a brand may be the most effective—the most creative—advertising of all.

Reading Time: _____
See Conversion Table.
Enter WPM Rate on the Progress Record Chart.

30 Creativity in the Advertising Mix

COMPREHENSION CHECK

Getting the Facts

1. Creativity was said to (a) dazzle, (b) entertain, (c) highlight, (d) separate.

1. ___

2. Specific mention was made of (a) using TV shorts, (b) outspending competitors, (c) double-page spreads, (d) video cassettes.

2. ___

3. A creative advertisement was said to (a) cost more, (b) rely on music, (c) stand out, (d) use shock.

3. ___

4. The most effective advertising has how many elements? (a) three, (b) two, (c) one, (d) no set number.

4. ___

5. Surprise was (a) related to color, (b) linked with music, (c) contrasted with creativity, (d) defined.

5. ___

Getting the Meaning

6. The main idea was to show, in discussing advertising, (a) the importance of creativity, (b) how creativity is achieved, (c) the key role of emotion, (d) the importance of surprise.

6. ___

7. The material is organized on what basis? (a) problem-solution, (b) important-to-less-important, (c) point-by-point, (d) cause-effect.

7. ___

8. You would infer that advertisers must appeal most strongly to (a) reason, (b) emotion, (c) value, (d) savings.

8. ___

9. Which of the following elements should apparently dominate attention? (a) relevance, (b) surprise, (c) emotion, (d) no one element

9 ___

10. This is primarily to (a) summarize, (b) raise questions, (c) entertain, (d) explain.

10. ___

10 Off for Each Mistake.
Comprehension Score: _____
Answer Key in Appendix.
Enter the Results on the Progress Record Chart.

PREFIX MINI-REVIEW

Here's a mini-review of the twenty prefixes, the most important shortcuts in the English language. They're so important you should know them all perfectly. And here's the review to insure that kind of mastery. Use it from time to time, as needed, to keep top-level performance. Try all three review patterns.

1. Cover the right-hand column with a 3 x 5 card. Try to supply the common meaning for each prefix, moving the card down for an immediate check of your answer. This is the easiest pattern.

2. Cover both right-hand columns for a more difficult check. See if you can supply both mnemonic and common meaning.

3. For the most difficult review, cover both left-hand columns and try to supply both mnemonic and prefix to fit each meaning, again checking your answers immediately.

Prefix	Suggested Mnemonic	Common Meaning
1. *pre-*	preview	before
2. *re-*	refund, reread	back, again
3. *pro-*	progress, prolabor	forward, for
4. *inter-*	intermission, interspersed	between, among
5. *non-*	nonresident	not
6. *de-*	depress, depart, defrost	down, away, reverse
7. *un-*	untidy	not
8. *trans-*	transport, transcend	across, beyond
9. *over-*	overpass, overseer	above, beyond
10. *mono-*	monopoly	one
11. *epi-*	epidemic, epidermis	upon, above
12. *mis-*	misspell	wrong, wrongly
13. *com-*	companion, connect	with, together
14. *in-*	insecure	not
15. *ex-*	exit	out
16. *dis-*	dissect, dispatch	apart, away
17. *ad-*	advance	to, toward
18. *ob-*	obstinate, objective	against, to
19. *in-*	inhale	in, into
20. *sub-*	submerge	under

31 Reading Entire Selections More Effectively

WORD POWER WORKOUT

A. Leaning on Context

In each of the blanks provided, place the letter that precedes the best definition of the underlined word in context to the left.

Words in Context	Definitions
1. ___ main and <u>subordinate</u> point	a. depend
2. ___ facts and <u>supporting</u> material	b. stylistic
3. ___ that word <u>captures</u> the primary role	c. minor
4. ___ to <u>extract</u> it	d. assist, help
5. ___ their <u>chief</u> function	e. substantiating
6. ___ <u>lean</u> heavily on paragraphing	f. seizes
7. ___ the <u>rhetorical</u> device of balance	g. remove
8. ___ from the <u>obscure</u> into the obvious	h. little known, vague
9. ___ will <u>facilitate</u> progress	i. main
10. ___ a split-second <u>glance</u> at an outline	j. brief look

Check your answers with the Key before going on. Review any that you have missed.

Pronunciation aids: 7. ri tor'i cul.

KEY: add, āce; end, ēven; it, īce; odd, ōpen; pōol; up.

B. Leaning on Parts

Ponere means "put" or "place." Whenever you see *pon, posit* or *pos(t)* in a word, look for that meaning. Supply a form of *ponere* in each blank below.

1. When a notice is placed on a bulletin board, it is _____ there.

2. If you'd put your shoulders back, you'd have better _____.

3. The meeting was post _____, putting it a week later.

4. Take this money to the bank and de_____ it in your account.

5. You'll need more _____ stamps to send your letters overseas.

C. Making the Words Yours

In each blank below, enter the most appropriate word from the ten words in context in the first exercise, substituting it for the word(s) in parentheses. Use these words: *captured, chief, extracted, facilitates, glance, lean, obscure, rhetorical, subordinate, supporting.*

1. A small child will (depend) _____ on his parents for help.

2. A telephone (assists) _____ speech communication.

3. He took a (brief look) _____ at the magazine before discarding it.

4. Teachers often use (stylistic) _____ devices when lecturing.

5. An answer that is (vague) _____ can cause misunderstandings.

6. Smoking is a (main) _____ cause of lung cancer.

7. The dentist (removed) _____ the man's wisdom tooth.

8. The police (seized) _____ the criminal.

9. The officials discussed the (minor) _____ issues first.

10. He did not give any (substantiating) _____ evidence for his opinion.

4 Off for Each Mistake.
Word Power Score: _____
Answer Key in Appendix.

31

Reading Entire Selections More Effectively

Begin Timing

FIDENITY. What does that mean? You don't know! Well, don't reach for your dictionary. You won't find it there. That word captures in a nutshell the primary role of organization. But you have to reorganize those letters. Rearrange them into IDENTIFY. Yes, the role of organization is to help you identify the essentials. It should help you spot all-important ideas, facts, and supporting material for an entire article, chapter, or unit.

But to identify is not enough. Visualize if you will a thousand pounds of crushed ore. It's not enough to identify the presence of gold in that ore. You need to extract it. After all, it's not the thousand pounds of ore that are important. It's the seventy ounces of gold it contains. But, can you imagine trying to extract something you don't even know is there? No. Keep both in mind. First, identify. Next, extract, the second of the two roles of organization.

What is the role of outlining? It's to make organization clear—to help you identify and extract essentials. The outline form sets major points out and shrinks supporting material into a clearly visible subordinate position. Take a split-second glance at an outline. You can determine the main points in no time.

Furthermore, notice what making an outline does. It forces you to think in terms of main and subordinate points. It forces you to go through the mental gymnastics needed to discover and identify the author's plan. Writing the outline proves how skillfully you can extract the essentials. Such a combination of reading and thinking contributes much to comprehension.

How is organization revealed? As you read, what signs or special devices mark the writer's plan? Reading is just the reverse of writing. The author sends; the reader receives. The author uses certain devices to help the reader. Just looking at them more closely will facilitate progress. There are three kinds: *typographical*, *rhetorical*, and *verbal*.

Take typographical devices. Think what can be done with type. You can put an important point in CAPITAL LETTERS. See how they stand out on the page. Something a bit less important can be set in **boldface** type.

This too stands out. Even *italics* differ enough from regular type to be spotted easily on the page.

Now for rhetorical devices, turn instead to *repetition, parallelism*, or *balance*.

Repeating a word or phrase helps the reader fit what is said into a more orderly, easily remembered pattern. Here's an illustration. Do you know the three secrets of a successful speech? Stand up! Speak up! Shut up! The repetition of *s*'s in *stand, speak*, and *shut* puts this advice into neat, orderly form.

Lincoln's government, "of the people, by the people, and for the people," relies on parallelism as well as on repetition. Each of these phrases is in parallel form—preposition-article-noun—to accent the threefold pattern he had in mind. Repetition of "the people" helps still further to make the phrase unforgettable.

With the rhetorical device of balance, think of the old-fashioned scales or balance. Or just think of what you do to balance a pencil across your finger. It has to be placed right in the middle in order to balance. Similarly, balance in a sentence has to have an exact middle spot, both sides equal. Patrick Henry did it nicely. Listen to him. "Give me liberty or give me death!"

That word *or* marks the middle, or fulcrum. And on either side exactly three words to balance three words. Furthermore, the repetition of "give me . . . give me" makes it even stronger. You know he's talking about two alternatives.

Verbal devices make up the third and last of these special road signs. Dozens of English words have the following as their chief function: marking transitions, indicating methods of development, or noting outline form. The word *another*, for example, moves the reader easily from one point to the next, a real help in outlining. *Consequently* suggests a cause-effect development. And such words as *first*, *next*, and *finally* strongly indicate outline form.

All these devices—typographical, rhetorical, and verbal—function as highway signs to a driver. They keep us on the road.

Still another major way to determine organization is through paragraph structure. In each paragraph look for (1) a topic sentence or idea and (2) supporting details. Don't look for two main points in one paragraph. Look for them in two. And if a writer mentions three reasons, expect three paragraphs, if the reasons are important. If one reason is complex or multisided, look for two or more paragraphs to suggest subdivisions of that major point. In short, lean heavily on paragraphing as you outline.

What does organization contribute? Why bother with it, anyway? Well, you get two sets of benefits. For one, you open the way to capturing main ideas and relationships between parts. For another, you gain improved aids to both understanding and remembering.

When you complete your outline, getting the main ideas is no longer a problem. You've reduced the 1,000-word chapter to a mere handful of essentials—the gold.

And the outline lets you see the relationship between parts very clearly. Subordinate parts are in subordinate position in outline form.

Finally, outlining does amazing things for understanding and remembering. Getting details and understanding them are not the same. Organization adds understanding to details. Furthermore, you will remember CAPITALS, **boldface type**, and *italics* better because they are grouped in orderly fashion under the heading *typographical*. If Patrick Henry had not used balance, think of the added difficulty of remembering exactly what he said. Suppose he said, "Give me liberty, or I'd just as soon be killed." That rephrasing doesn't remember itself. The other does.

So, to summarize, make outlining your follow-up for reading. It will help you identify and extract the essentials. It will help you understand and remember them much better. It will turn NEMAGIN into MEANING, the obscure into the obvious.

Reading Time: _____
See Conversion Table.
Enter WPM Rate on the Progress Record Chart.

31 Reading Entire Selections More Effectively

COMPREHENSION CHECK

Getting the Facts

1. You are told that the role of organization is to help you (a) identify the essentials, (b) note interrelationships, (c) speed your reading, (d) write better.

1. ___

2. Reading is referred to as (a) the be-all and end-all, (b) the reverse of writing, (c) drinking in information, (d) a mental adventure.

2. ___

3. Capital letters belong under the heading (a) typographical, (b) rhetorical, (c) verbal, (d) personal.

3. ___

4. Devices to reveal organization are likened to (a) code signals, (b) highway signs, (c) radar images, (d) recipes.

4. ___

5. Outlining is said to turn the obscure into the (a) obvious, (b) clear, (c) commonplace, (d) plain.

5. ___

Getting the Meaning

6. The main focus of the article is on (a) what organization contributes to reading, (b) how organization is revealed, (c) outlining techniques, (d) the role of rhetorical devices.

6. ___

7. The FIDENITY paragraph is primarily to show (a) one purpose of organization, (b) how to organize, (c) the simplicity of good organization, (d) the importance of organization.

7. ___

8. You would infer that Lincoln was a master in the use of (a) outlining, (b) parallelism, (c) balance, (d) personal appeal.

8. ___

9. The word *because* suggests what kinds of development? (a) logical, (b) personal, (c) factual, (d) detailed.

9 ___

10. To remember something it should help particularly to (a) outline it, (b) write it, (c) reread it, (d) recite it aloud.

10. ___

10 Off for Each Mistake.
Comprehension Score: _____
Answer Key in Appendix.
Enter the Results on the Progress Record Chart.

Making the Application

To practice applying what you learned about organization in this selection, try to fill in the blank outline of the selection, looking back as often as you like to clarify your thinking.

I. _____

   A. _____

   B. _____

II. _____

III. _____

   A. _____

      1. _____

         a. _____

         b. _____

         c. _____

      2. _____

         a. _____

         b. _____

         c. _____

      3. _____

         a. _____

         b. _____

         c. _____

B. _____

    1. _____

    2. _____

IV. _____

  A. _____

    1. _____

    2. _____

  B. _____

    1. _____

    2. _____

V. _____

Outline answers are on page 390.

32 The Dumbest Antelope

WORD POWER WORKOUT

A. Leaning on Context

In each of the blanks provided, place the letter that precedes the best definition of the underlined word in context to the left.

Words in Context	Definitions
1. ___ my woolly <u>chaps</u>	a. glue
2. ___ they're <u>bumbling</u> around	b. keep alive, preserve
3. ___ the <u>jangling</u> of my spurs	c. drooped
4. ___ sticks like <u>epoxy</u>	d. clanking
5. ___ as I <u>slouched</u>	e. jerked
6. ___ to help <u>perpetuate</u>	f. self-important floundering
7. ___ a perfect <u>offhand</u> shot	g. cowardly
8. ___ if I had <u>flinched</u>	h. casual
9. ___ thereby <u>dissuading</u> it	i. cowboy's seatless trousers
10. ___ its <u>dastardly</u> attack	j. persuading against

Check your answers with the Key before going on. Review any that you have missed.

Pronunciation aids: 4. e pok′sē; 9. di swād′ing.
KEY: add, āce; end, ēven; it, īce; odd, ōpen; pōol; up.

B. Leaning on Parts

Mittere means "send." When you see *mit(t)*, or *mis(s)* in a word, look for that meaning. Fill in the following blanks with forms of *mittere*.

1. When you send in a formal report, you are said to sub_____ it.

2. The _____ sent toward the armed camp was launched from a sub.

3. Our minister was sent to Africa as a _____.

4. Money sent to pay a bill is called a re_____.

5. Smoke sent out of a car exhaust is e_____ from it.

C. Making the Words Yours

In each blank below, enter the most appropriate word from the ten words in context in the first exercise, substituting it for the word(s) in parentheses. Use these words: *bumbling, chaps, dastardly, dissuaded, epoxy, flinched, jangling, offhand, perpetuate, slouched.*

1. You could hear the (clanking) _____ of the iron bars in the wind.

2. I used (glue) _____ to cement the mug pieces together again.

3. The riders wore (cowboy's seatless trousers) _____ for the round-up.

4. This bronze plaque was to (keep alive, preserve) _____ the memory of our first mayor.

5. Despite the (casual) _____ manner of the artist, you know how much effort had gone into the painting of the picture.

6. The (cowardly) _____ deed made headlines everywhere.

7. Were you (persuaded against) _____ from trying a parachute jump?

8. The hunter (jerked) _____ just as he pulled the trigger.

9. It was laughable to see their (self-important floundering) _____ around.

10. The newcomer (drooped) _____ against the door as he talked.

4 Off for Each Mistake.
Word Power Score: _____
Answer Key in Appendix.

32

The Dumbest Antelope

Patrick F. McManus

*Have you ever traveled around in McManus country? If not,
you're in for a special experience. It's hilarious and unforgettable territory, populated, as you'll soon see, with an unusually
dumb antelope. Hardly sportsmanlike to shoot a dumb one—or
is it? Head right out to the hunter's camp!*

Begin Timing

Let me give you the true facts about the antelope hunt.

To begin with, I flew into Rock Springs, Wyoming, rented a four-
wheel-drive vehicle, and drove eight hundred miles to Rawlins. True, the
normal driving distance between Rock Springs and Rawlins is less than one
hundred miles, but only if you make a right turn instead of a left turn
leaving Rock Springs. The left turn takes you to Rawlins by way of Montana,
a very scenic route, believe me, and one that definitely should be put on the
map.

An elderly rancher, who claimed mine was the first "strange face" he
had seen in that part of Wyoming in the last four years, finally got me
pointed in the general direction of Rawlins. He said just follow the signs.
All the signs, however, had been made by deer and antelope, few of which
had been heading for Rawlins. The rancher, by the way, complimented me
on my woolly chaps, after he got over his first impression that I was trying
to steal two of his sheep, or so he claimed. We both thought that very
amusing, he somewhat more than I. He warned me not to wear them into
any of the tougher Wyoming saloons, no doubt fearful that one of the cowboys there might try to make off with them for his own use, such is the rar-
ity of woolly chaps nowadays in Wyoming.

I eventually found Rawlins and made my way to the hunting camp
some miles north of the town. Right away I saw I was about to fall in with
bad company—Vin Sparano, editor and writer; Jim Zumbo, editor and
writer; Bill Rooney, editor and writer; Hal Nesbitt, editor and writer; Kathy
Etling, writer; and Bob Etling, a normal person. A rougher bunch probably
hadn't been assembled in Wyoming since the Hole-in-the-Wall gang broke

up. There were characters here who could quickdraw a library card and check out three books faster than the eye could follow. Others could split an infinitive with a single blow and not think twice about it. Sparano was said to smile while firing off rejection slips with both hands.

I got Zumbo aside. "This looks more like a literary convention than a hunting trip," I told him. "I don't want to show these people up, or you either. Sure, I don't mind giving everybody a few hunting tips, but it's embarrassing for them when I fill my tag right away and they're bumbling around day after day, hoping against hope that they might luck out and get a close, standing shot."

"You don't have to worry," Zumbo said. "They'll do fine. Besides, Hal and I have already gotten our antelopes."

"You have? Hal too?"

Harold "Hal" Nesbitt happens to be the administrative director of the Boone & Crockett Club. I was happy to hear he had already got his antelope because that would leave him free to score my antelope before any shrinkage occurred. Typically, my big game trophies shrink as much as 50 percent before they can be measured, thus denying me admission to the Boone & Crockett record book. With Hal right there, this problem was as good as solved.

As you might expect, Zumbo had selected the worst possible camping site in all of Wyoming, a knob of ground surrounded on all sides by wide-open spaces as far as the eye could see. Since the camp had no restroom facilities and the tallest bush was less than a foot high, any calls of nature could be answered only by hiking out toward the horizon until one was concealed by the curvature of the earth. Just going to the bathroom took up half the day.

Shelter consisted of a small camping trailer and a motor home. Sparano and Rooney slept on the bed in the camper and Nesbitt and I slept on the table. I slept with all my clothes on, not only because I didn't know Hal that well but because my sleeping bag is rated at only ten degrees below zero. The first night I scarcely got a wink of sleep. Hal tossed and turned all night, complaining about stabbing pains in his legs. I would have got up and slept on the floor, except I thought the jangling of my spurs might wake the others.

The next day's hunting proved thoroughly disappointing. Everyone but me got an antelope. Vin made a lucky long shot. I say lucky because the antelope in question was so far away as not to be visible to the naked eye. Vin explained—and explained and explained—how he had held 503 feet above the animal and led it by a quarter of a mile, working into his calculations the factors of wind, temperature, humidity, and level of suspended particles in the air. My theory is that Vin fired a shot to test his rifle and an antelope came by several minutes later and accidentally got into the line of fire. Nothing can be proved, however, so Vin sticks like epoxy to his story.

Then what does Bill Rooney do? From a mile away, he sneaks up on a big buck right in the middle of a herd without one of the antelope spotting him. Up until then I liked Rooney a lot, but I simply cannot tolerate a show-off. To make matters worse, a Wyoming game warden who checked us said it was the best antelope he had seen taken that year!

I thought the worst had to be over, but when we got back to camp, I discovered that Kathy and Bob Etling had each got an antelope. Never have I been on a hunt in which so many things went wrong.

I had been told that antelope are easy to hunt, but I daresay that is not the case. They are cunning beasts. Off in the far distance, streams of them flow hither and yon, waves of them wash across the prairie, and fringes of them decorate almost every ridgeline. Occasionally they will streak, zip, or flash past within rifle range. Not once, however, did I see any antelope play, as is reputed in the song. Show me an antelope playing and I'll show you some antelope chops. Personally, I doubt the songwriter ever even saw an antelope, let alone one that played.

That night as I slouched in a corner of the camper, with the din of Vin's endless account of his long shot assaulting my eardrums, Kathy Etling slipped over beside me.

"Pat," she whispered, "I saw some dumb antelope today. I know where you can probably get one of them."

Kathy is a very nice person, and I didn't want to let on that there was simply no way I, a sportsman, would take advantage of some poor creature lacking in normal intelligence.

"How dumb, Kathy?"

"Really dumb."

"Well, thanks anyway, but I'm really not interested," I said, patting her on the shoulder. "Just for the heck of it, though, could you draw me a map?"

She drew the map on the back of an envelope, sketching in various landmarks. "How's that?"

"Fine. But I don't see any antelope."

She put an X on the map. "There's one."

You may think I'm exaggerating, but I'm not. Kathy actually drew the map just as I've described it, right down to the X. Naturally, this is just between you and me, and Kathy, of course. I wouldn't want Sparano or Zumbo to find out about the map, because I would never hear the end of it.

The next day Zumbo, Sparano, and Rooney went out with me on my hunt, each of them offering suggestions as to where I might find antelope. I refused to listen.

"Turn here, by the green post," I told Zumbo. "Turn right after we cross that big culvert. Then drive straight ahead three-quarters of a mile until we come to a large open area with a low ridge off to the south of it."

"You been up here before?" Jim said.

"Nope," I said. "Why do you ask?"

"No reason."

"This is crazy!" Sparano said. "There aren't any antelope around here. An antelope would have to be stupid to be in a place like this."

"Stop here!"

"Here?" Rooney said. "We're right out in the open. Even if there were any antelope here they could see us from a mile away in any direction. But there aren't any antelope here."

I got out, loaded my rifle, and walked a couple hundred feet away from the rig. The little group of observers sprawled out on the ground, sighing, groaning, and occasionally snickering.

After waiting twenty minutes for the arrival of an antelope, I began to wonder if maybe the boys had put Kathy up to drawing the map. It would have been about like them. Still, Kathy didn't seem the type to help perpetrate a low-down, dirty, rotten practical joke, even though it struck me as a pretty good one and probably worth a try on Zumbo sometime.

Suddenly, a dot appeared at the top of the ridge. I put my riflescope on the dot. The dot was staring back at me. It was an antelope, with horns. It sees me, I thought. There's no way it's going to come within range. As if reading my mind, the antelope galloped down off the ridge—*straight toward me!* Incredible! Here, truly, was a dumb antelope! It stopped three hundred yards away, offering an easy target. I fired, kicking up a spout of dust a couple of feet to its right. This, I should mention, is a good way to test an animal's reflexes, but should not be attempted by beginners.

The antelope, displaying excellent reflexes, if a total lack of good judgment, bounded up in the air and took off, turning into one of the brown-and-white streaks for which the species is noted. But it was still streaking right at me! Cool as ice, I stopped its charge with a perfect off-hand shot at fifty yards. Indeed, if I had flinched even slightly, I might have hit the befuddled creature, but such was not my intent. I had, of course, perceived that the antelope was not only extraordinarily dumb but also malicious, and dead set on attacking us. For that reason, I had fired a warning shot across its bow and thereby dissuaded it from carrying out its dastardly assault. The antelope, obviously shocked by this impressive display of marksmanship, streaked to safety.

"Wow!" said Zumbo.

"Amazing!" cried Rooney.

"I never saw anything like it!" exclaimed Sparano.

"It was nothing," I responded modestly.

"It was less than nothing!" shouted Zumbo. "An easy shot like that, and you missed? I can't believe it!"

I tried to explain that I had accomplished my intended purpose, but unfortunately my associates chose to cling to their own interpretation of the event. Naturally, I was more than a little annoyed. Here I had just stopped an antelope in midcharge and saved myself and probably them from a bad goring—a pronghorn gore is one of the worst kinds, too. But what thanks did I get? Nothing but ridicule.

"I will admit," Rooney finally admitted, "that it would have been unsportsmanlike to shoot that antelope. It was just too dumb."

"Yeah," agreed Sparano. "The world's dumbest antelope!"

"What a day!" exclaimed Zumbo. "The world's worst shot meets the world's dumbest antelope!"

Reading Time: _____

See Conversion Table.

Enter WPM Rate on the Progress Record Chart.

32 The Dumbest Antelope

COMPREHENSION CHECK

Getting the Facts

1. Pat flew to where in Wyoming? (a) Casper, (b) Gardner, (c) Rock Springs, (d) Sheridan.

   1. ___

2. Most of the others on the hunting trip were (a) writers, (b) salesmen, (c) critics, (d) reviewers.

   2. ___

3. Pat's big game trophies shrank as much as (a) 20 percent, (b) 30 percent, (c) 40 percent, (d) 50 percent.

   3. ___

4. Vin shot an antelope (a) from his horse, (b) out of a large herd, (c) not visible to the naked eye, (d) on the other side of a big rock.

   4. ___

5. Who gave Pat the map? (a) Bob, (b) Rooney, (c) Zumbo, (d) Kathy.

   5. ___

Getting the Meaning

6. This is mainly about (a) hunting antelopes, (b) spotting antelopes, (c) Pat's hunting experience, (d) hunting dumb antelopes.

   6. ___

7. Pat is best described as (a) overly confident, (b) self-admiring, (c) a careful planner, (d) unlucky.

   7. ___

8. Pat's reaction to Rooney's shooting an antelope in a herd shows, (a) jealousy, (b) intolerance of a show-off, (c) disbelief, (d) amusement.

   8. ___

9. You would infer Hal's stabbing pains in his legs came from (a) ants, (b) below-zero cold, (c) mosquitoes, (d) Pat's spurs.

   9 ___

10. This is organized (a) on a time sequence, (b) around illustrations of a point, (c) on a problem-solution basis, (d) logically.

    10. ___

10 Off for Each Mistake.
Comprehension Score: _____
Answer Key in Appendix.
Enter the Results on the Progress Record Chart.

SUPPLEMENTARY PREFIX MINI-REVIEW

Here are twenty additional prefixes not covered elsewhere in this text. While not as useful as the twenty treated in Part B, they are next in usefulness and still very valuable shortcuts. Review them from time to time, using the following procedure.

Initially, cover the right-hand column with your 3 x 5 card. Try to supply the common meaning of each prefix, checking immediately by moving the card down to reveal the answer.

When you can do that perfectly, try a more difficult pattern, Cover both right-hand columns. Then try to supply both the suggested mnemonic and the common meaning, checking as before.

Finally, for the most difficult review, cover the two left-hand columns. Try to supply both prefix and mnemonic associations for each common meaning, checking again as usual. Review as often as needed to keep a perfect score.

Prefix	Suggested Mnemonic	Common Meaning
1. *homo-*	homogenized	same
2. *hydro-*	hydrant	water
3. *hypo-*	hypodermic	under
4. *hyper-*	hyperactive	over, beyond
5. *dia-*	diameter	through
6. *para-*	parallel	beside
7. *per-*	percolator	through
8. *ab(s)-*	absent	away
9. *poly-*	polygamy	many
10. *peri-*	periscope	around
11. *tele-*	telescope	far
12. *archi-*	archetype	first, original
13. *ante-*	antecedent	before
14. *anti-*	antiaircraft	against
15. *en-*	enclose	in
16. *bi-*	bicycle	two
17. *mal-*	maladjusted	bad, badly
18. *tri-*	tricycle	three
19. *syn-*	synthesis	with, together
20. *bene-*	benefactor	well

33 Mrs. Packletide's Tiger

WORD POWER WORKOUT

A. Leaning on Context

In each of the blanks provided, place the letter that precedes the best definition of the underlined word in context to the left.

Words in Context

1. ___ for her sudden <u>deviation</u>

2. ___ could successfully <u>counter</u>

3. ___ <u>ostensibly</u> in Loona Bimberton's

4. ___ circumstances proved <u>propitious</u>

5. ___ the favored <u>rendezvous</u>

6. ___ they might <u>curtail</u>

7. ___ a <u>morbid</u> dread

8. ___ by <u>senile</u> decay

9. ___ gladly <u>connived</u> at the fiction

10. ___ with seeming <u>irrelevance</u>

Definitions

a. meeting place

b. aged

c. detour

d. strike back at

e. curious, unwholesome

f. seemingly

g. favorable

h. unrelatedness

i. shorten

j. winked

Check your answers with the Key before going on. Review any that you have missed.

Pronunciation aids: 1. dē'vē ā'shun; 3. os ten'suh blē; 4. prō pish'us; 5. ron'dā vōō; 8. sē'nil.

KEY: add, āce; end, ēven; it, īce; odd, ōpen; pōōl; up.

B. Leaning on Parts

Capere means "take" or "seize." When you see *cept, cap, cip,* or *ceiv* in a word, look for that meaning. Use forms of *capere* in the blanks below.

1. A person seized by the police is their _____.

2. The executive was the re_____ of an honorary degree.

3. When you take your choice, you re_____ what you've chosen.

4. Seizing your opponent's forward pass is inter_____ it.

5. A slave taken out of bondage was said to be eman_____.

C. Making the Words Yours

In each blank below, enter the most appropriate word from the ten words in context in the first exercise, substituting it for the word(s) in parentheses. Use these words: *connived, counter, curtail, deviation, irrelevance, morbid, ostensibly, propitious, rendezvous, senile.*

1. The storm caused some businesses to (shorten) _____ their hours.

2. Where's the (meeting place) _____ for the caravan?

3. The nurse called the patient's death a case of (aged) _____ decay.

4. With what argument will you (strike back at) _____ your opponent?

5. This seems like the most (favorable) _____ moment to begin.

6. Well, such (unrelatedness) _____ seems typical of flighty persons.

7. They secretly (winked) _____ at getting someone to tape the concert.

8. Watch for any sudden (detour) _____ in the inmate's train of thought.

9. The dog's condition was (seemingly) _____ caused by inadequate diet.

10. I'd call that a (curious, unwholesome) _____ book.

4 Off for Each Mistake.
Word Power Score: _____
Answer Key in Appendix.

33

Mrs. Packletide's Tiger

Saki

Saki is, of course, a pen name—for Hector Hugh Munro. His stories attack the conventions of Society, most of them giving us the enjoyment of seeing someone get well-deserved comeuppance. It's not so much what happens to the tiger but what happens to Mrs. Packletide that draws your interest. On to tiger country!

Begin Timing

It was Mrs. Packletide's pleasure and intention that she should shoot a tiger. Not that the lust to kill had suddenly descended on her, or that she felt that she would leave India safer and more wholesome than she had found it, with one fraction less of wild beast per million of inhabitants. The compelling motive for her sudden deviation towards the footsteps of Nimrod was the fact that Loona Bimberton had recently been carried eleven miles in an aeroplane by an Algerian aviator, and talked of nothing else; only a personally procured tiger-skin and a heavy harvest of Press photographs could successfully counter that sort of thing. Mrs. Packletide had already arranged in her mind the lunch she would give at her house in Curzon Street, ostensibly in Loona Bimberton's honour, with a tiger-skin rug occupying most of the foreground and all of the conversation. She had also already designed in her mind the tiger-claw brooch that she was going to give Loona Bimberton on her next birthday. In a world that is supposed to be chiefly swayed by hunger and by love Mrs. Packletide was an exception; her movements and motives were largely governed by dislike of Loona Bimberton.

Circumstances proved propitious. Mrs. Packletide had offered a thousand rupees for the opportunity of shooting a tiger without overmuch risk or exertion, and it so happened that a neighbouring village could boast of being the favoured rendezvous of an animal of respectable antecedents, which had been driven by the increasing infirmities of age to abandon game-killing and confine its appetite to the smaller domestic animals. The prospect of earning the thousand rupees had stimulated the sporting and commercial instinct of the villagers; children were posted night and day on the outskirts of the local jungle to head the tiger back in the unlikely event of his attempting to roam away to fresh hunting-grounds, and the cheaper kinds of goats were left about with elaborate carelessness to keep him satisfied with his present quarters. The one great anxiety was lest he should die of old age before the date appointed for the memsahib's shoot. Mothers carrying their babies home through the jungle after the day's work in the fields hushed their singing lest they might curtail the restful sleep of the venerable herd-robber.

The great night duly arrived, moonlit and cloudless. A platform had been constructed in a comfortable and conveniently placed tree, and thereon crouched Mrs. Packletide and her paid companion, Miss Mebbin. A goat, gifted with a particularly persistent bleat, such as even a partially deaf tiger might be reasonably expected to hear on a still night, was tethered at the correct distance. With an accurately sighted rifle and a thumb-nail pack of patience cards the sportswoman awaited the coming of the quarry.

"I suppose we are in some danger?" said Miss Mebbin.

She was not actually nervous about the wild beast, but she had a morbid dread of performing an atom more service than she had been paid for.

"Nonsense," said Mrs. Packletide; "it's a very old tiger. It couldn't spring up here even if it wanted to."

"If it's an old tiger I think you ought to get it cheaper. A thousand rupees is a lot of money."

Louisa Mebbin adopted a protective elder-sister attitude towards money in general, irrespective of nationality or denomination. Her energetic intervention had saved many a ruble from dissipating itself in tips in some Moscow hotel, and francs and centimes clung to her instinctively under circumstances which would have driven them headlong from less sympathetic hands. Her speculations as to the market depreciation of tiger remnants were cut short by the appearance on the scene of the animal itself. As soon as it caught sight of the tethered goat it lay flat on the earth, seemingly less from a desire to take advantage of all available cover than for the purpose of snatching a short rest before commencing the grand attack.

"I believe it's ill," said Louisa Mebbin, loudly in Hindustani, for the benefit of the village headman, who was in ambush in a neighbouring tree.

"Hush!" said Mrs. Packletide, and at the moment the tiger commenced ambling towards his victim.

"Now, now!" urged Miss Mebbin with some excitement; "if he doesn't touch the goat we needn't pay for it." (The bait was an extra.)

The rifle flashed out with a loud report, and the great tawny beast sprang to one side and then rolled over in the stillness of death. In a moment a crowd of excited natives had swarmed on to the scene, and their shouting speedily carried the glad news to the village, where a thumping of tom-toms took up the chorus of triumph. And their triumph and rejoicing found a ready echo in the heart of Mrs. Packletide; already that luncheon-party in Curzon Street seemed immeasurably nearer.

It was Louisa Mebbin who drew attention to the fact that the goat was in death-throes from a mortal bullet-wound, while no trace of the rifle's deadly work could be found on the tiger. Evidently the wrong animal had been hit, and the beast of prey had succumbed to heart-failure, caused by the sudden report of the rifle, accelerated by senile decay. Mrs. Packletide was pardonably annoyed at the discovery; but, at any rate, she was the possessor of a dead tiger, and the villagers, anxious for their thousand rupees, gladly connived at the fiction that she had shot the beast. And Miss Mebbin was a paid companion. Therefore did Mrs. Packletide face the cameras with a light heart, and her pictured fame reached from the pages of the *Texas Weekly Snapshot* to the illustrated Monday supplement of the *Novoe Vremya*. As for Loona Bimberton, she refused to look at an illustrated paper for weeks, and her letter of thanks for the gift of a tiger-claw brooch was a model of repressed emotions. The luncheon-party she declined; there are limits beyond which repressed emotions become dangerous.

From Curzon Street the tiger-skin rug travelled down to the Manor House, and was duly inspected and admired by the county, and it seemed a fitting and appropriate thing when Mrs. Packletide went to the County Costume Ball in the character of Diana. She refused to fall in, however, with Clovis's tempting suggestion of a primeval dance party, at which every one should wear the skins of beasts they had recently slain. "I should be in rather a Baby Bunting condition," confessed Clovis, "with a miserable rabbit-skin or two to wrap-up in, but then," he added, with a rather malicious glance at Diana's proportions, "my figure is quite as good as that Russian dancing boy's."

"How amused every one would be if they knew what really happened," said Louisa Mebbin a few days after the ball.

"What do you mean?" asked Mrs. Packletide quickly.

"How you shot the goat and frightened the tiger to death," said Miss Mebbin with her disagreeably pleasant laugh.

"No one would believe it," said Mrs. Packletide, her face changing colour as rapidly as though it were going through a book of patterns before post-time.

"Loona Bimberton would," said Miss Mebbin. Mrs. Packletide's face settled on an unbecoming shade of greenish white.

"You surely wouldn't give me away?" she asked.

"I've seen a week-end cottage near Dorking that I should rather like to buy," said Miss Mebbin with seeming irrelevance. "Six hundred and eighty, freehold. Quite a bargain, only I don't happen to have the money."

Louisa Mebbin's pretty week-end cottage, christened by her "Les Fauves," and gay in summer-time with its garden borders of tiger-lilies, is the wonder and admiration of her friends.

"It is a marvel how Louisa manages to do it," is the general verdict.

Mrs. Packletide indulges in no more big-game shooting.

"The incidental expenses are so heavy," she confides to inquiring friends.

Reading Time: _____

See Conversion Table.

Enter WPM Rate on the Progress Record Chart.

33 Mrs. Packletide's Tiger

COMPREHENSION CHECK

Getting the Facts

1. Loona Bimberton had ridden in a plane piloted by (a) an African, (b) a Hindustani, (c) an Algerian, (d) an Egyptian.

   1. ___

2. Mrs. Packletide lived in a house in (a) Curzon Street, (b) Cornhill Street, (c) Regent Street, (d) Dover Street.

   2. ___

3. When the tiger first appeared, it (a) laid its ears back, (b) growled softly, (c) crept toward the goat, (d) lay flat.

   3. ___

4. Specific mention was made of the (a) *London Guardian*, (b) *Texas Weekly Snapshot*, (c) *Los Angeles Tabloid*, (d) *Manchester Register*.

   4. ___

5. Mrs. Packletide attended a costume ball dressed as (a) Ion, (b) Venus, (c) Niobe, (d) Diana.

   5. ___

Getting the Meaning

6. This is mainly to tell the story of Mrs. Packletide's (a) tiger hunt, (b) desire to best Loona Bimberton, (c) problem with Miss Mebbin, (d) attempts to conceal the truth.

   6. ___

7. Saki prepares for the death of the tiger by mentioning (a) its infirmities, (b) the villagers' worry about its dying of old age, (c) its snatching a short rest before attacking, (d) all the preceding.

   7. ___

8. Miss Mebbin's interest in money was pointed up by her comments about (a) an old tiger, (b) the tiger bait, (c) the thousand rupees, (d) all the preceding.

   8. ___

9. Chief attention is placed on (a) Mrs. Packletide, (b) Miss Mebbin, (c) Loona Bimberton, (d) all the preceding about equally.

   9 ___

10. Strongest interest was on (a) story, (b) characters, (c) setting, (d) dialogue.

    10. ___

10 Off for Each Mistake.
Comprehension Score: _____
Answer Key in Appendix.
Enter the Results on the Progress Record Chart.

34 Getting Better Grades

WORD POWER WORKOUT

A. Leaning on Context

In each of the blanks provided, place the letter that precedes the best definition of the underlined word in context to the left.

Words in Context	Definitions
1. ___ your <u>academic</u> success	a. cost, extent of damage
2. ___ will <u>pose</u> no problem	b. school
3. ___ this <u>insures</u> personal growth	c. efforts
4. ___ the fearful <u>toll</u> of forgetting	d. highest point
5. ___ slightly <u>modified</u> form	e. cause, create
6. ___ <u>culmination</u> of your efforts	f. changed, altered
7. ___ <u>frantic</u> all-night cramming	g. guarantees
8. ___ reading and listening <u>endeavors</u>	h. primary, highest degree of
9. ___ the <u>utmost</u> importance	i. makes known
10. ___ it <u>releases</u> all information	j. desperate, frenzied

Check your answers with the Key before going on. Review any that you have missed.

B. Leaning on Parts

Plicare means "fold." When you see *plic, plex, ply,* or *ploy* in a word, look for that meaning. Fill in the following with forms of *plicare*.

1. To state clearly or unfold meaning is to be ex_____.

2. It's not what you say but what you fold in or im_____.

3. To fold troops into position is to de_____ them.

4. There are two families in the big du_____ next door.

5. How would you re_____ to that question.

C. Making the Words Yours

In each blank below, enter the most appropriate word from the ten words in context in the first exercise, substituting it for the word(s) in parentheses. Use these words: *academic, culmination, endeavors, frantic, insures, modified, pose, released, toll, utmost.*

1. The (cost) _____ was 300 persons dead or missing.

2. The new product was (made known) _____ to the public.

3. The (highest point) _____ of the actor's success was reached in his last performance.

4. Her (efforts) _____ to acquire a high-paying job were successful.

5. My (school) _____ interests conflicted with my interest in sports.

6. The track star's ability to throw the javelin (guarantees) _____ his success.

7. The drama critic soon (changed) _____ her ideas about the play.

8. The meeting between the heads of states was a matter of the (highest degree of) _____ secrecy.

9. Last-minute cramming for an exam can be a (desperate) _____ experience.

10. If a young couple wants to get married, the parents may (cause) _____ a problem.

4 Off for Each Mistake.
Word Power Score: _____
Answer Key in Appendix.

34

Getting Better Grades

Did you hear about the student in the bookstore? He was failing and asked the clerk if there was a book to help him get better grades. The clerk picked up a how-to-study guide and said, "Here's one that will do half your work for you." The student brightened up immediately. "Fine!" A pause while he did some mental arithmetic. "Fine! I'll take *two*."

Sounds like another musical, doesn't it—*How To Succeed in College without Really Trying!* Well, if it weren't for all those quizzes, midterms, and finals, it might be that easy. Even those, however, with the right approach, will pose no problem.

Requirements

But what *is* the right approach? You want a substitute for that common frantic all-night cramming, that washing down of chapter after chapter with strong black coffee. By exam time that regimen means bleary eyes and fuzzy mind—means unwanted D's instead of hoped-for B's.

As a substitute, you need an approach that is comprehensive, simple, appealing, and, above all, effective.

1. *Comprehensive.* It must cover everything—lectures as well as reading.

2. *Simple.* A complex system may work well, judging from research. But it it's too complex, it just won't be used. Those good grades will be as elusive as ever.

3. *Appealing.* It must have sufficient appeal to be actually used. Take the SQ3R system, for example. Three weeks after its presentation in detail to one of our classes, the students were asked what SQ3R stood for. Only 3 percent knew exactly. Obviously, no more than that number could possibly be applying the system. Insufficient appeal.

4. *Effective.* It *must* work—and work better than other approaches. That's of the utmost importance, of course.

The Natural Approach

Actually every single chapter in this book contributes significantly to your academic success. Better readers *are* better grade-getters, other things being equal. And this book focuses on developing and refining a wide variety of reading and vocabulary-building skills.

Now is the time to fit parts together into a special grade-getting approach. Look on it as either a capstone or culmination of your efforts. Here it is.

Identify. This is a natural first move, lying at the very heart of all your reading and listening endeavors. You can't remember everything you read and hear. As mentioned earlier, you must learn to identify essentials and note meaningful relationships. This you should already know how to do efficiently.

Extract. This second step does involve something new. Mark each notebook page by drawing a line down the left side about two inches from the edge. When you finish reading a few pages, enter your summary of essential material on the right-hand portion of the page. Make your notes complete enough so you'll be able to understand them later. Continue in this way until you have finished your reading. Take lecture notes the same way, using the right-hand side.

Speaking of lectures, someone once described the lecture system as a way of getting information from the notes of the teacher to the notes of the student, without affecting the minds of either. This mustn't happen with you. Be sure, as you listen or read, to take notes in your own words. This insures personal involvement. This runs ideas through your mind and into your notes, putting your own mark upon them.

Label. After completing your notes, master the material. Go back to the beginning and write down a word or phrase in the left-hand margin opposite each idea or point in your notes. Use words that will best help you recall the full information. Think in terms of a computer. You feed it a key word. It releases all information it has on that point. Your key entries in the left-hand narrow margin will function the same way, providing a convenient handle for picking up the information. Treat lecture notes as you do your reading notes. After class, look them over, supplying key words in the left margin.

Recite. Here's where you can appreciate the full advantage of this approach. You see, it's not enough to read and comprehend. You must also remember. This above all! Research indicates that after two weeks, without recitation, you'll remember only about 20 percent. With recitation, however, that figure becomes 80 percent—*four times more*.

The review is simplicity itself. Just cover the notes on the right side of your notebook. Then start down, looking at each key word or phrase on the left. With that as a clue, recite aloud the full information on the right for which it stands. Uncover, then, to check how accurately and fully you know the material. Continue through in this way. Correct any mistakes. Add any omissions. Restudy any points not remembered.

Recognize this as a fact of life. Suppose that key word doesn't now trigger the information covered on the right. Don't expect that on an exam something—perhaps the same key word in one of the questions—will, like magic, bring the information flooding into your mind. It just doesn't work that way. If it works for your review, fine. You can expect it to work also during the exam. During review, restudy, if you can't recall the material on the right. That's your true, natural test of mastery—being able to recite your notes completely when seeing the key word.

Cautions

Don't use a formal outline as you take notes. Concentrate on content. Some things just don't lend themselves easily to outline form.

Don't misschedule your review-recite sessions. Remember—you forget most right after you've learned or reviewed something. For that reason, schedule your review immediately before the examination. At least minimize the time between review and exam to minimize the fearful toll of forgetting.

As you can see, this approach is indeed an easy, natural approach. It is a slightly modified form of one described and advocated by Dr. Walter Pauk. He says that "over 98 percent of the students instructed in this approach continue to use it and report unusual success." Why not join the ranks? Enjoy similar success yourself.

Reading Time: _____
See Conversion Table.
Enter WPM Rate on the Progress Record Chart.

34 Getting Better Grades

COMPREHENSION CHECK

Getting the Facts

1. How many copies of the how-to-study book did the
   student decide to buy? (a) one, (b) two, (c) three,
   (d) four.   1. ___

2. Specific mention was made of what system?
   (a) PQRST, (b) OARWET, (c) SQ3R, (d) SPD4.   2. ___

3. You were asked to think of the approach advocated
   here as a (a) capstone, (b) short-cut, (c) cure-all, (d)
   study-substitute.   3. ___

4. You are cautioned not to use (a) ink, (b) shorthand,
   (c) a formal outline, (d) a typewriter.   4. ___

5. About what percentage of the students taught this approach
   continued to use it? (a) 13%, (b) 36%, (c) 46%, (d) 98%.   5. ___

Getting the Meaning

6. The main focus is on (a) taking notes, (b) improving
   study techniques, (c) taking tests, (d) using recitation.   6. ___

7. Most emphasis is on (a) the simple, (b) the appealing,
   (c) the effective, (d) the comprehensive.   7. ___

8. What was the point of the lecture system definition?
   To make sure that notes are (a) complete, (b) not busy
   work, (c) translated into sounds, (d) not too detailed.   8. ___

9. Apparently it is most important to (a) involve yourself,
   (b) be efficient, (c) plan carefully, (d) practice often.   9 ___

10. Figures as to the numbers of students using this program 10. ___
    were to show (a) its effectiveness, (b) the degree
    of interest, (c) its simplicity, (d) the degree of need.

10 Off for Each Mistake.
Comprehension Score: _____
Answer Key in Appendix.
Enter the Results on the Progress Record Chart.

Making the Application

To learn how to do anything, even some very simple things, you have to try them yourself. Try this new system on the first page only of Selection 34, using the space marked off below.

Word or phrase labels	Fairly complete summary of essentials

Establish this as your system for both lectures and textbook reading. It works if you'll form the habit right now and put it to weekly use.

35 The Wonders of Water

WORD POWER WORKOUT

A. Leaning on Context

In each of the blanks provided, place the letter that precedes the best definition of the underlined word in context to the left.

Words in Context

1. ___ these <u>metabolic</u> wastes
2. ___ is also lost <u>insensibly</u>
3. ___ it <u>excretes</u> the excess
4. ___ death is usually <u>imminent</u>
5. ___ <u>compulsive</u> water drinking
6. ___ from the <u>depletion</u>
7. ___ and <u>dilution</u>
8. ___ by kidney <u>malfunction</u>
9. ___ may be <u>counterproductive</u>
10. ___ acts as a <u>diuretic</u>

Definitions

a. fast approaching
b. body-building
c. against one's will
d. imperceptibly
e. improper performance
f. discharges
g. draining
h. tending to defeat one's purpose
i. watering down
j. activator of increased urine flow

Check your answers with the Key before going on. Review any that you have missed.

Pronunciation aids: 1. met′uh bol′ic; 4. im′uh nunt; 10. dī′yuh ret′ik.
KEY: add, āce; end, ēven; it, īce; odd, ōpen; pōol; up.

B. Leaning on Parts

The Greek root *graphein*, which appears in English as *graph*, means "to write." Fill in each of the following blanks, using that root.

1. A written account of your own life is an autobio_____.

2. A list of source books at the end of an article is a biblio_____.

3. A device to wire written messages is called a tele_____.

4. A piece of writing treating a single subject is a mono_____.

5. A vivid written description of an event provides a _____ account.

C. Making the Words Yours

In each blank below, enter the most appropriate word from the ten words in context in the first exercise, substituting it for the word(s) in parentheses. Use these words: *compulsive, counterproductive, depletion, dilution, diuretic, excretes, imminent, insensibly, malfunction, metabolic.*

1. Apparently we have different (body-building) _____ rates.

2. One inmate was (against one's will) _____ about hand-washing.

3. War brings a rapid (draining) _____ of our natural resources.

4. The (improper performance) _____ of the machinery completely stopped production.

5. The slow-flowing liquid needed further (watering down) _____.

6. The doctor said I'd need something to serve as a (activator of increased urine flow) _____.

7. The black clouds suggested that a storm was (fast approaching) _____.

8. The body (discharges) _____ excess water through the kidneys.

9. Some are (imperceptibly) _____ losing their awareness of environmental change.

10. Eating rich food when trying to lose weight seems (tending to defeat one's purpose) _____.

35

The Wonders of Water

Jane Brody

How much water does your body contain? Guess! Now check up on yourself as you read. Don't let this selection plunge you into deep water or make you feel like a fish out of water. Just drink in every word of this fascinating account.

Begin Timing

Water, it may surprise you to know, is actually our most vital nutrient. It is also our most neglected one. Probably because it provides no calories, it rarely (if ever) appears on charts depicting basic nutrient requirements. Yet, we would all expire a lot sooner without water than without food.

Your insides are an internal sea. As solid as a person may look, the body is actually about two-thirds water—55 to 65 percent water for females, 65 to 75 percent water for males. The difference exists because fat, which makes up a larger proportion of a woman's body than a man's, holds less water than lean tissue does. Newborns of both sexes are about 85 percent water.

Every living cell in your body depends on water to carry out its essential functions. Through the blood and lymphatic system, water carries nutrients and oxygen to cells and removes waste products. The body eliminates these metabolic wastes through the water in sweat and urine. Water is essential to the digestion and absorption of food from the gastrointestinal tract as well as to the elimination of digestive wastes. In fact, the best treatment for constipation is to eat fibrous foods, which increase the water-holding capacity of the stool.

Water lubricates every joint in your body and keeps your soft tissues from sticking together. Water provides a protective cushion for your tissues and for the fetus during pregnancy. And water is the body's natural air-conditioning system. The loss of water through perspiration cools the body and prevents it from building up internal heat. Heat is required for the evaporation of water from your skin, and that heat comes from your body. When you're not sweating noticeably, you're probably losing what is called "insensible," or invisible, perspiration. Even if you're not moving a muscle, your body produces heat it may have to get rid of through metabolic processes. Some water is also lost insensibly through your lungs.

All told, the average adult body contains forty to fifty quarts of water, with 40 percent of it inside cells. The percentage of water varies with the tissue: blood, 83 percent; muscle, 75 percent; the brain, 74 percent; and bone, 22 percent.

The water within and outside your cells contains a variety of dissolved salts that regulate the distribution of water. If the concentration of salts outside cells is higher than that inside, water moves out of the cells to try to even things out. One way to visualize this is to think of what happens when you sprinkle salt on lettuce leaves or cucumber slices. The salt draws water from the cells, causing the vegetable to wilt. In the human body, wilted cells are not very effective at carrying out their required tasks, so it's very important to properly balance your intake of water and salts. When your body has more water than it needs, it excretes the excess through the kidneys, and when water is in relatively short supply, the kidneys hold more back. But no matter how little water you may consume, the kidneys must excrete a certain amount—about ten to seventeen ounces—each day to get rid of metabolic wastes.

Thus, neither your kidneys nor your cells can function properly unless you drink enough. You can live a long time without any food (just how long depends in part on how fat you were to begin with), but after two or three days without water, death is usually imminent. With a loss of 5 percent of body water, your skin shrinks and muscles become weak; the loss of just 15 to 20 percent of body water is fatal.

Although it's possible to drink enough water to kill yourself, this only occurs in an extremely rare psychiatric disorder called psychogenic polydipsia, which has as its primary symptom compulsive water drinking. Death results not from the water itself but from the depletion and dilution of sodium in body fluids. The more common problem is *dehydration*—insufficient water intake to compensate for the amount lost. This can be caused by kidney malfunction; the loss of a great deal of blood; repeated bouts of vomiting or diarrhea; high fever; extreme physical exertion; or living in a hot dry climate without sufficient water to replace what you lose as perspiration.

Your body lets you know when it needs more water through that well-known signal, *thirst*. At least two mechanisms are involved in this warning signal. When the blood becomes too salty, it draws water from the salivary glands. This dries your mouth and makes you feel as if you need a drink. Also, the salty blood signals the brain directly that more liquid is needed. But thirst is an imperfect signal. More than likely, it shuts off before you've drunk enough. Therefore, it's a good idea for everyone—and especially persons who are physically active—to continue drinking beyond the point of quenching thirst. Remember, *extra water can't hurt*; your body will simply get rid of whatever it doesn't need.

The average adult consumes and excretes about two and a half to three quarts of water a day. For persons living in hot climates or engaging in strenuous physical activity, this amount may exceed four quarts. But, you say, "I don't drink ten glasses of liquid a day." No, you probably don't (although it couldn't hurt). More likely, only about five or six glasses are consumed directly as liquids. Most of the rest comes from the solid foods you eat, and some is derived from metabolic processes within your body.

Just as most of your solid tissues are primarily water, water forms a large percentage of the weight of most solid foods. While milk—a liquid—is 87 percent water, green beans—a solid—are 89 percent water, and lettuce is 95 percent water. Even meat is half water and bread is about one-third water by weight. If you eat a lot of fruits and vegetables, you're probably consuming considerably more water than you realize, since most are more than 80 percent water.

It can be tricky trying to figure out if you're getting enough water to meet your body's needs. To be on the safe side, it's a good idea under ordinary circumstances to *drink at least six—and preferably eight—eight-ounce glasses of liquids a day*. These may include juices, soft drinks, milk, coffee, and tea as well as plain water (although coffee and tea may be counterproductive because the caffeine in them acts as a diuretic, causing the kidneys to give up more water than they would otherwise). The more physically active you are at work or at play and the hotter the climate, the more liquids you'll need.

Reading Time: _____
See Conversion Table.
Enter WPM Rate on the Progress Record Chart.

35 The Wonders of Water

COMPREHENSION CHECK

Getting the Facts

1. Our body is about (a) two-thirds water, (b) one-half water, (c) one-third water, (d) twenty % water.

2. In terms of water content, women's bodies contain (a) more than men's, (b) less than men's, (c) the same as men's, (d) no such comparisons given.

3. Blood is (a) 83% water, (b) 75% water, (c) 74% water, (d) an unspecified amount of water.

4. About how long can you live without water? (a) only a day, (b) two or three days, (c) four or five days, (d) six or seven days.

5. You were told to drink at least how many glasses of water a day? (a) 2 to 3, (b) 4 to 5, (c) 6 to 8, (d) 8 to 10.

1. ___

2. ___

3. ___

4. ___

5. ___

Getting the Meaning

6. This is mainly to make you aware of (a) how water functions in the body, (b) how thirst regulates intake, (c) the distinction between body water and water, (d) the body's need for water.

7. The paragraph about the water content of food was intended primarily to get you to (a) eat more fruit, (b) know where body water comes from, (c) plan a more healthful diet, (d) remember to supplement food with water.

8. This is primarily to get you to (a) enjoy, (b) understand, (c) act, (d) evaluate.

9. In style this is best described as (a) dramatic, (b) factual, (c) literary, (d) formal.

10. Points are developed largely through (a) details, (b) quoting research findings, (c) definition, (d) narration.

6. ___

7. ___

8. ___

9 ___

10. ___

10 Off for Each Mistake.
Comprehension Score: _____
Answer Key in Appendix.
Enter the Results on the Progress Record Chart.

36 Can't Get a Good Night's Sleep?

WORD POWER WORKOUT

A. Leaning on Context

In each of the blanks provided, place the letter that precedes the best definition of the underlined word in context to the left.

Words in Context	Definitions
1. ___ that <u>periodic</u> wakefulness	a. physiological
2. ___ begin to <u>deteriorate</u>	b. relieve, lighten
3. ___ over <u>eons</u>	c. gasping for breath
4. ___ a <u>circadian</u> rhythm	d. get worse
5. ___ apparently <u>incites</u>	e. intermittent
6. ___ a sleep <u>apnea</u>	f. general, nonspecific
7. ___ <u>nocturnal</u> breathing disorder	g. drives, moves
8. ___ <u>alleviate</u> depression	h. immeasurable ages
9. ___ such <u>generic</u> names	i. nightly
10. ___ <u>extraneous</u> noise	j. unassociated, foreign

Check your answers with the Key before going on. Review any that you have missed.

Pronunciation aids: 3. ē'ons; 6. ap nē'uh; 8. uh lē'vē āt; 9. ji ner'ik; 10. ik strā'ne us.

KEY: add, āce; end, ēven; it, īce; odd, ōpen; pōol; up.

B. Leaning on Parts

Legein means "speak" or "study of." When you see *logue, log,* or *loq* in a word, look for those meanings. Use a form of *legein* in each blank below.

1. Talk between two or more is known as a dia_____.

2. A person who gives a powerful speech is an e_____ speaker.

3. The study of myths is mytho_____.

4. A speech coming before a dramatic performance is called a pro_____.

5. Bio_____ is the study of the life processes of plants and animals.

C. Making the Words Yours

In each blank below, enter the most appropriate word from the ten words in context in the first exercise, substituting it for the word(s) in parentheses. Use these words: *alleviate, apnea, circadian, deteriorate, eons, extraneous, generic, incites, nocturnal, periodic.*

1. That long overseas flight disrupted my (physiological) _____ rhythm badly.

2. Don't get the name brand; the (general, nonspecific) _____ is much cheaper.

3. It took (immeasurable ages) _____ to form the Grand Canyon.

4. Improve your theme by eliminating (unassociated, foreign) _____ details.

5. This pill should (relieve, lighten) _____ your pain.

6. One's health tends to (get worse) _____ as one gets older.

7. They made (intermittent) _____ visits to each other.

8. Having a goal in life (drives, moves) _____ people to action.

9. Have you ever had a problem with sleep (gasping for breath) _____?

10. As you well know, the owl is a (nightly) _____ bird.

4 Off for Each Mistake.
Word Power Score: _____
Answer Key in Appendix.

36

Can't Get a Good Night's Sleep?

Changing Times

Shakespeare talks about "sleep that knits up the ravel'd sleave of care." But if, for you, sleep doesn't do a good job of knitting, what next? After all, you'll spend about a third of your life sleeping—or trying to! Doesn't it make sense to spend a few minutes learning more about that lifetime activity? Who knows what sage advice you'll find!

Begin Timing

Over a lifetime virtually all of us have a nodding acquaintance with insomnia. Now and then we find ourselves still battling the pillow at two or three o'clock in the morning or suddenly snapping wide awake long before dawn.

Ironically, a common cause of losing sleep is not a cause at all. Many people have the mistaken notion that they should fall asleep the minute their head hits the pillow and not wake up until morning. When sleep does not come readily, they develop full-blown worry, ignoring doctors' advice that periodic wakefulness is the last thing to lose sleep over.

Here are other points of medical agreement:

• The amount of wakefulness is often exaggerated unconsciously by the person who is having trouble sleeping.

• The amount of sleep needed at age 21—say eight hours—may not be normal at 50 or 60, when sleep patterns begin to deteriorate.

• Self-diagnosed insomnia may miss the real trouble—mental depression.

• Quality of sleep may be as important as quantity.

First, What Sleep Is

The tree shrew, a remarkably awake animal, sleeps very little, while the bat, a slugabed by any standard, sleeps away five-sixths of its life. Adult human beings, on the other hand by evolution and habit have developed sleep-wake cycles based on a need to be active two-thirds of the time. Put another way, over eons people have developed a circadian rhythm of 23 to 25 hours, a third of which is spent sleeping.

Research into normal sleep is science's way of creating a yardstick by which to gauge the abnormal. Doctors can tell whether you have true insomnia—or some other sleep disorder—by comparing your sleep cycle with a normal pattern.

Normal sleep is not an even and continuous slumber, as you might suspect. Human sleep is made up of separate stages of light and deeper sleep. Typically, only during the first hours of sleep do you reach stage four, the deepest slumber. The rest of the time is spent drifting between the other three lighter stages in specific patterns.

Sleep cycles, as they are called, range from 90 to 110 minutes each and end with a flurry of rapid eye movement (REM) sleep. These rapid eye movements are detected by electronic sensors near the eyes. In experiments in which sleepers are awakened from REM sleep, eight out of ten report they were dreaming at the time. While it was once thought that depriving sleepers of REM sleep was psychologically damaging, the theory has been largely discarded, along with the notion that a person's eye movements during sleep are following the action of his dreams.

The amount of time you spend in each stage of slumber varies. Children enjoy the deepest sleep, with 20% to 30% of the time in stage four. This tapers off to 10% to 16% in young adults, then declines and almost disappears in the elderly. As you grow older, the hope of recapturing the undisturbed sleep of youth is a dim prospect.

Actually, some insomniacs of all ages tend to overestimate how long it takes them to fall asleep and the number of times they awaken during the night. When those who are diagnosed in a sleep laboratory see the recorded electronic evidence that they have been unconsciously exaggerating their plight, the insomnia often clears up.

There is more to going to sleep than closing your eyes. When you start feeling drowsy, a number of bodily changes begin. During sleep muscles relax and tense and body temperature typically drops one and a half degrees. Heart rate slows and blood pressure drops, sometimes drastically, but it, too, fluctuates.

Scientists have long studied what happens during sleep, using electroencephalographs to measure brain waves, electronic sensors to record eye movements, analyses of body chemistry and other methods.

Investigators can now study the cells of the brain itself. Using tiny electrodes inserted into the brain of cats (which have sleep cycles similar to ours), they have shown that two specific groups of brain cells may play roles in the REM cycle of sleep. One group of cells, researchers report, apparently incites the electrical nerve impulses that start REM sleep, while the other shuts it off.

At a recent meeting on sleep disorders, sponsored by the Albert Einstein College of Medicine, the Montefiore Hospital and Medical Center, and the Upjohn Co., it was explained that the two cell groups may somehow connect to and interact with the hypothalamus, the part of the brain thought to contain the clock mechanism that controls human biological rhythms. If the specific properties of the cells can be uncovered, observed Harvard's Dr. J. Allan Hobson, the knowledge might become an important new clue that would help researchers understand the sleep-wake cycle in people.

Who's a Poor Sleeper?

You could qualify as a poor sleeper if you get less than six or six and a half hours of sleep, if you take half an hour or so to drop off, if you experience 30 minutes of more of wakefulness during the night, and then feel tired and jittery during the day. Even if you manage to piece together more than six hours, but sleep is fitful or broken off long before dawn, you probably have a legitimate complaint. The cure may be only a matter of adjusting your sleep-wake cycle—some people simply go to bed before they are tired.

Some forms of insomnia come from such problems as muscular jerking of the legs, arthritis, ulcers and hyperthyroidism. One of the most serious causes is sleep apnea, a nocturnal breathing disorder that afflicts an estimated 50,000 Americans and sometimes wakes its victims hundreds of time a night. So brief are the episodes (snorelike gasps for air) that apnea victims may be completely unaware of them and for years be unable to account for the source of their daily fatigue.

Insomnia can also result from a psychological disorder. Anxiety is a cause; another common one is mental depression, which often goes unrecognized until the patient takes his sleeping complaint to the doctor.

Sleep researchers speak of two main types of depression, reactive and endogenous. Reactive depression may follow a personal crisis—serious injury, loss of job or marriage problems. Endogenous depression creeps up gradually, emerging usually after age 40 from deep within the personality and often defying rational explanation.

The type of treatment for depression depends, of course, on the severity, but in serious cases the doctor may use a combination of psychotherapy and drugs called tricyclic antidepressants. Curiously, there appears to be a link between the way such antidepressants work and the timing of REM sleep in the depressed patient. It is known, for example, that REM slumber in people with endogenous depression starts within five to 15 minutes after they fall asleep, compared with 90 minutes in normal people. But if REM sleep is continuously delayed by waking the patient who has this depression, reports Dr. Gerald W. Vogel of Atlanta's Emory University, the patient's mood will eventually lift. It is thought that tricyclic drugs alleviate depression because they achieve a similar REM-delaying effect.

When You Have a Sleeping Problem

If getting to sleep seems like a real struggle night after night, the first step is to size up the actual extent of your discomfort. Keep a record for a week, noting bedtime, wake-up time and the periods of wakefulness in between.

If you think you do have a real sleep disturbance, talk to your doctor. He will want to determine whether a physical ailment is responsible.

In certain cases the doctor may for a time prescribe sleeping pills with such generic names as chloral hydrate or secobarbital. The idea is to give your body and nerves a rest while you try to get back on schedule.

You should know about the drawbacks of sleeping pills. They will not cure insomnia. And since it is easy to build up tolerance to them, the longer they are used, the bigger the dose you will need to get relief. This can lead to dependence and sometimes serious withdrawal symptoms when drug treatment is stopped.

Because of these problems, sleep experts generally discourage the use of sleeping pills. If you must have them, the advice is to limit intake to several days of any one spell of sleeplessness.

Here are other strategies for your campaign to get a good night's sleep:

• Exercise every day if you have your doctor's okay, but avoid vigorous calisthenics or sports at bedtime.

• Don't go to bed with a full stomach. Big meals should be eaten several hours before retiring because a heavy stomach can interfere with sleep.

• Avoid daytime napping.

• Avoid stimulants, such as coffee and tea, in the evening. A small amount of alcohol is sometimes recommended for elderly people.

• Sleep in a cool room, If the house is dry, you might find that a humidifier helps create a more comfortable environment.

• Develop a calming routine an hour or so before bed. Try to screen out extraneous noise, and read a book or watch a TV show requiring little mental involvement.

• Finally, go to bed only when you are sleepy, and try to blank out the day's worries and forget about tomorrow's.

If none of this works, don't lie there tossing and turning. Get up, find a comfortable chair and read or watch a dull TV program. The surest route to insomnia is to stay in bed stewing about whether you will ever get to sleep.

Reading Time: _____
See Conversion Table.
Enter WPM Rate on the Progress Record Chart.

36 Can't Get a Good Night's Sleep?

COMPREHENSION CHECK

Getting the Facts

1. You were told that periodic wakefulness (a) is a bad sign, (b) suggests mental depression, (c) is nothing to worry about, (d) is more typical with older people.

   1. ___

2. Usually the deepest sleep comes (a) during the first hours, (b) during the middle of the night, (c) toward morning, (d) at different times depending upon the individual.

   2. ___

3. Deepest sleep in enjoyed by (a) old people, (b) middle-aged people, (c) young adults, (d) children.

   3. ___

4. How many main types of depression were discussed? (a) only one, (b) two, (c) three, (d) four.

   4. ___

5. If you have a real sleep problem you were advised to (a) take sleeping pills as a cure, (b) read in bed until sleepy, (c) tire yourself with exercise before bedtime, (d) see your doctor.

   5. ___

Getting the Meaning

6. The main idea was to (a) define what sleep is, (b) describe a poor sleeper, (c) suggest how to improve sleep, (d) discuss sleep—its problems and remedies.

   6. ___

7. This is organized essentially on a (a) problem-solution pattern, (b) cause-effect pattern, (c) general-to-specific order, (d) more to less important order.

   7. ___

8. The purpose is apparently to (a) summarize, (b) make clear, (c) amuse, (d) raise questions.

   8. ___

9. Points were developed largely by (a) quoting experts, (b) logical reasoning, (c) citing research findings, (d) using individual case histories.

   9 ___

10. Apparently mention of the tree shrew and bat was to (a) reveal variations in sleep patterns, (b) contrast animal and human sleep patterns, (c) show the difficulty of defining sleep, (d) show the effects of evolution.

    10. ___

10 Off for Each Mistake.
Comprehension Score: _____
Answer Key in Appendix.
Enter the Results on the Progress Record Chart.

37 Generating New and Wider Interests

WORD POWER WORKOUT

A. Leaning on Context

In each of the blanks provided, place the letter that precedes the best definition of the underlined word in context to the left.

Words in Context	Definitions
1. ___ a <u>colleague</u> of mine	a. fame
2. ___ never yet <u>voluntarily</u> read a book	b. associate
3. ___ smiled <u>condescendingly</u> at his roommate	c. remarkable
4. ___ a <u>genuinely</u> interested student	d. unreasonable
5. ___ of world <u>renown</u>	e. sincerely
6. ___ <u>impersonal</u> objectivity	f. inefficiency
7. ___ killed by academic <u>restraint</u>	g. willingly
8. ___ showing off his <u>ineptitude</u>	h. disinterested
9. ___ almost <u>irrational</u> enthusiasm	i. control
10. ___ to bring <u>outstanding</u> achievement	j. with an air of superiority

Check your answers with the Key before going on. Review any that
you have missed.

Pronunciation aids: 1. kol'ēg; 3. kon di send'ing lē; 5. ri nown'; 8. in ep'tuh tōōd'.
KEY: add, āce; end, ēven; it, īce; odd, ōpen; pōōl; up.

B. Leaning on Parts

Tenere means "have" or "hold." When you see *ten(t)*, *tend*, *tain*, or *tin*, look for those meanings. Fill in the blanks below with a form of *tenere*.

1. Some people observe total abs_____ to control a drinking problem.

2. A person who rents real estates or property is a _____.

3. To hold someone from going is to de_____ the person.

4. To hold firmly to something is to hold on _____.

5. The star's discon_____ lessened everyone else's pleasure.

C. Making the Words Yours

In each blank below, enter the most appropriate word from the ten words in context in the first exercise, substituting it for the word(s) in parentheses. Use these words: *colleague, condescendingly, genuinely, impersonal, ineptitude, irrational, outstanding, renown, restraint, voluntarily.*

1. His (unreasonable) _____ plan was responsible for the loss of the battle.

2. A parent must sometimes be (disinterested) _____ when disciplining a child.

3. His (inefficiency) _____ at typing lost him the job.

4. A person's (control) _____ may disappear when he is being teased.

5. My hope was to achieve (fame) _____ in big league baseball.

6. The nurse was (sincerely) _____ interested in helping crippled children.

7. He (willingly) _____ accepted his responsibilities.

8. The baseball player's (remarkable) _____ success got him into the Hall of Fame.

9. My (associate) _____ was known for her humorous remarks.

10. The students asked only a few questions because the teacher answered (with an air of superiority) _____.

4 Off for Each Mistake.
Word Power Score: _____
Answer Key in Appendix.

37

Generating New and Wider Interests

Begin Timing

Why do some people reach their goals so quickly? What's their secret? That is, indeed, knowledge most worth knowing.

The Driving Force of Interest

The best car ever made still needs fuel to get you anywhere. Similarly, the best of minds needs a strong interest to bring outstanding achievement.

Interest led Napoleon to become a military leader of world renown. Interest led Charles Darwin to discover the origin of species. Interest led Glenn Cunningham to overcome a major physical handicap and become a record-breaking mile runner.

Interest led Thomas Edison to try 6,000 different substances in his attempt to find a suitable electric light filament. How many people do you know who would have sufficient interest to try even 1,000 substances? No wonder he is known the world over. Interest is the secret. Just as gunpowder speeds a bullet toward its mark, so interest can speed you toward any and every goal you have in mind.

Turn to reading. A comprehensive survey by Shaw of over 400 colleges and universities disclosed that an estimated 64 to 95 percent of all freshmen are handicapped by reading deficiencies.

Get the implication? Probably 64 to 95 percent are not as interested in reading as in other things. Put it another way. It also suggests that unless reading is the most interesting thing you ever do, you're not reading up to your full potential.

The Need to Enlist Interest

Let's have a closer look. You've noticed that people like to do those things that they do fairly well. A terrible swimmer doesn't really look forward to a swim. Who enjoys showing off his ineptitude?

It's equally true with reading. The better you read, the stronger your interest. *And*—the stronger your interest, the more you read. But there's the other side—the vicious circle side. The poorer you read, the less your interest. *And*—the less your interest, the less you read.

Take the 64 to 95 percent who don't read well. For them, the secret of improvement lies in enlisting the powerful force of interest.

The normal academic climate isn't always too helpful. To develop interest, you need almost irrational enthusiasm. And that kind of enthusiasm is all too often killed by academic restraint, cold reason, and impersonal objectivity. Together they may dampen completely the little spark of interest an individual has in developing desired skills. What's needed is sufficient enthusiasm to fan that spark into brilliant flame. Then you'll get results. Interest is your assurance.

Build Interest by Personalizing

As a first move, ask yourself this question: What can reading do for me, personally?

Specifically, list your present most important four or five goals. Next, find specific articles or books to help you reach each one. For example, one goal might be to improve your reading. List this book. It will help you attain that goal.

You'll find articles or books help you do anything better. Yes, *anything*. A colleague of mine beat me at handball. How? Reading a book on how to play winning handball tipped the close rivalry in his favor. You can get help from reading even if the goal is to play better handball. Once you connect reading to an important personal goal, that interest actively promotes your reading progress.

Build on Present Interests

As a second move, tap your current interests. Let them lead you to improved reading ability.

What three things are *you* most interested in? Whatever you put down—say, hunting, money, nutrition, scuba diving—be sure they reflect really strong interest. Suppose you have never yet voluntarily read an entire book. Only those required. But—there's a book about one of your strongest interests. That will be the easiest book of all to read.

Take such books as *Hunter* or *I Married a Hunter*. You'll find them fascinating reading. Why? Because of your strong interest in hunting. Or take Mark Skousen's practical book, *High Finance on a Low Budget*, or *Jane Fonda's Workout Book*, or *Jane Brody's Nutrition Book* or *Coping with Difficult People*. Such books focus on your strongest interests, making them much easier to read. Furthermore, each book you complete makes the next one that much easier.

Building New Interests

At this point, you're ready for the much more difficult problem—reading a book in a subject area where you have little or no interest. How do you manage that? Let's say you're required to take chemistry, whether you're interested or not. And that means reading the chemistry text.

Here are four suggestions.

First, cultivate the acquaintance of a genuinely interested student. In the chemistry course, for example, listen for a student who's talking with some enthusiasm about a point raised in class. Fall into step with him or her. Suggest a cup of coffee. You'll find that genuine enthusiasm rubs off on you. One student drew a bird-watcher for a roommate. At first he smiled condescendingly at his roommate's talk about birds. In two months, however, sufficient enthusiasm had rubbed off to make him buy binoculars and bird books and go on early morning bird-watching trips. Interest is contagious.

Second, read a popular book on the subject. To generate interest in painting or art, read Stone's book *Lust for Life*, a biography of Vincent Van Gogh. Stefansson, the arctic explorer, traced his lifelong interest in exploring to the reading of one book. Henri Fabre, the famous French entomologist, said the same thing happened to him. One book generated a lifelong interest.

Third, spend extra time on your dullest and most difficult subject. The more you know about any field, the stronger your interest. If you know nothing about football, you're not likely to watch any games.

Fourth, watch for educational TV shows or movies touching areas of your low interest. A movie about Pasteur should stimulate added interest in chemistry.

Now, get busy! Tap interests already present. Develop new ones. Let deepened interest turn study from work to pleasure, and turn a potential D into a B.

Reading Time: _____
See Conversion Table.
Enter WPM Rate on the Progress Record Chart.

37 Generating New and Wider Interests

COMPREHENSION CHECK

Getting the Facts

1. Which person is mentioned? (a) Napoleon, (b) Darwin, (c) Glenn Cunningham, (d) all of the preceding.

1. __

2. What percentage do not read too well? (a) up to 30%, (b) up to 65%, (c) up to 80%, (d) up to 95%.

2. __

3. One book title mentioned is (a) *Hunter*, (b) *Call of the Wild*, (c) *Into the Silk*, (d) *Between the Elephant's Eyes*.

3. __

4. What subject is mentioned? (a) physics, (b) chemistry, (c) zoology, (d) biology.

4. __

5. Fabre was (a) an entomologist, (b) an ecologist, (c) a painter, (d) a sculptor.

5. __

Getting the Meaning

6. The article's main focus is on (a) how to develop interest, (b) the uses of interest, (c) the personal factor in interest, (d) variations in interest.

6. __

7. The reference to well-known individuals is to show (a) how to develop interest, (b) how important interest is, (c) the different areas of interest, (d) the varying degrees of interest.

7. __

8. Mention of the normal academic environment is made to show (a) the importance of the right setting, (b) the way to fan a spark into a flame, (c) the way to supplement reason, (d) the need to add to the normal academic setting.

8. __

9. The handball illustration shows (a) the importance of experience, (b) the importance of reading, (c) the value of experience and reading, (d) the limitations of reading.

9 __

10. The bird-watching incident is to show (a) how inter-   10. ___
    ests are developed, (b) what strange interests we
    have, (c) the importance of interest, (d) the speed
    with which interest can be developed.

10 Off for Each Mistake.
Comprehension Score: _____
Answer Key in Appendix.
Enter the Results on the Progress Record Chart.

Making the Application

Interests—your own—deserve a close, careful scrutiny. Start by listing the five things you are presently most interested in. List them in order of interest—the most interesting first, the next most interesting second, and so on.

1. _____

2. _____

3. _____

4. _____

5. _____

Now list two things you think it would be most important to have as interests, in place of two in your first listing. Think in terms of your next five years and your personal growth and development. If your original five still seem most important for the next five years, just leave these spaces blank.

1. _____

2. _____

In terms of reading interest, what are the two most interesting books you have read recently?

1. _____

2. _____

What magazines do you usually read?

1. _____

2. _____

3. _____

Do you (a) read a news magazine, (b) read a newspaper, or (c) listen to the radio or TV for most of your news? a _____ b _____ c _____

Estimate the total time spent daily in reading, including required reading. _____

How many books, generally speaking, do you have of your own?
_____

How many books do you think you read in a year, excluding required textbooks? _____

Which two selections in this book have you found most interesting reading?

(titles)

1. _____

2. _____

You don't have to eat an entire cake to know whether or not you like it. No, you just need a sample. A single bite should answer your question. That's so with books also. You don't have to read an entire book to know if it's interesting. All you need is a taste.

That's the beauty of short samples, such as the eighteen in this book. If you like the sample, you'll want to read more. That's exactly why samples were included—to help you discover really enjoyable reading.

For example, if you liked Selection #2, "Instrument of Evil," chances are very good that you'll like the full-length book from which that chapter was taken. The author happened to have *two* books on the bestseller list at the same time—a very rare occurrence. You know he's exceptionally interesting. What do you need to know to get through life? His book—*All I Really Need to Know I Learned in Kindergarten*—tells you.

If you found #3, "Breaking the Sound Barrier," interesting reading, you should find Yeager's incredible life story equally so. *Yeager*—his autobiography—sold a million copies. It's a book to keep you up in the air for hours. How did he escape after being shot down over occupied France during World War II? It's a wide-open, full-throttle account which you've already had a sample of. Go for the full treatment.

Again, if you like the brief look into Bill Cosby's married life—Selection #14, "My Greatest Adventure"—you'll want to continue the whimsical tour he provides through his exhilarating world of romance—before and after marriage.

And don't forget textbooks. They're also interesting. For example, if you liked Selections #12 and #41, whether you're taking a course in government or not, you'll find the entire text—*A Preface to Politics*— fascinating reading. Professor Schuman, the author, was awarded the Distinguished Teacher Award by the University of Massachusetts.

Actually eight of the selections—#12, #15, #30, #39, #41, #42, #43, and #44—are drawn from college texts, giving you a rare opportunity to sample various subject matter areas for interest. The following additional samples also lead straight to books—(#6) "Look! No Words!" (#9) "Why 30 Seconds?" (#17) "Lincoln at Gettysburg," (#21) "Scientist at Work," (#32) "The Dumbest Antelope," and (#33) "Mrs. Packletide's Tiger."

38 How to Get the Job You Want

WORD POWER WORKOUT

A. Leaning on Context

In each of the blanks provided, place the letter that precedes the best definition of the underlined word in context to the left.

Words in Context	Definitions
1. ___ <u>motivated</u> for success	a. risking
2. ___ your <u>ultimate</u> success goal	b. unconscious
3. ___ <u>jeopardizing</u> your current job	c. spreads
4. ___ the <u>halo</u> effect	d. prompted, driven
5. ___ it <u>radiates</u> out	e. inclines
6. ___ an <u>engaging</u> smile	f. ring of light
7. ___ <u>predisposes</u> them to like Chet	g. final, last
8. ___ electronic <u>components</u>	h. deep-rooted
9. ___ important <u>subliminal</u> messages	i. elements
10. ___ so <u>ingrained</u> in them	j. pleasing

Check your answers with the Key before going on. Review any that you have missed.

Pronunciation aids: 3. jep'ur dīz ing; 4. hā'lō; 7. prē di spōz's; 9. sub lim'uh nl.

KEY: add, āce; end, ēven; it, īce; odd, ōpen; pool; up.

B. Leaning on Parts

Ferre means "bear" or "carry." When you see *fer* or *lat* in a word, look for those meanings. Fill in the blanks below with a form of *ferre*.

1. If you bear or endure pain, you can be said to suf_____.

2. If a company moves you from one city to another, it trans_____ you.

3. A boat carrying passengers from shore to shore is a _____ boat.

4. Rich soil that bears abundantly is known as _____ soil.

5. For this job you must be able to trans_____ from French to English.

C. Making the Words Yours

In each blank below, enter the most appropriate word from the ten words in context in the first exercise, substituting it for the word(s) in parentheses. Use these words: *components, engaging, halo, ingrained, jeopardizing, motivated, predisposes, radiates, subliminal, ultimate.*

1. The effect of a good deed (spreads) _____ out in every direction.

2. Some students seem (prompted, driven) _____ to special endeavor.

3. The child's early habits remained (deep-rooted) _____ for life.

4. Can you skip reviewing without (risking) _____ your grades?

5. The artist's representation of Christ had the typical (ring of light) _____ above his head.

6. The student's (final, last) _____ goal is a Ph.D.

7. Who will finally put these (elements) _____ together?

8. The speaker's (pleasing) _____ manner won immediate acceptance.

9. Reading upbeat books (inclines) _____ one to think optimistically.

10. The experimenter tried (subconscious) _____ cues to encourage sale of popcorn and candy.

4 Off for Each Mistake.
Word Power Score: _____
Answer Key in Appendix.

38

How to Get the Job You Want

Dr. Joyce Brothers

Churchill divided people into two groups—those for whom work is work and pleasure is pleasure, and those for whom work is pleasure. In lighter vein, there's Charlie McCarthy—"Hard work never killed anybody, but why take a chance?" You want the right job, of course. How do you get it?

Begin Timing

Getting the job you want requires motivation, energy and preparation. You may be superbly qualified, but there is tremendous competition these days for jobs that offer a future. There may be a dozen or more equally qualified candidates. You are going to have to convince your potential employer that *you* are that special person he has been looking for. And you can.

I am going to give you some psychological tools, based on psychologists' findings and techniques, that can give you a significant edge over your competitors. These tools are easy to use. And they are effective. But first, a few words about looking for a job.

I was shocked recently when I learned that the average person spends no more than five hours a week on his or her job search. The person who is truly motivated for success treats looking for a job like a job itself. Once you have the job, you are going to spend 40 hours a week working for someone else. If you invest the same amount of time a week in your hunt for that job, you will find it sooner and be that much closer to your ultimate success goal.

The exception to this rule is the person who already has a job. Don't leave it. It is much easier to go from one job to another than to quit and start from ground zero. This doesn't mean that you slack off on the work you are now doing. It does mean that you will have to put in extra time in your job search. One way to become known without jeopardizing your current job is to join a professional society in your field or the field you want to move into—and play an active role in it. This will bring you to the attention not only of your own management but also to that of top executives in other companies in the same field.

The Interview and the Halo Effect

You've looked long and hard and have lined up some appointments. The big obstacle now standing between you and the job you want is the interview. Don't underestimate its importance.

Psychologists have analyzed job interviews and found that they consist of two parts. If you mess up the first part, your chances of getting the job are extremely slim, no matter how brilliantly you handle the second. I call the first part the 30-Second Hurdle, because research has shown that most employers make up their minds about job applicants in the first 30 seconds. This 30-second decision is based on what psychologists call the Halo Effect. It has nothing to do with saints or godliness. As psychologists use the term "halo," it means the effect of a person's first impression of you. Unfortunately, first impressions are not always good impressions.

The Halo Effect can be negative or positive. Whichever it is, it radiates out in all directions from the initial effect or impression. At its best, it helps make people think we are even better than we are.

"Why work so hard to make a good impression?" Chet asked me one day. Chet is head of his own electronics firm, which he started from scratch 25 years ago, and I have known him most of my life. "It's what you know and whom you know and what you do that count," he declared. "I always judge a man on the basis of his work, not on how good or bad an impression he makes or how he looks."

I did not want to contradict him bluntly, although I could have pointed out several ways in which he used the Halo Effect himself to good advantage. Chet has an engaging smile and a firm handshake. People meeting him for the first time always have the impression that he is absolutely delighted to meet them. That first impression predisposes them to like Chet and to want to do business with him.

His office suite is a showplace of contemporary design, with a Mies van der Rohe glass table and Le Corbusier chairs. His desk is a slab of highly polished black Italian marble on chrome legs. A sculpture of electronic components stands in one corner. And behind the desk hangs a photograph of Chet with a United States President. Visitors can't help getting some important subliminal messages to the effect that electronics is a modern growth industry and Chet is prospering—and has very good connections. The office is designed to impress just the kind of sophisticated technologists with whom Chet does business. It creates a positive Halo Effect.

I decided to bide my time and not to point out his unconscious and very effective mastery of the Halo Effect. A couple of weeks later, I was able to show Chet that he did indeed judge people on the basis of first impressions. When I heard Roland, a young psychology instructor, mention that he planned to shave off his moplike beard, I asked him to help me.

I called Chet and said I knew two bright young men who were interested in getting into the electronics field, perhaps as salesmen. Would he, as a favor, be willing to spend 10 minutes with each of them?

He agreed. "If they're really bright," he said, "I might have a spot for them."

Roland showed up for his interview on time. His hair was long and shaggy, just like his beard. He wore sneakers, jeans and a blue work shirt. He was clean but rumpled. He was courteous and spoke intelligently about his interest in his field.

The next day, Roland appeared for the second interview. He introduced himself as "Hobart." His hair had been cut, and his beard was gone. He word a gray flannel suit with a white shirt and a striped tie. The effect was pressed and crisp. (If Chet were to remark about his resemblance to Roland, "Hobart" was prepared to say they were cousins.)

Chet telephoned me the next day and thanked me for sending Hobart to see him. "That's the kind of young man I like to hire," he said. "But that other guy. What's his name? Roland. I was surprised you asked me to see him. He's a real hippie."

I laughed. "Hippie is out of date, Chet," I told him. Then I explained the trick I had played on him. And apologized.

"Good Lord!" he exclaimed. "You don't mean it!" "Yes, I do," I told him. "I just had to show you that you do judge people on the basis of first impressions. Everybody does. It's the Halo Effect." If Chet had not been an old and dear friend, I would never have done this. But he was, and he thanked me. And he made me explain the Halo Effect once more—in detail.

So put your best foot forward, smile, have a firm and dry handshake, sit slightly to the left of the interviewer and look him in the eye. You'll clear the 30-Second Hurdle with flying colors.

Three Key Questions

There are three questions that almost every interviewer asks. It is a good idea to think out your answers to them a couple of days before your interview is scheduled. The man or woman who decides just to wing his way through an interview will never make as good an impression as the person who has thought through what he or she wants to say. The questions are:

1. So you are interested in the lab assistant job (or whatever the opening is)?

The answer is *not* "yes." The answer is yes plus—as in, "Yes, I am very interested in the lab assistant job. It's exactly the kind of opening I've been hoping to find." Keep your answer short, but never reply with a naked yes or no.

2. Why do you want this job?

One personnel executive told me that when applicants answer this question with "I think it will be interesting" or "I like working with people," he crosses them off his list immediately. "I know they haven't any idea of what they really want to do and haven't given any thought to what the job involves."

3. What can you tell me about yourself?

He does not want your life history. What he is looking for are clues to your character, ambitions and motivation. A good answer could be, "Ever since I sold more Girl Scout cookies than anyone else in our troop, I've known what I wanted—a sales career. To me, getting people to buy something is a wonderful game." Or: "I used to work in a hardware store after school, and I learned how important it is not just to sell the customer a hammer or a screwdriver but to make sure you sell him the right hammer or screwdriver for his purpose. People used to ask for me to wait on them, because they knew I'd make sure they got exactly what they needed. I'm pretty competitive too. It means a lot to me to be the best."

An answer like this shows ambition, an understanding of what the job involves and a competitive spirit. It is short—less than a minute—and to the point. If the interviewer wants to know more, he will ask.

Basic Training—the Edge You Need

When you have worked out your answers to the three key questions, ask someone to help you rehearse them. Have him or her read this article and take the role of the interviewer. The two of you should go through a mock interview from the first handshake to the last. Then talk about how it went. Perhaps the "interviewer" has some suggestions. Perhaps you feel you could have done better. Then run through the whole thing again.

Don't skip this double rehearsal. Think of it as basic training, a method rooted in a solid psychological concept. Soldiers could learn all there is to know about basic training in a matter of days. The reason it takes so long is to give them a chance to do things over and over until it becomes automatic. When the soldiers are actually in combat, the knowledge of what has to be done will be so ingrained in them that they won't panic but will just go ahead and do what they were trained to do.

Unless you are truly exceptional, you are going to be nervous during the interview. You may forget some of the points you want to make. The way to assure a good performance is to rehearse beforehand.

Rehearsals are not just for beginners. Success-oriented people always run through a mental rehearsal before an important meeting or interview. They think about the points they want to make, the impression they want to create and the result they want to get from the meeting or interview. So don't try to wing it. Give yourself that important rehearsal edge.

You now have the psychological tools that can help you do better than your competitors. Use them, and you will have the best chance of handling the interview like a pro and getting that job you want. Good luck!

Reading Time: _____
See Conversion Table.
Enter WPM Rate on the Progress Record Chart.

38 How to Get the Job You Want

COMPREHENSION CHECK

Getting the Facts

1. In searching for a job the average person spends no more than how many hours a week? (a) ten, (b) seven, (c) six, (d) five.

   1. ___

2. If you have a job and want another, you're told (a) to leave it immediately, (b) not to leave it, (c) to get another opinion, (d) to start collecting new leads.

   2. ___

3. Chet headed a firm that dealt with (a) computers, (b) software, (c) electronics, d) plastics.

   3. ___

4. Chet's desk top was of (a) black marble, (b) Danish teak, (c) polished ebony, (d) hand-rubbed walnut.

   4. ___

5. Before the interview, you were told to (a) read about the firm, (b) do a double rehearsal, (c) do something relaxing, (d) write out answers to key questions.

   5. ___

Getting the Meaning

6. The main idea was to (a) provide the psychological tools to get the job, (b) help you understand the Halo Effect, (c) clarify job-hunting procedures, (d) point up the difficulties.

   6. ___

7. The purpose of the Chet illustration was primarily to show (a) how unobservant Chet was, (b) the importance of dress, (c) how Chet used the Halo Effect himself, (d) the importance of first impressions.

   7. ___

8. You would infer that getting the job you want depends primarily on your (a) qualifications, (b) motivation, (c) preparation, (d) energy.

   8. ___

9. The photograph of Chet and the President was mentioned to emphasize Chet's (a) good connections, (b) use of the Halo Effect, (c) pride in his firm, (d) respectability.

   9. ___

10. Most emphasis was on (a) reducing nervousness,
    (b) rehearsing, (c) managing first impressions,
    (d) taking enough time.

    10. ___

39 Women in Management

WORD POWER WORKOUT

A. Leaning on Context

In each of the blanks provided, place the letter that precedes the best definition of the underlined word in context to the left.

Words in Context	Definitions
1. ___ up the <u>corporate</u> ladder	a. harmful
2. ___ problem of <u>stereotyping</u>	b. requires
3. ___ male <u>chauvinism</u>	c. features
4. ___ be just as <u>detrimental</u>	d. company
5. ___ age <u>discrepancies</u>	e. respectful
6. ___ <u>trend</u> signals improvement	f. glaring
7. ___ tend to be <u>deferential</u>	g. differences
8. ___ now <u>mandates</u> such practices	h. tendency
9. ___ not as <u>blatant</u>	i. conventional patterning
10. ___ positive <u>aspects</u>	j. contempt for opposite sex

Check your answers with the Key before going on. Review any that you have missed.

Pronunciation aids: 2. ster'ĕ uh tĭp'ing; 3. shō'vun iz um; 5. dis krep'un sĕs; 9. blā'tant.

KEY: add, āce; end, ĕven; it, īce; odd, ōpen; pōōl; up.

B. Leaning on Parts

Facere means "make" or "do." When you see *fac(t)*, *fec*, *fic*, *fas*, or *fea* in a word, look for those meanings. Use a form of *facere* in each blank below.

1. The washer still won't work; I think the motor is de_____.

2. They had suf_____ help to finish the project on time.

3. The tennis team was not de_____ even once all season long.

4. The artist _____ a beautiful sculptured figure of Venus.

5. To do a task with ease is to do it with great _____.

C. Making the Words Yours

In each blank below, enter the most appropriate word from the ten words in context in the first exercise, substituting it for the word(s) in parentheses. Use these words: *aspects, blatant, chauvinism, corporate, deferential, detrimental, discrepancies, mandates, stereotyping, trend.*

1. If this inflationary (tendency) _____ continues, we're in trouble.

2. Are there (differences) _____ in the two sets of figures?

3. Male (contempt for opposite sex) _____ will not be tolerated here.

4. She moved up in the (company) _____ ranks with unbelievable speed.

5. What (features) _____ of this situation seem most important?

6. The driver showed a (glaring) _____ disregard of traffic rules.

7. Leaded fuel has a (harmful) _____ effect on my car operation.

8. The law (requires) _____ that you pay the fine immediately.

9. The manager expected (respectful) _____ treatment from all employees.

10. In casting the play, the director had to rely on some (conventional patterning) _____.

4 Off for Each Mistake.
Word Power Score: _____
Answer Key in Appendix.

39

Women in Management

Jerry Kinard

What's your goal in life? What do you want to be? If you want to be a manager, reading one book should do wonders in speeding you on your way. After all, the one who looks ahead, gets ahead! The comprehensive text, Management, *gives you a rare mixture of theory and practice—and opens a future for you.*

Begin Timing

Women managers can expect to confront a number of barriers as they struggle up the corporate ladder. Several surveys of female managers in all types of industries show that the one obstacle standing out above all others is male prejudice.

Stereotypes

Actually, such prejudice is manifested in a number of ways. Women managers may be excluded from social activities: golf on Saturday mornings, for instance. Or male executives may not take female managers seriously. And, of course, there is the problem of stereotyping. Too many males still view women as being overly emotional and temperamental. Such attitudes can hurt the chances of promotion and virtually eliminate the acceptance of females in policy-making circles.

But men can prove helpful to women in their careers, too. Women managers readily acknowledge that men have been instrumental in helping them perform well and in getting them recognition. An overwhelming majority of survey respondents say that the single person who has been most helpful to them in their careers has been a man. Many female executives, in fact, blame other women for many of their problems. Women, they say, can be jealous, petty, and too critical. While acknowledging that male chauvinism can hinder their progress, they maintain that female jealousy can be just as detrimental. This partly explains why a majority of female managers prefer their senior executives to be male.

Family Demands

Contrary to popular belief, female managers do not view family responsibilities and a lack of formal education as major stumbling blocks. In one study, only 3 percent of the female respondents cited family obligations as their most serious obstacle, and only 12 percent mentioned the lack of formal training. To make certain that family responsibilities don't interfere with their careers, many families of female executives employ part-time domestic workers to help with family and household chores. Although the costs of employing maids and housekeepers can greatly cut into take-home pay, many female managers feel that this is the only way that they can balance both spheres.

Age Discrepancies

Older female managers are finding that working under the supervision of younger female managers can be particularly frustrating. While older women generally have long accepted the inevitability of working for younger men, some are having difficulty coming to grips with the idea that younger women are occupying more and more managerial positions.

Today, nearly 1.5 million women under the age of thirty-five hold managerial jobs, up from 322,000 in the early 1970s. On one hand, this trend signals improvement in the status of career-minded women. On the other, it can stifle progression and lead to dissatisfaction.

Older women tend to be deferential with coworkers and maternal with supervisors. Such behavior can infuriate young female executives and can cause stressful working conditions. Conflict often arises because older workers frequently feel that they know how things ought to be done. Their advice is sought in some cases, but most of the time they are perceived as a source of the "problem" by younger, career-oriented female managers.

Pay Differential

On the average, women earn about two-thirds of what men do for similar work. In the past, this differential has been explained away by citing seniority and educational differences. But things may be changing in the private sector, just as they changed in government a few years ago. Business firms may be charged with the responsibility of developing "comparable pay" guidelines.

For years, women struggled to achieve "equal pay for equal work." Federal law now mandates such practices. But now there is a move on to establish "equal pay for comparable work." Essentially, this means that companies will have to determine which jobs are comparable in skill, effort, responsibility, and conditions; they will then group comparable jobs into pay categories. Thus, jobs that traditionally have been filled by women may be judged as being comparable to those traditionally filled by men.

Most employers insist that their salary programs are already fair and equitable and that federal law does not apply to "comparable" jobs. The Equal Employment Opportunities Commission (EEOC) seems to agree. In its first ruling on the subject, the EEOC said that unequal pay for work of comparable value does not in itself constitute pay discrimination.

Fearful that the government will ultimately require equal pay for comparable work, some firms are beginning to devise their own comparable work plans. For example, AT&T has developed its own plan using fourteen measurements of job-related factors for twenty major categories of employment. For the most part, the company is pleased with what it found when jobs were surveyed. Although a few jobs were found to be undervalued, the company discovered that just as many male-held jobs were underpaid as female-held jobs.

A Look to the Future

Although female managers will be required to overcome a host of barriers as they pursue their corporate careers, the payoffs appear to justify the effort. Salaries for young, aggressive, career-oriented women are on the rise; and pay discrimination is not as blatant as it once was, thanks in part to government intervention and to an awareness of the value of excellent female managerial talent. In addition, their personal satisfaction and achievement are at an all-time high. While job-related stress affects women just as it does men, the majority of female managers contend that the positive aspects of their jobs outweigh the negative.

Most female managers plan to continue their climb up the corporate ladder. Younger female managers will find a more favorable environment than their predecessors simply because their presence has been accepted. Surveys conducted to assess the opportunities for female managers in the future reveal that the opportunities are increasing. In one survey, 75 percent of the respondents stated that they believed the opportunities for women starting out today are better than they have ever been. Even so, the road will be bumpy. Unfortunately, perhaps the best advice that could be offered is that given by a lower-level female bank executive: "Work twice as hard and three times as long as a man in the same position."

Reading Time: _____

See Conversion Table.

Enter WPM Rate on the Progress Record Chart.

39 Women in Management

COMPREHENSION CHECK

Getting the Facts

1. The author said that women managers are sometimes
   excluded from (a) cocktail parties, (b) weekend out-
   ings, (c) Saturday morning golf, (d) gourmet clubs.

   1. ___

2. Most female managers prefer what kind of senior executives? (a) male, (b) female, (c) college-trained,
   (d) company-trained.

   2. ___

3. How many female respondents cited family obligations
   as their most serious obstacle? (a) 3%, (b) 9%, (c) 12%,
   (d) 16%.

   3. ___

4. How many women under the age of thirty-five hold managerial jobs? (a) 1.1 million, (b) 1.3 million, (c) 1.5
   million, (d) 1.8 million.

   4. ___

5. The author specifically mentioned (a) Ford, (b) AT&T,
   (c) General Electric, (d) Honeywell.

   5. ___

Getting the Meaning

6. The main focus was on (a) age differentials, (b) training,
   (c) opportunities, (d) difficulties.

   6. ___

7. Points were developed largely through (a) statements of
   experts, (b) personal experience, (c) specific details,
   (d) generalities.

   7. ___

8. The point of view is best described as (a) realistic,
   (b) personal, (c) visionary, (d) theoretical.

   8. ___

9. The author seems primarily interested in (a) raising
   questions, (b) explaining, (c) persuading, (d) entertaining.

   9 ___

10. The discussion of age discrepancies was apparently
    intended to (a) indicate the rapidity of change,
    (b) reveal an encouraging aspect, (c) criticize older
    managers, (d) point up a problem.

    10. ___

10 Off for Each Mistake.
Comprehension Score: _____
Answer Key in Appendix.
Enter the Results on the Progress Record Chart.

PART

V

The Round-up

40 Reading for School and Life

WORD POWER WORKOUT

A. Leaning on Context

In each of the blanks provided, place the letter that precedes the best definition of the underlined word in context to the left.

Words in Context	**Definitions**
1. ___ the <u>boundaries</u> of the human mind	a. attic
2. ___ a poor man in the <u>garret</u>	b. search
3. ___ your most important <u>quest</u>	c. occupation
4. ___ those about your <u>vocation</u>	d. tasted
5. ___ a <u>surplus</u> of about 2 million teachers	e. limits
6. ___ they supply <u>assurance</u>	f. confidence
7. ___ the <u>ideal</u> supplement	g. shock
8. ___ before being properly <u>savored</u>	h. excess
9. ___ Greeks <u>epitomized</u> that problem	i. perfect
10. ___ avoid the <u>trauma</u>	j. typified

Check your answers with the Key before going on. Review any that you have missed.

Pronunciation aids: 8. sā′vur′d; 9. i pit′uh mīz′d; 10. traw′muh.

KEY: add, āce; end, ĕven; it, īce; odd, ōpen; pōōl; up.

B. Leaning on Parts

Specere means "see" or "look." When you see *spec(t)* or *spic* in a word, look for those meanings. Enter a form of *specere* in each blank below.

1. A person looking at a sporting event is called a _____.

2. To look on someone with honor and esteem is to show re_____.

3. To see better, the teacher got a new pair of _____.

4. You must look into all a_____ of the situation before acting.

5. On such an au_____ occasion, everyone seemed overjoyed.

C. Making the Words Yours

In each blank below, enter the most appropriate word from the ten words in context in the first exercise, substituting it for the word(s) in parentheses. Use these words: *assurance, boundaries, epitomized, garret, ideal, quest, savored, surplus, trauma, vocation.*

1. The damp condition of the (attic) _____ made the clothes mildew.

2. A dry, warm day is (perfect) _____ for a car race.

3. His actions (typified) _____ those of a jealous husband.

4. The United States no longer has (excess) _____ grain to give away.

5. Because of his interest in helping others, he chose social work as his (occupation) _____.

6. The three-year-old boy's (search) _____ for his dog led him into the woods.

7. To write an appealing ad, a person must set (limits) _____ on what to include.

8. After you have studied a word carefully, you can than use it with real (confidence) _____.

9. The unsuccessful artist finally (tasted) _____ the rewards of success.

10. The father's death put his daughter into a state of (shock) _____.

4 Off for Each Mistake.
Word Power Score: _____
Answer Key in Appendix.

40

Reading for School and Life

Round-up time! Only it's not for cattle—it's for all the things you've learned so far to improve your reading and vocabulary. Now's the time to put your personal touch on everything you've covered. The next four readings after this one come from textbooks—school reading—essential reading. They make perfect additional practice. And, as you well know, without practice you don't get any nearer to perfection. Then the last four readings are samples of the reading you'll be doing after school. So—round up all you've learned. Put your brand on it, apply it—then enjoy to the full the satisfaction that successful progress brings.

Begin Timing

Today is the first day of the rest of your life. How can reading fill it to overflowing with adventures, richness, and fullness?

Your Pleasure-Giving Skill

Skills are skills. Pleasures are pleasures. *But*—some skills are lasting pleasures. Such is reading. Listen to Hazlitt: "The greatest pleasure in life is that of reading." Or Macaulay: "I would rather be a poor man in a garret with plenty of books than a king who did not love reading." To them and countless others all over the world, reading is a source of deepest and fullest enjoyment. That's true from early school days to days of leisure and retirement.

Your Fountain of Youth

Reading is more than that. It can be your fountain of youth. Virginia Woolf said, "The true reader is essentially young." One of your major problems is how to stay alive as long as you live. Some die at 30 but are not buried until they're 70. With some, youth slips away before being properly savored. Reading provides a spring of living water, refreshing and life-giving. Stay young for life with reading.

Your Dream-Fulfillment Aid

Part of youth lies in dreaming—dreaming impossible dreams that you can sometimes make possible. Robert F. Kennedy said this: "Some men see things as they are and say 'Why?' I dream things that never were and say 'Why not?' " Certain books push the boundaries of the human mind out beyond belief. After all, a little bit of greatness hides in everyone. Let books bring it into full bloom.

Your Know-Thyself Aid

What's your most important quest? Finding yourself. Finding your own identity. The Greeks epitomized that problem in two words: Know thyself. Well, articles and books help in that all-important search. They supply assurance of the power and worth of your own life, a measure of your possibilities.

To see yourself in proper perspective, you need detailed pictures of real people in real situations. We need to see three-dimensional characters, with all the typical human fears and limitations. Then, and only then, can you begin to see and know yourself as you should.

Your Vocational Counselor and Consultant

What about practical questions, such as those about your vocation? Will reading help you decide more intelligently (1) what to do, (2) how to prepare yourself, and (3) how to succeed on the job?

To answer the first question, you have to know your own talents, abilities, and interests well. You must also, however, know the opportunities in the world around you. Some Bureau of Labor statistics, for example, predicted a surplus of approximately two million school teachers. Still another source indicated that right now "the health fields are the only fields in which we have shortages." Balance such information with self-knowledge and you have some of the ingredients needed to make intelligent, perceptive choices.

Second. You've decided on a career. How and where do you get the required preparation? Again, turn to reading. You'll probably find a listing of school programs to choose from. You may even find them rated. If so, you'll know exactly where to go for the best possible preparation.

Third. Don't stop yet. You've selected a career and trained yourself. Lean on reading now to help you succeed on the job. A variety of magazines and books will provide guidance and help.

But that's not all. The days of only one lifetime career may be almost over. All too often, change throws hundreds out of work. Change hit the aircraft industry, for example. Result? Hundreds of well-qualified engineers suddenly out on the street.

If you manage things well, keeping a close eye on changing conditions, you can avoid the trauma of waking up to find yourself out of a job. Through reading develop some new skills and interests. Then if conditions change, you can slip with comparative ease from one field into another, hardly breaking stride.

Most of the things taught in school—typing, shorthand, key punching, languages, farming, business management—are readily available in interesting self-help articles and books. Let them smooth your path in any new direction you decide to take.

Your Experience Extender

What's the best teacher? Experience, of course! It's priceless. It comes from what you yourself have seen, heard, tasted, smelled, and felt—what you yourself have lived through.

Take a closer look. Look at our limitations. No wonder experience is so precious. We can't begin to get enough of it. We can't even experience again what we just lived through. We're not born with instant replay. We can't actually relive any moment. And, obviously, we're limited to one lifetime.

Space and time! How they limit us. Who has a time machine to carry him back into history? No one. It's the same with space. We can't literally be in two places at the same time. Right now you can't be sitting where you are and at the same time be strolling down the famed Champs Elysées in Paris.

And there's so much experience we need. What's it really like to work on an assembly line? What's it really like to be a secretary?

Here's where reading fits. It can bring us, personally, almost unlimited additional experience. To be sure, it's secondhand experience. But it's often so vivid it seems firsthand, just as if we're living through it ourselves, being moved to tears, laughter, or suspense. That rich range of experience provides the ideal supplement to our own limited experience. In this way, reading becomes one of our most profound mind-shaping activities.

Furthermore, all this experience is available when we want it. Books never impose on us. When we want them, we reach out and pull them off the shelf or table. At our convenience we invite them to share their unbelievable wealth with us.

Carlyle sums this all up nicely. "All that mankind has done, thought, gained, or been; it is lying as in magic preservation in the pages of books." Help yourself! Make reading your experience extender for the rest of your life.

Reading Time: _____
See Conversion Table.
Enter WPM Rate on the Progress Record Chart.

40 Reading for School and Life

COMPREHENSION CHECK

Getting the Facts

1. One quotation is from (a) the Bible, (b) Hazlitt,   1. ___
   (c) Shakespeare, (d) Alexander Pope.

2. Complete this quotation: "The true reader is essen-   2. ___
   tially . . ." (a) busy, (b) well informed, (c) young,
   (d) creative.

3. Specific mention is made of the (a) aircraft industry,   3. ___
   (b) automotive industry, (c) electronic industry,
   (d) plastic industry.

4. The best teacher is said to be (a) experience, (b) books,   4. ___
   (c) friends, (d) TV.

5. What place is mentioned? (a) Madison Avenue,   5. ___
   (b) Champs Elysées, (c) State Street, (d) Main Street,
   U.S.A.

Getting the Meaning

6. This article is mainly about how to make reading   6. ___
   (a) a normal habit, (b) contribute to living, (c) fulfill
   your dreams, (d) stimulate thought.

7. To die at thirty but be buried at seventy uses the word   7. ___
   die in the sense of to (a) lose purpose, (b) lose incen-
   tive, (c) stop growing, (d) die spiritually.

8. Kennedy's quote implies that (a) we all do less than   8. ___
   we could, (b) we need to be prodded to act, (c) we
   need interest to get us going, (d) we need frequent
   stimulus to get a response.

9. The talk about several careers is to show (a) the need   9. ___
   for variety, (b) how uncertain life is, (c) the need for
   stability, (d) the need for broad planning.

10. The talk about limitations of time and space is intended   10. ___
    to point up what? (a) the need to do different things,
    (b) the need to do a few things well, (c) the need for
    thorough training, (d) the need to supplement our
    experience with that of others.

10 Off for Each Mistake.
Comprehension Score: _____
Answer Key in Appendix.
Enter the Results on the Progress Record Chart.

Making the Application

A carefully planned reading program can help you reach about any personal goal you can think of. Try your hand at drawing up a specific reading plan for the next year to help with the following two goals:

1. Describe a specific plan for continuing your improvement in reading, in rate, comprehension, and development of broader interests.

2. Describe a specific plan for continuing your vocabulary development. It might be a word-a-day plan, words drawn from your reading. It might be a prefix-a-day plan, or a dictionary-study plan.

Now, set down a purpose of your own choice. List the books and articles that will help you reach this goal.

41 Work and Leisure

WORD POWER WORKOUT

A. Leaning on Context

In each of the blanks provided, place the letter that precedes the best definition of the underlined word in context to the left.

Words in Context	Definitions
1. ___ <u>incidentally</u>, to earn money	a. disappointments
2. ___ <u>deflect</u> or obscure meaning	b. beliefs
3. ___ the <u>tempo</u> is no longer ours	c. top people
4. ___ involved with <u>therapy</u>	d. by the way
5. ___ fool our <u>frustrations</u>	e. medical treatment
6. ___ <u>extensions</u> of each other	f. turn away
7. ___ all kinds of <u>alienation</u>	g. in accord, agreeing
8. ___ of manager <u>elites</u>	h. pace
9. ___ work <u>compatible</u> with creativity	i. withdrawal, detachment
10. ___ the clarity of <u>dogma</u>	j. stretchings, increasings

---

Check your answers with the Key before going on. Review any that you have missed.

Pronunciation aids: 8. ā lēts'.

KEY: add, āce; end, ĕven; it, īce; odd, ōpen; pōōl; up.

B. Leaning on Parts

Tendere means "stretch." When you see *tent*, *tend*, or *tens* in a word, look for those meanings. Use forms of *tendere* to fill the blanks below.

1. If it's interesting, it's bound to hold your at_____.

2. When you take care of a certain matter, you at_____ to it.

3. In a dangerous situation you are likely to feel _____.

4. Comets are regarded by many as por_____ of evil.

5. If you're too in_____ on talking, your driving may suffer.

C. Making the Words Yours

In each blank below, enter the most appropriate word from the ten words in context in the first exercise, substituting it for the word(s) in parentheses. Use these words: *alienation, compatible, deflect, dogma, elite, extensions, frustrations, incidentally, tempo, therapy.*

1. In any marriage, the (withdrawal, detachment) _____ of affection is traumatic.

2. What church (beliefs) _____ do you find the most difficult to accept?

3. To recover use of your leg, go into (medical treatment) _____.

4. Toward final exam time, the (pace) _____ of student life picks up.

5. I'm going—and, (by the way) _____, so will my roommate.

6. Is the software for my computer (in accord, agreeing) _____ with that for yours?

7. You certainly belong among the (top people) _____ of the campus.

8. These (stretchings, increasings) _____ of conference costs pose a problem.

9. Just bear up under all those (disappointments) _____.

10. This tempered steel will even (turn away) _____ a bullet.

4 Off for Each Mistake.
Word Power Score: _____
Answer Key in Appendix.

41

Work and Leisure

David F. Schuman with Bob Waterman

Work! Jerome K. Jerome put it nicely—"I like work; it fascinates me. I can sit and look at it for hours." Leisure! Here's what Gilbert, of Gilbert and Sullivan fame, said about it: "He did nothing in particular and did it very well." But work and leisure are serious matters—not to be taken lightly. So—read on.

Begin Timing

Work and leisure, two everyday economic topics, are almost too close to us to figure out. They are givens—facts of life. They are so common and commonplace that we really don't or maybe even can't, think very clearly about them.

After all, we know that there is work-time and play-time: You do one and enjoy the other, and that is just the way it is, so why worry about it. What I want to argue is that somehow work and leisure are important—things that we should make an effort to understand.

Following the logic of the topic, the order will be work now, and leisure next.

I thought it would be interesting to see how a textbook defined work. Interesting to see what the scholars had to say. I quote: Work is a "form of activity that has social approval and satisfies a real need of the individual to be more active. To produce, to create, to gain respect, to acquire prestige, and incidentally, to earn money . . . the paycheck must mean different things to different people."

So that is what work is in serious language. One of the truly fantastic things about textbooks is that they often hide, deflect, or obscure meaning. Sometimes they just lie—and teach us a great deal by what they systematically miss. We still have our problem: What does work mean to a person? In a most serious way, maybe it means this: To many people, most of the time, a job is a job is a job.

Work is what you do eight hours a day to get money to buy things. If you do not work, society will shun you. You will not be able to participate, you will not be able to do or make or buy. Let's face it: Work is one way society has to keep you off the streets.

Cheaper than jail and very effective.

The tempo is no longer ours. It is not of people, but it is made by people. Ours is an environment genuinely not human. We serve the rhythm of mechanical movement. Labor might have been noble, for it was our own relationship with ourselves—but what we get instead is work, and the brutal logic of the time clock.

In our crazy, complex, capitalist, consuming setting—in our work and leisure life—the individual comes unglued.

Think about it. There is no clear relationship between a job and a finished product. That just no longer exists. One person does one small thing: We are a nation of experts, full of sound and fury, separately signifying nothing. Certainly we know that raw materials are transformed—dead trees or high school graduates are turned into the finished products of paper or consumers. What is magical is that no person involved in that organized work process ever seems either involved or responsible.

We get separated from our very own work. And we get separated from people around us. And we get separated from our own imaginations.

So here we are. Work fills time and space; it displaces our self-worth for money; it divides us from others for material reward; it speeds us up in order to satisfy the logic of machinery.

That is hard work. Enough. Enough. It's time to relax, take a break, get into leisure.

The other day, after a graduate seminar, we were talking about the differences between the modest incomes of graduate students and the much larger incomes of the very wealthy. One student was quiet for a while, and then told this story.

He had met and talked with a person of about his age, and later was invited to this person's home. He accepted the invitation and went. What he found was surprising. The new acquaintance and his wife lived in a huge house filled with very expensive things. Neither worked. Both were bored. Life was gray.

They were both very involved with therapy.

The student, a little uncomfortable and with nothing to say, did not stay long. As he told us the story he just shrugged and said: "They blew it."

In a real sense, that may be a key issue to leisure: "We blew it."

What do we do when we are free from work? One thing, of course, is that we fill our social and economic obligations. We spend money to fill time, to fulfill our ego, to try and fool our frustrations. We spend and consume, spend and are consumed.

Then we're broke—spent, if you will—and we go back to the highly structured situation of work. So we repeat ourselves.

It is more involved than that. We watch television, see a movie, get drunk, chase men or women. Essentially, just escape. Get our minds off things, off school or work or whatever. Dull ourselves. Become mindless and meaningless in our "off" hours. Leisure, to be sure.

What the hell good is it, is leisure, if it does not somehow relate to work? We work so we can escape it, but our escape is all too often uninterestingly blah. Our work and leisure should be extensions of each other. To put it differently, without meaningful labor we cannot expect meaningful leisure. To isolate the two leads directly to all kinds of alienation.

We should feel cheated. We need work and play in order to feel good about ourselves, in order to feel needed. Easy times, it seems, aren't necessarily easy in the long run, and not necessarily a blessing if you use time poorly.

To talk about economics, to get right down to it, we might want to begin with saving our lives—socially and spiritually. A reasonable economic question would be: How do we make the world safe for itself and for its people? A reasonable way to begin to answer is to do what we can to ignore corporate capitalist/socialist/Marxist economics. While it is clear that these systems do not go out of their way to abuse common sense, it certainly *seems* that way. Some kinds of capitalism can be good and some kinds of Marxism bad, and it works just as easily the other way around. To get into the details is not worth our time just now.

In an essay entitled "Buddhist Economics," E. F. Schumacher writes that work should fill these three functions: "to give a man a chance to utilize and develop his faculties; to enable him to overcome his ego-centeredness by joining with other people in a common task; and to bring forth the goods and services for a becoming existence."

More gets built into that kind of work. It makes sense to continue to use Schumacher's words.

> Wisdom demands a new orientation of science and technology towards the organic, the gentle, the non-violent, the elegant and beautiful. . . . We must look for a revolution in technology to give us inventions and machines which reverse the destructive trends now threatening us all.
>
> . . . We need methods and equipment which are
> * cheap enough so that they are accessible to virtually everyone;
> * suitable for small-scale application; and
> * compatible with man's need for creativity.

It is not difficult to see what is left out of these calculations. No talk of manager elites and of the masses. They simply have no place when economics becomes a serious affair for individuals. Nor is there the false calculation that large size is more "economical" than small, or the desire to try to quantify the concepts of gentleness, elegance, and beauty.

The way we choose to operate our material relationships, our economics, is a basic question of how we live our lives and how we do our politics. The important value questions we ask for ourselves should be asked of our economics.

If we try tying labor with leisure, producing in a nondestructive way, making work compatible with creativity, making goods and services accessible in a more equitable way—if we decide on these kinds of values, we can only expect a world radically different (and probably much more wonderful) than we have now.

It seems safe to assume that there will be no one best way to answer the new set of questions, no one set of people, no single class or council or committee or board of directors that will give us folks the word. The way we choose to organize and to create should take its directions from our self, our physical surroundings, and our social setting. As each gets mixed in different amounts for different reasons, and as we relearn the uses of our imaginations, our economic dealings and our politics and our lives will line up in ways to make all of those things more interesting.

I can think of no way to make the notion clear and understandable. When there are no single answers, but only sets of multiple answers, one is forced to sacrifice the clarity of dogma.

Reading Time: _____
See Conversion Table.
Enter WPM Rate on the Progress Record Chart.

41 Work and Leisure

COMPREHENSION CHECK

Getting the Facts

1. There was specific mention of (a) year-end bonuses, 1. ___
   (b) work-time, (c) getting fired, (d) job-hunting.

2. In our life it was said the individual (a) cracks up, 2. ___
   (b) comes unglued, (c) burns out, (d) collapses.

3. The student, talking about his wealthy acquaintances, 3. ___
   said, (a) They blew it, (b) They missed the boat, (c) They
   let it slip through their fingers, (d) They let it go up
   in smoke.

4. The selection mentioned (a) Darwinism, (b) Marxism, 4. ___
   (c) Leninism, (d) Mohammedanism.

5. Schumacher said work should fill how many functions? 5. ___
   (a) one, (b) two, (c) three, (d) four.

Getting the Meaning

6. The main idea was to point up the need to (a) know 6. ___
   how work undermines self-worth, (b) understand work
   and leisure, (c) know how leisure undermines self-worth,
   (d) understand how work affects leisure.

7. Apparently the authors consider textbooks (a) incom- 7. ___
   plete (b) authoritative, (c) misleading, (d) serious.

8. The authors felt the textbook definition should focus 8. ___
   more on (a) the individual, (b) what work involved,
   (c) how society looked on work, (d) the work itself.

9. The illustration of the graduate student and wealthy 9. ___
   couple was primarily intended to show the (a) importance of work, (b) importance of leisure, (c) need to
   plan, (d) need to think.

10. Both work and leisure need primarily to focus on   10. ___
    (a) proper balance, (b) creativity, (c) individual and
    social development, (d) individual self-development.

10 Off for Each Mistake.
Comprehension Score: _____
Answer Key in Appendix.
Enter the Results on the Progress Record Chart.

42 Your Career Strategy

WORD POWER WORKOUT

A. Leaning on Context

In each of the blanks provided, place the letter that precedes the best definition of the underlined word in context to the left.

Words in Context	**Definitions**
1. ___ a career <u>strategy</u>	a. movable
2. ___ achieve that <u>objective</u>	b. counselors
3. ___ teachers, and <u>mentors</u>	c. plan
4. ___ with specific <u>criteria</u>	d. goal, aim
5. ___ searching for <u>options</u>	e. dedication
6. ___ including present, <u>pending</u>	f. business person
7. ___ how <u>mobile</u> am I	g. standards, guidelines
8. ___ become an <u>entrepreneur</u>	h. choices
9. ___ the work <u>ethic</u>	i. savingness
10. ___ work, thrift, <u>frugality</u>	j. undecided

Check your answers with the Key before going on. Review any that you have missed.

Pronunciation aids: 1. strat'uh jē; 4. krī tēr'ē uh; 8. on'truh pruh nur'; 10. frōō gal'uh tē.

KEY: add, āce; end, ēven; it, īce; odd, ōpen; pōōl; up.

B. Leaning on Parts

Stare means "stand." When you see *sist*, *sta(t)*, or *sti*, look for those meanings. Fill in each blank below with some form of *stare*.

1. The bronze equestrian _____ of the captain stood in the plaza.

2. To stand firmly on a point you've made is to in_____ on it.

3. If the car stands perfectly still, it is _____.

4. All hostilities ended when the armi_____ was signed.

5. If you can't do that by yourself, get an as_____.

C. Making the Words Yours

In each blank below, enter the most appropriate word from the ten words in context in the first exercise, substituting it for the word(s) in parentheses. Use these words: *criteria, ethic, entrepreneur, frugality, mentors, mobile, objective, options, pending, strategy.*

1. What (guidelines, standards) _____ will insure success?

2. The group gave only two (choices) _____ for release of the hostages.

3. Now prepare a workable (plan) _____ for getting a job.

4. The course (goal, aim) _____ was to improve vocabulary.

5. Turn to (savingness) _____ to cope with money shortages.

6. We just rented temporarily so as to be more (movable) _____.

7. The Protestant work (dedication) _____ seems still very much alive.

8. I always need (counselors) _____ close at hand.

9. Do you plan on being the (business person) _____ in the family?

10. I'll check with the judge to see which actions are (undecided) _____.

4 Off for Each Mistake.
Word Power Score: _____
Answer Key in Appendix.

42

Your Career Strategy

Leon C. Megginson, Lyle R. Trueblood, and Gayle M. Ross

The three authors of Business *bring an incredibly rich combination of experience to their task. They could have called their text "How to Succeed in Business Without Really Trying"—except they know that isn't true. Their text contains information of immediate, practical use to all students. The following sample passage is typical—invaluable help for anyone thinking of a career in business.*

Begin Timing

Assuming that you want a career in business, what's the best way to pursue it? One good way is to plot out a career strategy and follow it through in seeking your first meaningful job. "You will be what you resolve to be," begins a practical book on career development. This simple observation is quite true. When you resolve to reach a certain position, you'll begin to prepare to achieve that objective. You'll read about the position and study the courses leading to it. Your spouse, children, parents, friends, teachers, and mentors will help you reach your goal. You may change your goal as you progress, but you'll have a strategy to follow.

There are some fairly well defined steps to follow in narrowing down a career strategy. Regardless of how it's actually formulated, a career strategy should consider at least the following:

1. *Your opportunities.* The things you *might* do.
2. *Your competencies and resources.* A list of abilities, time, money, skills, and the aid you can expect from others will help you determine what you *can* do.
3. *Your ambitions and hopes.* What you *want* to do.
4. *Your obligations.* The moral, emotional, and financial obligations you owe to your family and other groups to which you belong will determine what you *ought* to do.

5. *Your personal values*. The things you believe in will largely dictate what you are *willing* or *unwilling* to do.

You should set realistic dates for completing specific phases of your career strategy, along with specific criteria for measuring progress. Make these measurements of career objectives (time limitations, job titles, and actual rewards) specific, and it will be easier to determine whether or not you've achieved them.

Opportunities

"If you don't know where you're going, you'll probably end up somewhere else" is the theme of a book with some sound principles to guide you in searching for options and opportunities. In considering your options, you shouldn't forget the technological, economic, political, and sociocultural environments in which you live.

Undoubtedly, new businesses and jobs will develop for technological reasons. Some questions you might ask about the economic environment are: What kinds of resources (skills, values, and abilities) are in demand in the economy? What's the current, short-run, and long-run extent of this demand? What areas of the economy—such as manufacturing, finance, and services—are most likely to use these resources? What's the reward for someone with these resources? What costs will be involved in upgrading present skills? The political environment, including present, pending, and probable legislation, also affects career decisions. New opportunities are available for women, minorities, the handicapped, and older workers in the present sociocultural environment.

Competencies and Resources

Next, you should determine the strengths you can build on and weaknesses you can overcome. A good match of your strengths with crucial factors needed for success in a given job should lead to success. Some questions to consider are: Which tasks do I perform well? What are my distinctive competencies?

Probably the future will demand a different set of competencies, but the basic one—such as the ability to communicate well orally and in writing, to analyze rationally, to work well with people, and to plan in a systematic and orderly way—will still be important. Therefore, you should make an effort to overcome, or at least diminish, any weaknesses, while searching for competencies to emphasize. There are various testing services that can indicate which of your abilities need improvement.

Some other key questions to ask yourself are: Can my strengths be utilized in a variety of situations or only in limited areas? How mobile am I? Am I limiting myself to a certain location? How well do I manage myself? Do I set measurable standards of performance to be met in reaching objectives? Do I seek performance feedback in order to determine how well I'm doing?

A part of identifying one's abilities is going through a self-analysis. Knowing your talents and vocational interests well will help you determine the type of work that suits you best.

Ambitions and Hopes

It's easy enough to dream of fame and fortune, but you should be realistic, too. What would you *really* like to do or become? What are you willing to sacrifice to achieve your dreams? Do you want to become an entrepreneur and found a company for your children and grandchildren? Do you want to be a top executive in someone else's business? Or would you be satisfied with some other position?

Obligations

We usually try to live up to the expectations of other people, for they help us to satisfy some of our needs and to develop a sense of identify and self-worth. Therefore, those people deserve some of our time, energy, and other resources. For instance, your family might want you to return home to help run the family business. Or one of your parents may need you to help him or her physically or financially. Remember that you need not plan to accomplish all of your desired goals on the job; some can be achieved at home or elsewhere.

Personal Values

Although talents, interests, ambitions, hopes, and obligations are important in the choice of a career, personal values must also be considered. Values are the relative worth or importance we place on people, ideas, or events. These greatly influence the choice of what we want to do because the work we do also affects the way we feel about ourselves. Some key questions to ask are: What is my personal concept of success, and how important is it to me to achieve it? How much risk am I willing to take? What's the basis of my values? Do I believe in the work ethic or in a more leisurely approach?

The work ethic is a principle emphasizing hard and diligent work, thrift, frugality, and dedication to work as a life interest.

Reading Time: _____
See Conversion Table.
Enter WPM Rate on the Progress Record Chart

42 Your Career Strategy

COMPREHENSION CHECK

Getting the Facts

1. One quotation was, "You will be what you (a) will to be," (b) resolve to be," (c) dream of being," (d) grow to be."

    1. ___

2. In planning, you were told to (a) get an MBA, (b) check want ads routinely, (c) read about current research, (d) set realistic dates for yourself.

    2. ___

3. Specific mention was made of what factor affecting career decisions? (a) age, (b) foreign competition, (c) legislation, (d) community size.

    3. ___

4. Among basic competencies listed was the ability to (a) communicate well, (b) do computations well, (c) use a computer, (d) adjust.

    4. ___

5. Specific mention was made of (a) getting an advanced degree, (b) establishing a partnership, (c) helping with the family business, (d) seeing a vocational counselor.

    5. ___

Getting the Meaning

6. The main idea with respect to career strategy was to (a) stress its importance, (b) formulate desired steps, (c) explain why it should be done, (d) indicate when to do it.

    6. ___

7. Central focus is on (a) how, (b) what, (c) when, (d) why.

    7. ___

8. Most emphasis was placed on (a) personal values, (b) obligations, (c) self-analysis, (d) ambitions and hopes.

    8. ___

9. This is organized (a) on a point-by-point basis, (b) on a problem-solution pattern, (c) on a cause-effect pattern, (d) logically.

    9. ___

10. Primary purpose was to (a) persuade, (b) raise questions, (c) stimulate interest, (d) inform.

    10. ___

10 Off for Each Mistake.
Comprehension Score: _____
Answer Key in Appendix.
Enter the Results on the Progress Record Chart.

ROOT MINI-REVIEW

Here's your speed review for the fourteen roots you are studying. Use your 3 x 5 card as before. Remember the three review patterns: cover the right-hand column first; then cover both right-hand columns; finally, cover the two left-hand columns to insure perfect mastery.

Root	Suggested Mnemonic	Common Meaning
1. ducere	duct	lead
2. scribere	inscribe	write
3. ponere	deposit	put, place
4. mittere	missile	send
5. capere	capture	take, seize
6. plicare	reply	fold
7. graphein	autograph	write
8. legein, logos	geology, travelogue	study of, speech
9. tenere	tenant	have, hold
10. ferre	ferry	bear, carry
11. facere	manufacture	make, do
12. specere	inspect	see
13. tendere	distend	stretch
14. stare	stationary	stand

43 Why We Behave as We Do

WORD POWER WORKOUT

A. Leaning on Context

In each of the blanks provided, place the letter that precedes the best definition of the underlined word in context to the left.

Words in Context	**Definitions**
1. ___ called <u>operant</u> conditioning	a. course
2. ___ <u>instrumental</u> conditioning	b. theorizes
3. ___ delivers a small <u>pellet</u>	c. nourished, promoted
4. ___ the normal <u>procedure</u>	d. ball
5. ___ with a <u>tidbit</u> of grain	e. developed gradually
6. ___ superstition is <u>fostered</u>	f. facilitating
7. ___ ritual ceremonies have <u>evolved</u>	g. inclined trough
8. ___ Skinner <u>speculated</u>	h. relevancies
9. ___ down the <u>chute</u>	i. delicate morsel
10. ___ with the <u>implications</u>	j. stimulus-reinforced

Check your answers with the Key before going on. Review any that you have missed.

Pronunciation aids: 1. op′ur unt.
KEY: add, āce; end, ēven; it, īce; odd, ōpen; pōōl; up.

B. Leaning on Parts

Now for some suffixes, those useful parts you fit on the end of words. Take *describe*. How do you turn it into "one who describes"? Just add an *-er* to make *describer*. In each blank below, add the required suffix.

1. One who helps is a help_____.

2. One who is young is youth_____.

3. If you work without tiring, you are a tire_____ worker.

4. A female lion is a lion_____.

5. Of or pertaining to an infant is infant_____.

C. Making the Words Yours

In each blank below, enter the most appropriate word from the ten words in context in the first exercise, substituting it for the word(s) in parentheses. Use these words: *chute, evolved, fostered, implications, instrumental, operant, pellet, procedure, speculates, tidbit.*

1. To evacuate the plane, passengers must slide down the (inclined trough) _____.

2. Just follow the normal (course) _____ in ordering the supplies.

3. Rewarding the good behavior (nourished, promoted) _____ immediate improvement.

4. The (relevancies) _____ of accepting the bribe were disturbing.

5. The small (ball) _____ lodged in the leg had to be removed by surgery.

6. Do you know how this procedure has (developed gradually) _____?

7. The recommendation of the teacher was the (facilitating) _____ factor in the scholarship award.

8. Give your child a (delicate morsel) _____ to encourage good behavior.

9. The reporter (theorizes) _____ about the reliability of the statements.

10. The subject of (stimulus-reinforced) _____ conditioning deserves special attention.

4 Off for Each Mistake.
Word Power Score: _____
Answer Key in Appendix.

43

Why We Behave as We Do

Morris K. Holland

Why do you behave as you do? For example, do you believe in luck?—carry a lucky pocket piece? Garrison Keillor says, "Some luck lies in not getting what you thought you wanted but getting what you have, which once you have got it you may be smart enough to see is what you would have wanted had you known." Now if you have that sorted out, you're ready for this compara-tively simple textbook passage from Introductory Psychology. *Be careful! You may find your natural interest in human behavior so stimulated, you'll want to read the whole book.*

Begin Timing

A dog is told to "sit," is encouraged to sit by pressing down on its hindquar-ters, and then is fed a dog biscuit. After a few such trials, when the dog is told to sit, it sits. By rewarding it with grain, a chicken is taught to dance when music is played. When any behavior is rewarded, it tends to be repeated. This kind of conditioning by consequences is called operant con-ditioning, or instrumental conditioning.

An infant is lying in its crib making babbling noises, and its mother is working nearby. By chance, the infant babbles "ma-ma, ma-ma"; smiling, the mother picks the baby up and snuggles it. The baby receives attention and affection as a consequence of babbling in a particular way; such rewards make it likely that "ma-ma" will be said more often in the future. The response of saying "ma-ma" in the presence of its mother will be learned through *operant conditioning*.

The key to operant conditioning is controlling the consequences of behavior. When behavior has favorable consequences, it tends to be repeated. When behavior has unfavorable consequences, it tends to be abandoned. Therefore, by controlling the consequences of behavior, the behavior itself can be controlled.

One of the most influential figures in modern psychology was B. F. Skinner, a man who devoted his life to the study of operant conditioning. One of Skinner's early contributions was the invention of a special box for studying animal learning. When a rat, pigeon, or other small animal is placed in this box and it pushes a lever, a mechanism delivers a small pellet of food to the animal. The Skinner box automatically rewards the animal for pressing the lever; lever pressing is learned through operant conditioning. The Skinner box makes it possible for psychologists to study the effects of various kinds of rewards and reward schedules on the behavior of animals. For example, it has been learned that responses rewarded occasionally but not consistently do not weaken easily. They become very persistent habits.

Pigeons have been used extensively in operant-conditioning studies. A pigeon can be put into a Skinner box and taught to peck at a small disk or key in order to receive a reward of grain. In the normal procedure, the pigeon works for its reward by pecking at the key in the box; the reward is not given unless the pigeon pecks at the key.

Skinner wondered what pigeons would do if they were reinforced with grain no matter what they did. Several pigeons were put into Skinner boxes and rewarded every fifteen seconds with a tidbit of grain; the delivery of the grain was not dependent upon what any bird was doing. In effect, these birds were put on welfare; they did not have to work in order to be fed. After some time had passed, Skinner looked into the boxes to see what the birds were doing. He found that each bird was performing some highly patterned act. One bird was turning counterclockwise around the cage, making two or three turns between each feeding; another was repeatedly thrusting its head into the far upper corners of the cage; a third was rocking with a pendulum motion; another bird developed a kind of rhythmic dance. Skinner described the behavior as *superstitious*.

The birds seemed to be repeating what they were doing when they received their reward of grain. Their responses were irrelevant, but they had been conditioned by the reward. The rewards actually appeared by chance and had nothing to do with what the pigeons did.

Human behavior is also sometimes superstitious. Whenever the connection between human activity and significant rewards is uncertain, superstition is fostered. In many parts of the world, rain is a most significant event but is not very predictable to the average person. Although the coming of rain does not depend on what people do, rain dances and other ritual ceremonies have evolved to "bring the rain." Skinner speculated that such ceremonies may have origins in some distant time in the past when, by chance, rain followed some human activity.

What are your superstitions?

For many students, receiving a good grade on an exam is a highly important but rather unpredictable event. By chance, you may have worn a particular shirt one day when you made an unusually high grade; thereafter, this may become your "good luck" shirt. By chance, you may have sat in a particular place one day when you made a high grade on a test; thereafter, you feel more confident taking exams while sitting in that part of the room. Wearing a certain shirt or sitting in a particular place in the room on exam day are examples of what Skinner would call superstitious behavior—

behavior that is acquired because of a past accidental association with reward.

Skinner contended that the world is like the Skinner box. People are like pigeons or rats: their behavior is controlled by the environment, which rewards some activities and not others. As Skinner put it in an interview:

> The world at large is a laboratory. Take the people in Las Vegas, pulling levers on slot machines. They are in a laboratory situation, and very willingly. The slot machines simply use a schedule of conditioning and reinforcement similar to those we use in the laboratory—with money dropping down the chute instead of food.

Skinner argued that in this "Skinner-box" world freedom is an illusion. People are not free; their behavior is controlled by their environment. The problem for people to solve is how to gain control over the rewards and punishments in their environment by applying the principles learned in the Skinner box to the design of future society.

To those who are concerned about the excessive control of our lives, Skinner replied, "What we need is more control, not less, and this is itself an engineering problem of the first importance." Skinner believed that we cannot avoid controls, and that therefore our problem is to design a society with good controls rather than bad ones. He said:

> What is needed is a new conception of human behavior which is compatible with the implications of a scientific analysis. All men control and are controlled. The question of government in the broadest possible sense is not how freedom is to be preserved but what kinds of control are to be used and to what ends.

If, as Skinner believed, we are all controlled by external environmental forces, then there is no freedom. Freedom in only an illusion we have, resulting from our ignorance of the forces that control us.

Reading Time: _____
See Conversion Table.
Enter WPM Rate on the Progress Record Chart.

43 Why We Behave as We Do

COMPREHENSION CHECK

Getting the Facts

1. Operant conditioning and instrumental conditioning (a) are the same, (b) are different, (c) have slight differences, (d) have many differences.

1. ___

2. What specific animals were mentioned? (a) dogs, (b) rats, (c) pigeons, (d) all the preceding.

2. ___

3. In one experiment, how often were pigeons rewarded with grain? (a) every fifteen seconds, (b) every thirty seconds, (c) every minute, (d) every five minutes.

3. ___

4. It was said that luck sometimes gets connected with a student's (a) slacks, (b) tie, (c) shirt, (d) pen.

4. ___

5. Skinner connected his beliefs expressly with (a) education, (b) laws, (c) government, (d) all the preceding.

5. ___

Getting the Meaning

6. This is mainly about (a) the Skinner box, (b) animal learning, (c) the effects of rewards, (d) the controls of external environmental forces.

6. ___

7. The paragraph dealing with the baby and "ma-ma" was used to illustrate how (a) language is learned, (b) mothers control children, (c) early conditioning begins, (d) conditioning works.

7. ___

8. The behavior of the pigeons "on welfare" was used to show (a) how superstitious behavior develops, (b) how psychologists do research, (c) how irrelevant pigeon responses were, (d) how quickly pigeons learned.

8. ___

9. The discussion of students and exam grades was introduced primarily to (a) get readers to identify their own superstitions, (b) illustrate the need for further research, (c) relate animal and human behavior, (d) contrast animal with human behavior.

9. ___

10. Skinner apparently believed our behavior is primarily   10. ___
    (a) conditioned by laws, (b) controlled by will and reason,
    (c) conditioned by environment, (d) controlled by social
    custom.

44 America's Industrial Revolution

WORD POWER WORKOUT

A. Leaning on Context

In each of the blanks provided, place the letter that precedes the best definition of the underlined word in context to the left.

Words in Context	Definitions
1. ___ steel <u>tentacles</u>	a. devices
2. ___ the early <u>contraptions</u>	b. prominence
3. ___ the mechanized <u>colossus</u>	c. collision, crash
4. ___ was <u>phenomenal</u>	d. flexible appendages
5. ___ the <u>impact</u>	e. showy display
6. ___ this <u>infectious</u> prosperity	f. extraordinary
7. ___ <u>ostentation</u> seemed more important	g. giant
8. ___ its later <u>notoriety</u>	h. punishing, fatiguing
9. ___ in a <u>grueling</u> thirty-three hours	i. deadly
10. ___ a <u>lethal</u> new weapon	j. contagious

Check your answers with the Key before going on. Review any that you have missed.

Pronunciation aids: 1. ten'tuh kuls; 3. kuh los'us; 4. fi nom'uh nul;
7. os tun tā'shun; 8. nō tuh rī'uh tē.

KEY: add, āce; end, ēven; it, īce; odd, ōpen; po͞ol; up.

B. Leaning on Parts

Try getting acquainted with a few more suffixes. In the following, fill in each blank with the suffix that provides the right meaning.

1. A very small glob of water would be a glob_____.

2. If it happens every hour, it's an hour_____ occurrence.

3. If the bottles can be returned, they are return_____.

4. Someone with the qualities of a child is child_____.

5. To make a room dark is to dark_____ it.

C. Making the Words Yours

In each blank below, enter the most appropriate word from the ten words in context in the first exercise, substituting it for the word(s) in parentheses. Use these words: *colossus, contraptions, grueling, impact, infectious, lethal, notoriety, ostentation, phenomenal, tentacles.*

1. With its strong (flexible appendages) _____ the octopus seized its prey.

2. One of the seven wonders of the world was the (giant) _____ of Rhodes.

3. Do you know how to operate all these (devices) _____?

4. What about banning the most (deadly) _____ weapon of all?

5. You need the (extraordinary) _____ ability of a genius to use the latest computer.

6. The (collision, crash) _____ of the two cars could be heard for blocks.

7. Don't get near me. What I have is very (contagious) _____.

8. With some people, (showy display) _____ makes more difference than practicality.

9. The bicycle race was a (punishing) _____ forty miles long.

10. My roommate's escapade gained too much (prominence) _____.

4 Off for Each Mistake.
Word Power Score: _____
Answer Key in Appendix.

44

America's Industrial Revolution

Thomas A. Bailey and David M. Kennedy

When did we begin rolling around on rubber tires or sprouting wings? Back in industrial revolution days! American history makes fascinating reading, provided you go to The American Pageant. *This text—one of the most popular of its kind—gives you a vivid, entertaining look back at our "good old days." See how they're brought to life!*

Begin Timing

A new industrial revolution slipped into high gear in America in the 1920s. Thrusting out steel tentacles, it changed the daily life of the people in unprecedented ways. Machinery was the new messiah—and the automobile was its principal prophet.

Of all the inventions of the era, the automobile cut the deepest mark. It heralded an amazing new industrial system, based on assembly-line methods and mass-production techniques.

Americans adapted rather than invented the gasoline engine; Europeans can claim the original honor. By the 1890s a few daring American inventors and promoters, including Henry Ford and Ransom E. Olds (Oldsmobile), were developing the infant automotive industry. By 1910 there were sixty-nine companies, with a total annual production of 181,000 units. The early contraptions were neither speedy nor reliable. Many a stalled motorist, profanely cranking a balky car, had to endure the jeer "Get a horse" from the occupants of a passing dobbin-drawn carriage.

An enormous industry sprang into being, as Detroit became the motorcar capital of America. The mechanized colossus owed much to the stopwatch efficiency techniques of Frederick W. Taylor, a prominent inventor, engineer, and tennis player, who sought to eliminate wasted motion. His epitaph reads: "Father of Scientific Management."

Best known of the new crop of industrial wizards was Henry Ford, who more than any other individual put America on rubber tires. His high and hideous Model T ("Tin Lizzie") was cheap, rugged, and reasonably reliable, though rough and clattering. The parts of Ford's "flivver" were highly standardized, but the behavior of this "rattling good car" was so individualized that it became the butt of numberless jokes.

Lean and silent Henry Ford, who was said to have wheels in his head, erected an immense personal empire on the cornerstone of his mechanical genius, though his associates provided much of the organizational talent. Ill educated, this multimillionaire mechanic was socially and culturally narrow; "History is bunk," he once testified. But he dedicated himself with one-track devotion to the gospel of standardization. After two early failures, he grasped and applied fully the techniques of assembly-line production— "Fordism." He is supposed to have remarked that the purchaser could have his automobile any color he desired—just as long as it was black. So economical were his methods that in the mid-1920s he was selling the Ford roadster for $260—well within the purse of a thrifty worker.

The flood of Fords was phenomenal. In 1914 the "Automobile Wizard" turned out his five hundred thousandth Model T. By 1930 his total had risen to 20 million, or, on a bumper-to-bumper basis, more than enough to encircle the globe. A national newspaper and magazine poll conducted in 1923 revealed Ford to be the people's choice for the presidential nomination in 1924. By 1929, when the great bull market collapsed, there were 26 million motor vehicles registered in the United States. This figure, averaging 1 for every 4.9 Americans, represented far more automobiles than existed in all the rest of the world.

The impact of the self-propelled carriage on various aspects of American life was tremendous. A gigantic new industry emerged, dependent on steel, but displacing steel from its kingpin role. Employing directly or indirectly about 6 million people by 1930, it was a major prop of the nation's prosperity. Thousands of new jobs, moreover, were created by supporting industries. The lengthening list would include rubber, glass, and fabrics, to say nothing of highway construction and thousands of service stations and garages. America's standard of living, responding to this infectious prosperity, rose to an enviable level.

New industries boomed lustily; older ones grew sickly. The petroleum business experienced an explosive development. Hundreds of oil derricks shot up in California, Texas, and Oklahoma, as these states expanded wondrously and the new frontier became an industrial frontier. The once-feared railroad octopus, on the other hand, was hard hit by the competition of passenger cars, buses, and trucks. An age-old story was repeated: one industry's gains were another industry's pains.

Other effects were widely felt. Speedy marketing of perishable foodstuffs, such as fresh fruits, was accelerated. A new prosperity enriched outlying farms, as city dwellers were provided with produce at attractive prices. Countless new roads ribboned out to meet the demand of the American motorist for smoother and faster highways, often paid for by taxes on gasoline. The era of mud ended as the nation made haste to construct the finest network of hard-surfaced roadways in the world. Lured by new seductiveness in advertising, and encouraged by the perfecting of installment-plan buying, countless Americans with shallow purses acquired the habit of riding as they paid.

Zooming motorcars were agents of social change. At first a luxury, they rapidly became a necessity. Essentially devices for needed transportation, they soon developed into a badge of freedom and equality—a necessary prop for self-respect. To some, ostentation seemed more important than transportation. Leisure hours could now be spend more pleasurably, as tens of thousands of cooped-up souls responded to the call of the open road on joyriding vacations. Women were further freed from clinging-vine dependence on men. Isolation among the sections was broken down, while the less attractive states lost population at an alarming rate. By the late 1920s, Americans owned more automobiles than bathtubs. "I can't go to town in a bathtub," one housewife explained.

Other social by-products of the automobile were visible. Autobuses made possible the consolidation of schools and to some extent of churches. The sprawling suburbs spread out still farther from the urban core, as American became a nation of commuters.

The demon machine, on the other hand, exacted a terrible toll by catering to the American mania for speed. Citizens were becoming statistics. Not counting the hundreds of thousands of injured and crippled, the one millionth American had died in a motor vehicle accident by 1951—more than all those killed on all the battlefields of all the nation's wars to that date. "The public be rammed" seemed to be the motto of the new age.

Virtuous home life partially broke down as joyriders of all ages forsook the ancestral hearth for the wide-open spaces. The morals of flaming youth sagged correspondingly—at least in the judgment of their elders. Even the disgraceful crime waves of the 1920s and 1930s were partly stimulated by the motorcar, for gangsters could now make quick getaways.

Yet no sane American would plead for a return of the old horse and buggy, complete with fly-breeding manure. The automobile contributed notably to improved air and environmental quality, despite its later notoriety as a polluter. Life might be cut short on the highways, and smog might poison the air, but the automobile brought more convenience, pleasure, and excitement into people's lives than almost any other single invention.

Gasoline engines also provided the power that enabled man to fulfill the age-old dream of sprouting wings. After near-successful experiments by others with heavier-than-air craft, the Wright brothers, Orville and Wilbur, performed "the miracle at Kitty Hawk," North Carolina. On a historic day— December 17, 1903—Orville Wright took aloft a feebly engined plane that stayed airborne for 12 seconds and 120 feet (37 meters). Thus, the air age was launched by two obscure bicycle repairmen.

As aviation gradually got off the ground, the world slowly shrank. The public was made increasingly air-minded by unsung heroes—often martyrs—who appeared as stunt fliers at fairs and other public gatherings. Airplanes—"flying coffins"—were used with marked success for various purposes during the Great War of 1914–1918. Shortly thereafter private companies began to operate passenger lines with airmail contracts, which were in effect a subsidy from Washington. The first transcontinental airmail route was established from New York to San Francisco in 1920.

In 1927 modest and skillful Charles A. Lindbergh, the so-called Flyin' Fool, electrified the world by the first solo west-to-east conquest of the Atlantic. Seeking a prize of $25,000, the lanky stunt flier courageously piloted his single-engined plane, the *Spirit of St. Louis*, from New York to Paris in a grueling thirty-three hours and thirty-nine minutes.

Lindbergh's exploit swept Americans off their feet. Fed up with the cynicism and debunking of the jazz age, they found in this wholesome and handsome youth a genuine hero. They clasped the fluttering "Lone Eagle" to their hearts much more warmly than the bashful young man desired. "Lucky Lindy" received an uproarious welcome in the "hero canyon" of lower Broadway, as eighteen hundred tons of ticker tape and other improvised confetti showered upon him. Lindbergh's achievement—it was more than a "stunt"—did much to dramatize and popularize flying, while giving a strong boost to the infant aviation industry.

The impact of the airship was tremendous. It provided the soaring American spirit with yet another dimension. At the same time, it gave birth to a giant new industry. Unfortunately, the accident rate in the pioneer stages of aviation was high, though hardly more so than on the early railroads. But by the 1930s and 1940s, travel by air on regularly scheduled airlines was markedly safer than on many overcrowded highways.

Humanity's new wings also increased the tempo of an already breathless civilization. The floundering railroad received another sharp setback through the loss of passengers and mail. A lethal new weapon was given to the gods of war; and with the coming of city-busting aerial bombs, people could well debate whether the conquest of the air was a blessing or a curse. The Atlantic was shriveling to about the size of the Aegean Sea in the days of Socrates, while isolation behind ocean moats was becoming a bygone dream.

Reading Time: _____
See Conversion Table.
Enter WPM Rate on the Progress Record Chart.

44 American's Industrial Revolution

COMPREHENSION CHECK

Getting the Facts

1. Our new industrial revolution slipped into high gear
   gear in the (a) 1900s, (b) 1910s, (c) 1920s, (d) 1930s.

   1. ___

2. The Father of Scientific Management was (a) Frederick W.
   Taylor, (b) Ransom E. Olds, (c) Henry Ford, (d) Charles
   Hanna.

   2. ___

3. When the bull market collapsed, one out of every how
   many Americans had a car? (a) 3.8, (b) 4.2, (c) 4.7,
   (d) 4.9.

   3. ___

4. At one time Americans were said to own more automobiles
   than (a) ice boxes, (b) bathtubs, (c) flush toilets,
   (d) washing machines.

   4. ___

5. The prize for solo-flying the Atlantic was (a) $10,000,
   (b) $15,000, (c) $20,000, (d) $25,000.

   5. ___

Getting the Meaning

6. This was chiefly to describe (a) the growth of automobile
   manufacturing, (b) major aspects of our new industrial
   development, (c) changes resulting from automobile transportation, (d) the development of mass assembly-line
   methods.

   6. ___

7. How many major organizational divisions were there?
   (a) only one, (b) two, (c) three, (d) four.

   7. ___

8. In style this is best described as (a) formal, (b) literary,
   (c) lively, (d) simple.

   8. ___

9. Points were developed largely by (a) logical reasoning,
   (b) figures, (c) concrete details, (d) quoting of experts.

   9. ___

10. This is primarily to (a) evaluate evidence, (b) explain,
    (c) draw conclusions, (d) summarize.

    10. ___

10 Off for Each Mistake.
Comprehension Score: _____
Answer Key in Appendix.
Enter the Results on the Progress Record Chart.

SUFFIX MINI-REVIEW

Follow the same procedures as you have with the preceding mini-reviews, again using your 3 x 5 card to cover the answers until you have supplied them. Then check immediately by drawing the card down to uncover the answers.

	Suffix	Suggested Mnemonic	Common Meaning
1.	-able, -ible	readable	capable or worthy of
2.	-er	singer	one who
3.	-al	denial	pertaining to
4.	-ous, -ose	joyous	full of, involving
5.	-ful	hopeful	full of
6.	-ess	goddess	female
7.	-ile	servile	subject to, similar to
8.	-ish	childish	like or inclined to
9.	-less	pitiless	without, unable to
10.	-ory	illusory	serving to
11.	-ule	globule	little
12.	-ly	harshly	in a specified manner
13.	-en	darken	cause to be
14.	-esque	picturesque	like
15.	-ate	directorate	office or agent

45 Next

WORD POWER WORKOUT

A. Leaning on Context

In each of the blanks provided, place the letter that precedes the best definition of the underlined word in context to the left.

Words in Context	Definitions
1. ___ gradually <u>atrophied</u>	a. crush, subdue
2. ___ <u>proliferation</u> of computers	b. common
3. ___ of <u>menial</u> labor	c. theme
4. ___ support the <u>thesis</u>	d. inborn
5. ___ <u>intuitive</u> abilities	e. form, put into
6. ___ how to <u>encode</u> words	f. withered, wasted away
7. ___ way to <u>squelch</u> a child	g. spread, increase
8. ___ remove <u>scut</u> work	h. death
9. ___ the <u>demise</u> of schools	i. unconfined, unrestrained
10. ___ <u>untrammeled</u> in their relationship	j. worthless

---

Check your answers with the Key before going on. Review any that you have missed.

Pronunciation aids: 1. at′ruh fēd; 2. prō lif′uh rā shun; 3. mē′nē ul; 5. in tōō′uh tiv; 9. di mīz′.

KEY: add, āce; end, ēven; it, īce; odd, ōpen; pōol; up.

B. Leaning on Parts

Try working with a few more suffixes. In the following sentences, fill in the blanks with the suffixes that provide the right meaning.

1. A scheme full of grandeur is grandi_____.

2. If it's worth commending, it's commendat_____.

3. If the action tends to remedy the situation, it's remed_____.

4. If it's like a picture, it's pictur_____.

5. If you show affection, you're affection_____.

C. Making the Words Yours

In each blank below, enter the most appropriate word from the ten words in context in the first exercise, substituting it for the word(s) in parentheses. Use these words: *atrophied, demise, encode, intuitive, menial, proliferation, scut, squelch, thesis, untrammeled.*

1. They had a servant to do the (common) _____ tasks.

2. What do you think about the (spread, increase) _____ of foreign cars?

3. They supported the (theme) _____ that everyone should have a computer.

4. To write anything you need to be able to (form, put into) _____ words.

5. Some students have the (inborn) _____ sense to get along well.

6. We need to rid ourselves of (worthless) _____ work completely.

7. The muscles (withered, wasted away) _____ from disuse.

8. The (death) _____ of a dictatorship is cause for celebration.

9. Their (unconfined, unrestrained) _____ efforts paid off handsomely.

10. That look of contempt would (crush, subdue) _____ anyone!

4 Off for Each Mistake.
Word Power Score: _____
Answer Key in Appendix.

45

Next

Isaac Asimov

Ever read any science fiction? If so, the name Asimov should be familiar. After all, he's one of the big three, along with Arthur C. Clarke and Robert A. Heinlein. Asimov started reading science fiction at age nine and sold his first story at age eighteen. He's kept it up for nearly fifty years. But, for a change, he sometimes deserts science fiction for a science-related article, such as this one. Try it!

Begin Timing

The chief consequence of the computer revolution is that humans are being relieved of the dull and stultifying labor to which they have been subjected for all of history. Until this present generation, there have always been myriad tasks that required too much intelligence for anything but a human being to do—yet required far less intelligence than the human brain was capable of delivering.

The result was that most human beings earned their livings in ways that seriously underused their brains and gradually atrophied them. If, for years, a person has no occasion to indulge in creative thought, one cannot expect that person to be creative on demand.

That is why the proliferation of computers (and robots, which after all are merely computerized machines) may create a crisis as jobs inevitably disappear. Those who lose their jobs to computers cannot easily obtain other, more creative jobs, for they have seldom been called upon to be creative before. Society will have to engage in large-scale retraining, reeducation, welfare, and make-work projects.

However, the disappearance of menial labor will make it possible for human beings to switch to more appropriate work—the kind of work that cannot be done by computers, whose abilities may never match the complexity and versatility of the human brain, with its billions of cell-units, each enormously complex in itself and all arranged in intricate combinations. After relatively few years of reeducation, then, a new generation will arise that will be trained from the start for new kinds of work—far more humanly creative work.

This may seem hopelessly idealistic to those who feel that creativity, although a human attribute, is the province of only a fortunate few, while the vast majority of human beings simply don't and can't possess creativity.

This seems to me a misreading of human capacity brought about by ignoring the existence of a vicious cycle. We have always had a social system that condemned virtually all human beings to the underuse and atrophy of the brain, and we have surveyed the broken results and used them to support the thesis that, with some exceptions, human beings are brainless.

If computers rescue human beings from brain-destroying work, and if we then proceed to develop new and revolutionary forms of education, we many discover that creativity is a common human trait and that the intellectual, artistic, and intuitive abilities of humanity will make an enormous leap.

This may seem impossible to achieve, but humanity accomplished something of this sort earlier in its history. For all the centuries before the Industrial Revolution, literacy was the province of a very few. It was easy to suppose that most people simply lacked the mental equipment to learn how to encode words readily and easily into the intricate symbols of writing, and how to decode them just as readily and easily once written.

And yet when the Industrial Revolution came and people had to deal with new and complex machinery, mass literacy became necessary. For that reason, education was revolutionized, free public schools were organized, and youngsters were *forced* to attend. And behold! We discovered that most human beings could be taught to read and write after all.

But how can education be revolutionized in such a way that people can learn to be creative? How do you teach creativity?

Creativity does not have to be taught: it already exists in the normal human brain. But it seems to me that the present form of education, far from simply failing to teach creativity, actually brings about the destruction of the creativity that is already there.

This is not done deliberately. I'm not talking of villains. It's just that the only way of bringing about mass education in a noncomputerized society is to teach children in large groups according to the dictates of a uniform curriculum—to teach them the same things at the same time in the same manner. And yet every child is an individual with interests and curiosities of his own. What better way to squelch a child and turn him forever against the delights of learning than by introducing him to a system of learning that denies him his individuality?

However, the very computers that will remove scut work from the world can also transfer enormous libraries into their memories. The complex and versatile computers of the future will therefore have the capacity to be teaching machines of satisfying complexity.

We can imagine outlets in every home, so that people young and old can ask for information: books, pamphlets, technical directions, art, music. The products of thousands of years of human culture and knowledge will be readily available. The computer can locate answers to questions, can suggest further directions for research.

This will not lead to the demise of schools. Schools are places where certain basics can be taught, and where more important, person-to-person interactions can take place. There, youngsters will learn how to use computer outlets properly.

Mind you, I am not suggesting that the computer be merely another school tool, a fancier kind of pen-and-paper, a more elaborate textbook. A computer that is tied to school becomes merely part of the curriculum. It may be a convenience, but it won't be a revolution.

No, it is of the essence that a computer and a human being be untrammeled in their relationship; that the person who wishes information, however trivial or "unimportant," can indulge that wish in his own way, in his own place, at his own time; that he can switch interests without warning, drop certain subjects, pick up others; in short, that he can experience the ecstasy of learning. Give the owners of brains a chance to learn *in their own way, not necessarily in yours*, and they will love it. They may unleash their inherent creativity in the process.

And that is exactly what computers will allow them to do.

But then, to those who look into the future, it may seem that as computers advance and gain more capacity, they will take over more and more jobs we consider human and creative and thus render us obsolete.

I don't think so. Automobiles can go much faster than feet can go, but feet have not been rendered obsolete for the purpose of traveling. In the same way, even if the computer apes "intelligence," it is not necessarily the *same* intelligence we have. I am writing this essay on a word processor, but unless I strike the proper keys, it can't do a thing. Nor can I ever expect to be able to program a word processor to make up its own essay by telling it exactly which word to choose next and how to organize the essay as a whole.

I can't program a computer to do this because I don't know how *I* do it. The essence of human creativity in every field is that we don't really know how we create; we just do it. We can retain that nonunderstood ability—and we can leave it to the computer to do those jobs so simple that they can be analyzed and taught to a machine.

In that way, human beings won't be competing with computers; we'll be *cooperating* with them. The cooperation of two kinds of intelligence will make person/computer a far more powerful agency for understanding the universe than either alone would be.

And even as we continually improve and sharpen the computer's abilities, so we can use the computer more effectively to sharpen our own abilities and continually heighten our creative faculties.

The future might then prove a marvelous one.

Reading Time: _____
See Conversion Table.
Enter WPM Rate on the Progress Record Chart.

45 Next

COMPREHENSION CHECK

Getting the Facts

1. Most human beings were said to earn a living in ways
   that (a) were too routine, (b) required little education, (c) underused their brains, (d) demanded too
   little.

   1. ___

2. Specific mention was made of (a) fax machines, (b) copy
   machines, (c) talking typewriters, (d) robots.

   2. ___

3. Asimov expressly called himself hopelessly (a) idealistic (b) optimistic, (c) short-sighted, (d) pessimistic.

   3. ___

4. Computers were said to be able to store (a) whole libraries, (b) voluminous research findings, (c) all textbook
   information, (d) daily world and local news.

   4. ___

5. Asimov refers to (a) eyes, (b) ears, (c) arms, (d) feet.

   5. ___

Getting the Meaning

6. The main idea was to explain how computers (a) are
   presently misused, (b) should be used in the future,
   (c) should compete with schools, (d) have to be changed.

   6. ___

7. Asimov's ideas primarily require changes in (a) technology, (b) government, (c) workers, (d) education.

   7. ___

8. Asimov seemed chiefly concerned over our lack of
   (a) creativity, (b) intelligence, (c) word power,
   (d) the ability to communicate.

   8. ___

9. Major emphasis was on (a) using a word processor,
   (b) learning at home, (c) learning your own way,
   (d) developing stronger interests.

   9. ___

10. The author's chief purpose was to (a) warn, (b) amuse,
    (c) convince, (d) inform.

    10. ___

10 Off for Each Mistake.
Comprehension Score: _____
Answer Key in Appendix.
Enter the Results on the Progress Record Chart.

46 Future Shock's Doc

WORD POWER WORKOUT

A. Leaning on Context

In each of the blanks provided, place the letter that precedes the best definition of the underlined word in context to the left.

Words in Context	Definitions
1. ___ walked out in a <u>huff</u>	a. doubters
2. ___ many <u>skeptics</u> question	b. range
3. ___ to remain <u>anonymous</u>	c. limitless
4. ___ he has kept <u>tabs</u>	d. nameless
5. ___ an almost <u>cult</u> following	e. outline, script
6. ___ <u>purveyor</u> of futuristic facts	f. checking, track of
7. ___ protrude <u>impishly</u>	g. stew
8. ___ runs the <u>gamut</u> from	h. mischievously
9. ___ appetite is <u>insatiable</u>	i. supplier
10. ___ if the <u>scenario</u>	j. worshiping

Check your answers with the Key before going on. Review any that you have missed.

Pronunciation aids: 3. uh non'uh mus; 6. pur vā'ur; 9. in sā'shē uh bul; 10. sin är'ē ō.

KEY: add, āce; end, ēven; it, īce; odd, ōpen; pōol; up.

B. Leaning on Parts

Try this new kind of review exercise. Fit the appropriate word into each of the five numbered blanks below. Select from the following list of words derived from *stare*, meaning "to stand": *exist, restate, persist, constant, obstacles, constitute, stationary, assistance, substantial, establishing, circumstance.*

If, despite (1) _____, you (2) _____ in your efforts,

you'll soon see (3) _____ gains. These exercises provide positive

(4) _____ in (5) _____ improved word power habits.

C. Making the Words Yours

In each blank below, enter the most appropriate word from the ten words in context in the first exercise, substituting it for the word(s) in parentheses. Use these words: *anonymous, cult, gamut, huff, insatiable, impishly, purveyor, scenario, skeptics, tabs.*

1. Who will keep (checking, track of) _____ on what we spend?

2. My dog's (limitless) _____ appetite is bankrupting me!

3. I just found this (nameless) _____ letter under my door.

4. Just follow the (outline, script) _____ that I've laid out.

5. In that one day, the student ran the whole (range) _____ of emotion from complete desolation to unbelievable ecstasy.

6. Some (doubters) _____ stayed on to hear more.

7. Don't leave in a (stew) _____ just because you didn't get your way.

8. Who is the (supplier) _____ of such different ideas?

9. The misguided leader had a strong (worshiping) _____ following.

10. The practical joker grinned (mischievously) _____ after pulling the chair out from under his friend.

46

Future Shock's Doc

Nancy Spiller

Have you ever met anyone who predicted robots would replace spouses by 2010? Anyone who irritates his listeners so much that they throw chairs and cups of coffee? Would you believe that despite such reactions, he gets a minimum lecture fee of $3,000? You'd better read on!

Begin Timing

"The biggest sin of the new age is to be boring," says Canadian futurist Frank Ogden from amid a high-tech circus on his Vancouver houseboat. Video screens, VCRs, computers and shortwave radios compete for attention with primitive Polynesian tools and carvings. Lurking near his feet is Nabu, the guard robot. Outside on the dock, two satellite dishes are his umbilical cord to the world.

No one ever has accused Ogden, a.k.a. "Dr. Tomorrow," of being boring. Outrageous—yes. When he has told teachers their methods are obsolete, labor unions they're dinosaurs and big business it's asleep at the wheel, there have been those, he says proudly, who've thrown chairs and cups of coffee and walked out in a huff. When he predicts that robots will replace human spouses by the year 2010 and suggests China buy Australia as a site for its population overflow, many skeptics question his seriousness. His favorite reply is: "All ideas are serious when their times come."

But a growing number of businesses—including the British Columbia Medical Association, Century 21 Real Estate of Canada, Canada's Waste Management Ltd. and the British Columbia Utilities Commission—private investors and even countries (which prefer to remain anonymous) are looking to Ogden as a prime source for information on the latest global trends.

In an age in which Ogden claims knowledge is doubling every 20 months, he has kept tabs on the flow for the past 10 years. Working from his peanut-shaped boat (a converted grain-storage shed), Ogden tirelessly tracks some 200 international television stations and regularly taps into 3,700 databases in search of the latest high-tech developments. He spreads the word as lecturer, consultant, syndicated columnist, television producer and host (his *Hi-Tech, Hi-Touch Japan* airs on the Discover Channel), and head of his own electronic clipping service: 21st Century Communications.

"Shock value," Frank Klassen says of Ogden's appeal. Klassen publishes Ogden's column in the *Sunday News*, a biweekly Vancouver tabloid with a circulation of 400,000. "He's one of the few columnists in the country who's on the leading edge of what might happen. He keeps people on their toes." In so doing, Klassen adds, Ogden has developed an "almost cult following."

"Frank is plugged into all that's happening in the free world," says Peter Thomas, president of Century 21 Real Estate of Canada. Thomas uses Ogden as a lecturer and futurist consultant. "He keeps me in touch with concepts and ideas which I otherwise might miss."

"North Americans don't know what's going on," Ogden says of his mission. In wire-framed glasses and well-worn flannel and wool, the 69-year-old self-styled visionary looks more like a retired professor than a purveyor of futuristic facts. A lopsided grin tilts a dimpled mustache, and jug ears protrude impishly from his egg-shaped head.

"I show what's happening in the world that we're not even aware of," he says. Typical ignorance was encountered at a recent gathering for the North American Food Manufacturers and Processors Association, he says. "The presidents of the two biggest tomato companies were there, and they were not aware that the Japanese were growing 15,000 tomatoes from a single seed—*inside and in the shade*. They were just shocked."

Ogden claims to have 40,000 such revelations on file and features about 100 of them in his talks. The collection of gosh-gollies runs the gamut from apple trees that look like flagpoles to robot nurses and grocery clerks. He barely can let a minute go by without introducing something new.

"You know about the Forum Phone?" he asks, plucking one from a desk-side pile of gadgets and launching into the virtues of the British-made phone. It fits in the palm of the hand, is as thin as a pocket calculator, costs one-tenth the price of a cellular phone and works from public tele-points in airports, subway stations and convenience stores.

Then there's the Norwegian Gamma-knife, a gamma-ray device that excises brain tumors. Other items include airplanes with computer, fax, and phone centers at each seat; a Japanese ceramic house that's fire- and earthquake-proof and takes just 2½ hours to build; and French robots that make the highest grade of Camembert cheese.

And though some of those news items sound like "Buck Rogers meets the *National Enquirer*" (one column on cloning is headlined "Amazon Women Created"), he assures that everything is his lectures is backed up "with videotape, slides or the actual product." Like the clip of musical robots that play Simon and Garfunkel tunes. "If 10 percent of the audience has heard 10 percent of what I say, there's no charge." So far, he says, he has had no requests for refunds of his $3,000-minimum lecture fee.

Much of his information comes from Japan. "It's where all the action is," he says. A Tokyo contact mails weekly cassettes of the evening news, which is simulcast in English and Japanese. "Our news is emotionally and politically oriented. Theirs is technologically and economically oriented."

In the same way the British have ruled the age of empire and the United States has led the industrial age, Ogden is convinced the Japanese are leading the age of communications.

"Information means more to the Japanese than it does to us," he says. "They know it's the new ore of the future. We get some information: we say that's no good. They know it's good if they can find out how to use it."

Their appetite is insatiable, he says. "The Japanese are translating 700 documents from English to Japanese for every one we translate from Japanese to English. Every tourist here is a spy—not deliberately; they just absorb information." And, Ogden says with a shrug, "they're smarter than us."

The fact that the Japanese have been able to turn their collective vision toward the future while the West lingers in the industrial age has tremendously helped them get ahead. "They were a nation of ancestor-worshippers," he says. "They were always looking backwards. They've decided to go forward. Almost overnight, they're now looking through the windshield instead of in the rear-view mirror."

A similar decision led Ogden to an interest in futurism. After a World War II tour of duty with the Royal Canadian Air Force, he enrolled in college—then promptly quit. "Everyone was looking backward," he says. "It was damaging my brain. Even then, what they were teaching didn't match reality. I just started looking forward.

"If schools were factories," he continues, repeating a line he often delivers to teachers' groups, "we would have closed them 10 years ago because they're not producing a salable product. Kids can't get jobs because they don't know what's happening." The Japanese, he says, send their teachers to summer school to keep up with the changing information in their fields.

"You've got to live with uncertainty, be comfortable with it," he says. To survive the future, we'll have to "learn to walk on quicksand and dance with electrons." Those who can't will be left behind. "You're gonna have the growth of the techno-peasant—incapable of doing anything other than what they know from the industrial age."

If the scenario sounds anarchic, don't be alarmed. "Chaos is coming," he says, ever the optimist, "but chaos is the most creative environment. I can't wait."

With that, he fires another barrage of entertaining predictions. High-rise office towers are the "ghost towns of the future. You don't need the hierarchy that you had in the industrial age, and you don't need the storage space." With optical crystals, the history of the United States can fit in a shoe box. Secretaries will be replaced by "voicewriters" that turn dictation into electronic mail. Cars will be equipped with microwave ovens. Knowledge will flow into homes with the push of a button, like water from the tap.

What happens when the sink backs up? The phrase "information overload" doesn't exist in Ogden's vocabulary. "I don't believe there is such a thing. We're only using 1 percent of our brain." You may think you're reached your limit, he says, but "there is no limit. We're in a time not only revolutionary," Ogden pronounces, "but evolutionary."

Catching the weary look of a visitor who's seen one too many video clips on dancing robots, Ogden can't help but chide, "No one ever told you evolution was going to be easy."

Reading Time: _____

See Conversion Table.

Enter WPM Rate on the Progress Record Chart.

46 Future Shock's Doc

COMPREHENSION CHECK

Getting the Facts

1. Ogden claims knowledge is doubling every (a) 20 months, (b) 25 months, (c) 30 months, (d) 35 months.

   1. ___

2. Ogden lives and works (a) in a motor home, (b) in a small office, (c) in his house, (d) on a houseboat.

   2. ___

3. Japanese were said to grow how many tomatoes from one seed? (a) 5,000, (b) 10,000, (c) 15,000, (d) 20,000.

   3. ___

4. Specific mention was made of (a) Mighty Mouse, (b) Batman, (c) Buck Rogers, (d) Superman.

   4. ___

5. Ogden said we're using how much of our brain? (a) 1 percent, (b) 2 percent, (c) 10 percent, (d) 25 percent.

   5. ___

Getting the Meaning

6. This is mainly to (a) characterize Ogden, (b) present his ideas, (c) show how people react to him, (d) show where he gets his information.

   6. ___

7. Ogden's particular concern was about our (a) short-sightedness, (b) future, (c) schools, (d) problems.

   7. ___

8. Ogden seems most impressed with (a) Japan, (b) France, (c) England, (d) Taiwan.

   8. ___

9. What would you infer Ogden considered of most importance? (a) industry, (b) technology, (c) communication, (d) education and training.

   9. ___

10. You'd call Ogden's attitude primarily (a) scientific, (b) reflective, (c) pessimistic, (d) radical.

   10. ___

10 Off for Each Mistake.
Comprehension Score: _____
Answer Key in Appendix.
Enter the Results on the Progress Record Chart.

47 Deadly Danger in a Spray Can

WORD POWER WORKOUT

A. Leaning on Context

In each of the blanks provided, place the letter that precedes the best definition of the underlined word in context to the left.

Words in Context   **Definitions**

1. ___ were first <u>synthesized</u>   a. make certain

2. ___ are nontoxic and <u>inert</u>   b. influenced

3. ___ because they <u>vaporize</u>   c. inactive

4. ___ and <u>propellant</u> gases   d. upset

5. ___ thus <u>disrupt</u> the workings   e. formed by
                                                           combining things

6. ___ by <u>banning</u> their use   f. favorable

7. ___ environmentally <u>benign</u> substitutes   g. propulsive,
                                                           driving

8. ___ governments should <u>ensure</u>   h. evaporate

9. ___ offered cash <u>incentives</u>   i. prohibiting

10. ___ for <u>affected</u> products   j. rewards

Check your answers with the Key before going on. Review any that you have missed.

Pronunciation aids: 7. bē nīn'.

KEY: add, āce; end, ĕven; it, īce; odd, ōpen; pōōl; up.

B. Leaning on Parts

Here's another context-root review exercise—this one over *tendere*, meaning "to stretch." Fit the appropriate word into each of the five numbered blanks below. Select from the following list of words derived from *tendere*: *tent, tends, extend, tension, pretend, portent, extensive, intention, attention, superintend*.

Anything that makes words more interesting (1) _____ to

(2) _____ your vocabulary. (3) _____ to derivation has

that effect. So your present (4) _____ efforts with derivation are a

(5) _____ of increased interest and better results.

C. Making the Words Yours

In each blank below, enter the most appropriate word from the ten words in context in the first exercise, substituting it for the word(s) in parentheses. Use these words: *affected, banning, benign, disrupt, ensure, incentives, inert, propellant, synthesized, vaporize*.

1. The experiment resulted in a totally new (formed by combining parts) _____ plastic.

2. Authorities soon began (prohibiting) _____ the use of the spray.

3. The brochures called the island climate particularly (favorable) _____.

4. Don't let that rock music (upset) _____ your study time.

5. What (propulsive, driving) _____ fuel does the rocket use?

6. The (influenced) _____ document will have to be rephrased.

7. Does that short-term position offer any special (rewards) _____?

8. Intensive study should (make certain) _____ best results.

9. Fortunately, the gases we use are all (inactive) _____.

10. The solution will (evaporate) _____ if not tightly covered.

4 Off for Each Mistake.
Word Power Score: _____
Answer Key in Appendix.

47

Deadly Danger in a Spray Can

Michael D. Lemonick

Some say the word <u>news</u>—as news itself—comes from <u>N</u>orth, <u>E</u>ast, <u>W</u>est and <u>S</u>outh. Where do you get your news, usually? From TV? From the radio? From newspapers? Or from a news magazine? Each source gives you a somewhat different picture of what's going on. Try this Time *news story, for example.*

Begin Timing

When they were first synthesized in the late 1920s, chlorofluorocarbons (CFCs for short) seemed too good to be true. These remarkable chemicals, consisting of chlorine, fluorine and carbon atoms, are nontoxic and inert, meaning they do not combine easily with other substances. Because they vaporize at low temperatures, CFCs are perfect as coolants in refrigerators and propellant gases for spray cans. Since CFCs are good insulators, they are standard ingredients in plastic-foam materials like Styrofoam. Best of all, the most commonly used CFCs are simple, and therefore cheap, to manufacture.

There is only one problem. When they escape into the atmosphere, most CFCs are murder on the environment. Each CFC molecule is 20,000 times as efficient at trapping heat as is a molecule of CO_2. So CFCs increase the greenhouse effect far out of proportion to their concentration in the air.

A more immediate concern is that the chlorine released when CFC molecules break up destroys ozone molecules. The ozone layer, located in the stratosphere, between 10 and 30 miles up, is vital to the well being of plants and animals. Ozone molecules, which consist of three oxygen atoms, absorb most of the ultraviolet radiation that comes from the sun. And ultraviolet is extremely dangerous to life on earth.

The small amount that does get through to the earth's surface inflicts plenty of damage: besides causing sunburn, the rays have been linked to cataracts and weakened immune systems in humans and other animals. Ultraviolet light carries enough energy to damage DNA and thus disrupt the workings of cells, which is why excessive exposure to sunlight is thought to be the primary cause of some skin cancers.

When scientists first warned in the 1970s that CFCs could attack ozone, the United States responded by banning their use in spray cans. (Manufacturers switched to such environmentally benign substitutes as butane, the chemical burned in cigarette lighters.) But the rest of the world continued to use CFC-based aerosol cans, and overall CFC production kept growing. The threat became far clearer in 1985, when researchers reported a "hole" in the ozone layer over Antarctica. Although the size of the hole varies with the seasons and weather patterns, at times Antarctic ozone has been depleted by as much as 50 percent in some spots. As a result of this disturbing development, 24 nations, including the United States and the Soviet Union, met in Montreal some time ago and agreed to cut back on CFCs. The so-called Montreal Protocol is designed to achieve a 35 percent net reduction in worldwide CFC production by 1999.

That is not good enough, however. The same stability that makes CFCs so safe in industrial use makes them extremely long-lived: some of the CFCs released today will still be in the atmosphere a century from now. Moreover, each atom of chlorine liberated from a CFC can break up as many as 100,000 molecules of ozone.

For that reason, governments should ensure the careful handling and recycling of the CFCs now in use. Said Senator Albert Gore of Tennessee: "Much of what reaches the atmosphere is not coming from industrial sources. It's things like sloppy handling of hamburger containers." When plastic-foam burger holders are broken, the CFCs trapped inside escape. Discarded refrigerators release CFCs as well, and, noted Gore, a significant part of the U.S. contribution to CFC emissions comes from "draining automobile air conditioners and leaving the stuff in pans where it boils off." Such release of CFCs could be prevented if consumers and businesses were offered cash incentives to return broken-down air conditioners and refrigerators to auto and appliance dealers. Then the units could be sent back to the manufacturers so that the CFCs could be reused.

While recycling will help, the only sure way to save the ozone is a complete ban on CFC manufacture, which should be phased out over the next five years. Fortunately, as the Montreal Protocol demonstrates, banning CFCs will be far simpler than reducing other dangerous gases. "The CFC producers are a small club of countries," said Brice Lalonde, France's Environment Secretary. But a ban could admittedly be economically disruptive to the entire world: the annual market for CFCs is some $2.2 billion. The Soviet Union, which is a heavy user of CFCs, will have a particularly tough time phasing out the chemicals. "I agree with the ban in principle," said Vladimir Sakharov, a member of the Soviet State Committee for Environmental Protection, "but in practice it will be extremely difficult. Our economy is not as flexible as others."

To make the transition easier, chemical companies are working hard to find practical substitutes for CFCs. The most promising approach so far is to use CFC family members that are chemically altered to make them less dangerous to the environment. The chlorine-free substance HFC–134a, for example, is most likely to be used in refrigeration devices.

The major drawback to CFC substitutes is the high cost of making them. It may be that until better manufacturing techniques are developed, consumers will have to pay more for affected products. The prospect is not a pleasant one, but it is a small price to pay for curbing the greenhouse effect and saving the life-preserving ozone layer.

Reading Time: _____
See Conversion Table.
Enter WPM Rate on the Progress Record Chart.

47 Deadly Danger in a Spray Can

COMPREHENSION CHECK

Getting the Facts

1. CFCs were first synthesized in the late (a) 1910s, (b) 1920s, (c) 1930s, (d) 1940s.

1. ___

2. When CFC molecules break up they release (a) chlorine, (b) fluorine, (c) carbon, (d) all the preceding.

2. ___

3. Where did the twenty-four nations meet to discuss this problem? (a) New York, (b) Chicago, (c) Washington, (d) Montreal.

3. ___

4. What senator was quoted? (a) DeConcini, (b) Glenn, (c) Gore, (d) Durenberger.

4. ___

5. The annual market for CFCs is about (a) 1.2 billion, (b) 1.7 billion, (c) 2.2 billion, (d) 2.7 billion.

5. ___

Getting the Meaning

6. This is mainly to alert us to (a) the dangers of CFC, (b) its increasing use, (c) its ozone-destroying effect, (d) its accenting of the greenhouse effect.

6. ___

7. Mention of the Russian economy was to (a) show their unwillingness to cooperate on this problem, (b) point up their need for CFCs, (c) reveal their difficulty in phasing CFCs out, (d) suggest the detrimental effect on world economy.

7. ___

8. The organization goes (a) from advantages to disadvantages, (b) in a strict chronological order, (c) on a general-to-specific order, (d) on an effect-to-cause order.

8. ___

9. With respect to CFCs, chief emphasis is on (a) recycling, (b) additional controls, (c) banning, (d) achieving a 35% reduction in production.

9. ___

10. Sunburn and cataracts were mentioned primarily to illus-   10. ___
    trate, (a) the dangers of sun rays, (b) the need for ozone,
    (c) a problem growing out of the greenhouse effect, (d) the
    need for further research.

48 A Stinking Mess

WORD POWER WORKOUT

A. Leaning on Context

In each of the blanks provided, place the letter that precedes the best definition of the underlined word in context to the left.

Words in Context	**Definitions**
1. ___ <u>spectral</u> Flying Dutchman	a. foul, putrid
2. ___ <u>brazenly</u> dumped	b. ghostly
3. ___ its <u>noxious</u> cargo	c. huge
4. ___ <u>indiscriminate</u> dumping	d. wealth, richness
5. ___ urgent global <u>dilemma</u>	e. boldly, shamelessly
6. ___ the <u>gargantuan</u> waste	f. impenetrable
7. ___ <u>festering</u> industrial landfills	g. predicament
8. ___ with its <u>affluence</u>	h. wholesale
9. ___ most <u>profligate</u> offender	i. poisonous
10. ___ with <u>impermeable</u> clay	j. reckless

Check your answers with the Key before going on. Review any that you have missed.

Pronunciation aids: 2. brā′zun lē; 3. nok′shus; 4. in dis krim′uh nit; 5. di lem′uh; 6. gar gan′cho͞o un; 9. prof′luh git; 10. im pur′mē uh bul.

KEY: add, āce; end, ēven; it, īce; odd, ōpen; po͞ol; up.

B. Leaning on Parts

This context-root review exercise focuses on *ducere*, meaning "to lead." Fit the appropriate word into each of the five numbered blanks below. Select from the following list of words derived from *ducere: reduce, deduct, conduct, produce, educated, conducive, reproduce, introduce, abduct, productiveness.*

When you (1) _____ your learning effectively, you

(2) _____ the time needed to (3) _____ results. By now

you should be well (4) _____ in the managing of prefix, root, and

suffix elements. Such an accomplishment is (5) _____ to further

progress.

C. Making the Words Yours

In each blank below, enter the most appropriate word from the ten words in context in the first exercise, substituting it for the word(s) in parentheses. Use these words: *affluence, brazenly, dilemma, festering, gargantuan, impermeable, indiscriminate, noxious, profligate, spectral.*

1. The (poisonous) _____ waste may pollute the nearby stream.

2. The writer dreamed about a (ghostly) _____ form—a headless horseman.

3. The gang leader was the most (reckless, vicious) _____ of them all.

4. A layer of (impenetrable) _____ clay must be found to keep noxious waste from the water table below.

5. The United States is known for its (wealth, richness) _____.

6. For a long time the (foul, putrid) _____ insult kept the artist from his work.

7. A (huge) _____ figure suddenly loomed up in the darkness.

8. To study or go to the game—that posed a real (predicament) _____.

9. The thief (boldly, shamelessly) _____ claimed ignorance.

10. Such (wholesale) _____ disregard for the rights of others should not go unpunished.

4 Off for Each Mistake.
Word Power Score: _____
Answer Key in Appendix.

48

A Stinking Mess

John Langone

*As the old saying goes—"Haste makes waste." Perhaps that
needs updating, say to—"Plenty makes waste." But that's not so
catchy. For rhyme's sake, what about—"Disgraced by waste"?
And, if we don't do something about it, it may become "Encased
by waste"! See what you think.*

Begin Timing

Like the journey of the spectral *Flying Dutchman*, the legendary ship condemned to ply the seas endlessly, the voyage of the freighter *Pelicano*
seemed destined to last forever. For more than two years, it sailed around
the world seeking a port that would accept its cargo. Permission was
denied and for good reason: the *Pelicano's* hold was filled with 14,000 tons
of toxic incinerator ash that had been loaded onto the ship in Philadelphia
in September 1986. It was not until October that the *Pelicano* brazenly
dumped 4,000 pounds of its unwanted cargo off a Haitian beach, then
slipped back out to sea, trailing fresh reports that it was illegally deep-sixing
the rest of its noxious cargo. A month later, off Singapore, its captain
announced that he had unloaded the ash in a country he refused to name.

The long voyage of the *Pelicano* is a stark symbol of the environmental
exploitation of poor countries by the rich. It also represents the single most
irresponsible and reckless way to get rid of the growing mountains of
refuse, much of it poisonous, that now bloat the world's landfills. Indiscriminate dumping of any kind—in a New Jersey swamp, on a Haitian beach
or in the Indian Ocean—simply shifts potentially hazardous waste from one
place to another. The practice only underscores the enormity of what has
become an urgent global dilemma: how to reduce the gargantuan waste by-
products of civilization without endangering human health or damaging the
environment.

Scarcely a country on earth has been spared the scourge. From the
festering industrial landfills of Bonn to the waste-choked sewage drains of
Calcutta, the trashing goes on. A poisonous chemical soup, the product of
coal mines and metal smelters, roils Polish waters in the Bay of Gdansk.

Hong Kong, with 5.7 million people and 49,000 factories within its 400 square miles, dumps 1,000 tons of plastic a day—triple the amount thrown away in London. Stinking garbage and human excrement despoil Thailand's majestic River of Kings. Man's effluent is more than an assault on the senses. When common garbage is burned, it spews dangerous gases into the air. Dumped garbage and industrial waste can turn lethal when corrosive acids, long-lived organic materials and discarded metals leach out of landfills into ground water supplies, contaminating drinking water and polluting farmland.

The United States, with its affluence and industrial might, is by far the most profligate offender. Each year Americans throw away 16 billion disposable diapers, 1.6 billion pens, 2 billion razors and blades and 220 million tires. They discard enough aluminum to rebuild the entire U.S. commercial airline fleet every three months. And the country is still struggling to clean up the mess created by the indiscriminate dumping of toxic waste. Said David Rall, director of the National Institute of Environmental Health Sciences: "In the old days, waste was disposed of anywhere you wanted—an old lake, a back lot, a swamp."

How to handle all this waste? Many countries have made a start by locating and cleaning up acres of landfills and lagoons of liquid waste. But few nations have been able to formulate adequate strategies to control the volume of waste produced. Moreover, there are precious few methods of effective disposal, and each has its own drawbacks. As landfills reach capacity, new sites become scarcer and more expensive. Incinerators, burdensome investments for many communities, also have serious limitations: contaminant-laden ash residue itself requires a dump site. Rising consumer demands for more throwaway packaging add to the volume.

Few developing countries have regulations to control the output of hazardous waste, and even fewer have the technology or the trained personnel to dispose of it. Foreign contractors in many African or Asian countries still build plants without including costly waste-disposal systems. Where new technology is available, it is too often inappropriate. In Lagos, Nigeria, five new incinerator plants stand idle because they can only treat garbage containing less than 20 percent water; most of the city's garbage is 30 percent to 40 percent liquid.

Even in highly industrialized countries, there are formidable social obstacles to waste management; not-in-my-backyard resistance by many communities to new disposal sites and incinerators is all too common. In the United States 80 percent of solid waste is now dumped into 6,000 landfills. Their number is shrinking fast: in the past five years, 3,000 dumps have been closed; by 1993 some 2,000 more will be filled to the brim and shut. "We have a real capacity crunch coming up," said J. Winston Porter, an assistant administrator of the Environmental Protection Agency. In West Germany 35,000 to 50,000 landfill sites have been declared potentially dangerous because they may threaten vital groundwater supplies.

What can be done to prevent the world from wallowing in waste? Most important is to reduce trash at its source. At the consumer level, one option is to charge households a garbage-collection fee according to the amount of refuse they produce. Manufacturers too need more prodding. Higher fines, taxes and stricter enforcement might force offending industries to curb waste. Industry must also re-examine its production processes. Such an approach already has a successful track record. The Minnesota Mining and Manufacturing Co. has cut waste generation in half by using fewer toxic chemicals, separating out wastes that can be reused and substituting alternative raw materials for hazardous substances. 3M's savings last year: an astonishing $420 million. In the Netherlands, Duphar, a large chemical concern, adopted a new manufacturing process that decreased by 95 percent the amount of waste created in making a pesticide.

Recycling, of course, is perhaps the best-known way to reduce waste. Some countries do it better than others. Japan now recycles more than 50 percent of its trash, Western Europe around 30 percent. The United States does not fare nearly so well: only 10 percent of American garbage—or 16 million tons a year—is recycled, and only ten states have mandatory recycling laws.

Some experts believe local governments should hike cash refunds to people who return disposable items. Said Nicholas Robinson, who teaches environmental law at Pace University School of Law: "If we could persuade legislatures to increase the recycling price for a bottle from, say, a nickel to maybe a quarter or 50¢, then that bottle would be a very valuable commodity."

But even with more efficient recycling, there will still be refuse. That means landfills and incinerators, however harmful their emissions, will be needed as part of well-managed waste-disposal systems for the foreseeable future. Where possible, landfills should be fitted with impermeable clay or synthetic liners to contain toxic materials, and with pumps to drain liquid waste for treatment and disposal elsewhere. Landfill waste can also be burned to generate electricity, but the United States uses only 6 percent of its rubbish to produce energy. By comparison, West Germany sends more than 30 percent of its unrecycled wastes to waste-to-energy facilities.

Knowledge of the whole refuse cycle is imperative. Of the more than 48,000 chemicals listed by the EPA, next to nothing is currently known about the toxic effects of almost 38,000. Fewer than 1,000 have been tested for acute effects, and only about 500 for their cancer-causing, reproductive or mutagenic effects. Funding must be increased for such research.

In the last analysis, the waste crisis is almost always most effectively attacked close to the source. There should be an international ban on the export of environmentally dangerous waste, especially to countries without the proven technology to dispose of it safely. In the past two years, some 3 million tons of hazardous waste have been transported from the United States and Western Europe on ships like the *Pelicano* to countries in Africa and Eastern Europe. Observed Saad M. Baba, third secretary in the Nigerian mission to the United Nation: "International dumping is the equivalent of declaring war on the people of a country." And if such wastes continue to proliferate, man will have all but declared war on the earth's environment—and thus, in the end, on his own richest heritage.

Reading Time: _____
See Conversion Table.
Enter WPM Rate on the Progress Record Chart.

48 A Stinking Mess

COMPREHENSION CHECK

Getting the Facts

1. The waste was loaded on the *Pelicano* in (a) New York, (b) Philadelphia, (c) Boston, (d) Portland.

   1. ___

2. While looking for a dumping place the *Pelicano* sailed around for about (a) 5 months, (b) 9 months, (c) 1 year, (d) 2 years.

   2. ___

3. We discard enough aluminum to rebuild our entire U.S. commercial airline fleet every (a) 3 months, (b) 7 months, (c) 9 months, (d) year.

   3. ___

4. The article specifically mentioned (a) Firestone, (b) Honeywell, (c) Minnesota Mining, (d) General Motors.

   4. ___

5. What nation does the best job of recycling? (a) England, (b) America, (c) Belgium, (d) Japan.

   5. ___

Getting the Meaning

6. The main idea was to (a) prove the need for recycling, (b) point up the waste problem, (c) discuss a solution, (d) indicate which nation has the greatest problem.

   6. ___

7. The opening part about the *Pelicano* was primarily to illustrate the (a) need for a solution, (b) magnitude of the problem, (c) guilty party to blame, (d) exploitation of poor countries.

   7. ___

8. In general this was organized in a (a) chronological order, (b) simple-to-complex order, (c) problem-solution order, (d) general-to-specific order.

   8. ___

9. The points were developed largely through use of (a) logical reasoning, (b) contrast and comparison, (c) facts and figures, (d) opinions of experts.

   9. ___

10. Chief emphasis was placed on what to curb waste?   10. ___
    (a) recycling, (b) government regulation, (c) laws,
    (d) research and knowledge.

Appendix

Index According to Difficulty

Average difficulty level for these thirty-four selections is 63.3—standard level. According to Flesch this is the level of the average American, the typical reader of mass-circulation magazines and newspapers.

*These selections were all taken from college-level textbooks.

Progress Record Charts

For each selection enter a dot to indicate your comprehension score and, on the next page, a dot to indicate your wpm (word-per-minute) rate. If you read the selections in the exact order given in the text, the numbers in the *Reading Order* will be identical with the *Selection Numbers*. If, however, the third reading you do is not Selection #3 but Selection #8, enter 8 under 3 to indicate that you read that selection third.

COMPREHENSION SCORE

Reading Order	1 2 3 4 5 6 7	8 9 10 11 12 13 14	15 16 17 18 19 20 21 22
Selection #			
Comprehension Score: 100			
90			
80			
70			
60			
50			
40			
30			
20			
10			
0			

Reading Order	23 24 25 26 27 28 29	30 31 32 33 34 35 36	37 38 39 40 41 42 43 44 45
Selection #			
Comprehension Score: 100			
90			
80			
70			
60			
50			
40			
30			
20			
10			
0			

WPM Rate

Reading Order	1 2 3 4 5 6 7	8 9 10 11 12 13 14	15 16 17 18 19 20 21 22
Selection #			
Word-per-minute			
Rate: 1200			
1175			
1150			
1125			
1100			
1075			
1050			
1025			
1000			
975			
950			
925			
900			
875			
850			
825			
800			
775			
750			
725			
700			
675			
650			
625			
600			
575			
550			
525			
500			
475			
450			
425			
400			
375			
350			
325			
300			
275			
250			
225			
200			

WPM Rate

Reading Order	23 24 25 26 27 28 29	30 31 32 33 34 35 36	37 38 39 40 41 42 43 44 45
Selection #			
Word-per-minute			
Rate: 1200			
1175			
1150			
1125			
1100			
1075			
1050			
1025			
1000			
975			
950			
925			
900			
875			
850			
825			
800			
775			
750			
725			
700			
675			
650			
625			
600			
575			
550			
525			
500			
475			
450			
425			
400			
375			
350			
325			
300			
275			
250			
225			
200			

Conversion Tables

To convert your reading time in minutes and seconds to a word-per-minute rate figure, use the following tables. For the selection read, locate your reading time figure in the column headed *Time*. To get your reading rate, look to the right of the reading time figure, to the column headed *Rate*. Suppose you read Selection 1 in four minutes and ten seconds (4:10). Find that figure in the *Time* column, then look to the right. You will see the figure 240—your word-per-minute reading rate for that selection.

If your reading time for any selection is *less* than fifty seconds (or one minute for subsequent selections) *double* your reading time figure before using the table. Then double the figure in the table to get your rate. For example, if you read Selection #40 in forty seconds, double that figure to get eighty seconds—1:20. Then look in the table and double the 750 figure there to get your rate—1,500 wpm.

Use the following table
for Selections 1, 4, 7, 10, 13, 16, 19, 22, 25, 28,
31, 34, 37, and 40—the instructional selections

Time (Min)	Rate (wpm)	Time (Min)	Rate (wpm)	Time (Min)	Rate (wpm)	Time (Min)	Rate (wpm)
0:50	1200	1:55	522	3:00	333	5:10	194
0:55	1091	2:00	500	3:10	316	5:20	188
1:00	1000	2:05	481	3:20	300	5:30	182
1:05	923	2:10	461	3:30	286	5:40	176
1:10	857	2:15	445	3:40	273	5:50	171
1:15	800	2:20	428	3:50	261	6:00	167
1:20	750	2:25	414	4:00	250	6:20	158
1:25	706	2:30	400	4:10	240	6:40	150
1:30	667	2:35	387	4:20	231	7:00	143
1:35	632	2:40	375	4:30	222	7:20	136
1:40	600	2:45	364	4:40	214	7:40	130
1:45	571	2:50	353	4:50	207	8:00	125
1:50	545	2:55	343	5:00	200	8:20	120

If your reading time is more than six minutes for the selections that follow (pp. 386–389), divide your reading time in half before using the conversion table. Then divide the figure in the table by half to get your reading rate. For example, if it takes you eight minutes to read Selection #11, divide by half and look at the entry for four minutes. Then divide the 490 figure by half to get your rate—245 wpm.

Time (Min)	Sel. 2	Sel. 3	Sel. 5	Sel. 6	Sel. 8	Sel. 9	Sel. 11	Sel. 12	Sel. 14
1:00	940	970	1280	1030	1290	1380	1960	1130	820
1:05	867	895	1172	950	1191	1274	1808	1042	757
1:10	806	832	1097	882	1106	1183	1680	966	702
1:15	752	776	1024	824	1032	1104	1568	901	656
1:20	705	726	960	772	968	1035	1468	846	615
1:25	663	684	904	726	911	974	1382	798	578
1:30	626	648	853	686	860	920	1306	752	546
1:35	593	612	808	650	814	872	1236	714	518
1:40	564	582	768	618	774	828	1176	678	492
1:45	537	555	731	588	738	789	1120	648	468
1:50	513	528	698	562	704	753	1068	618	447
1:55	490	506	667	536	673	720	1022	589	427
2:00	470	485	640	515	645	690	980	565	410
2:05	451	466	610	494	619	662	940	542	394
2:10	434	448	581	475	595	636	904	521	378
2:15	418	432	566	458	573	613	870	512	365
2:20	403	416	548	441	553	592	840	484	352
2:25	389	402	528	426	534	571	810	467	340
2:30	376	388	512	412	516	552	784	451	328
2:35	364	376	496	398	499	534	758	437	318
2:40	352	364	480	386	484	518	734	424	308
2:45	342	352	462	374	469	502	712	410	299
2:50	332	342	452	363	455	486	691	399	289
2:55	322	334	436	352	442	473	672	387	281
3:00	313	323	427	343	430	460	653	376	273
3:10	297	306	406	325	407	436	618	357	259
3:20	282	291	384	309	387	414	588	339	246
3:30	268	278	367	294	369	396	560	324	235
3:40	256	264	349	281	351	376	534	309	224
3:50	245	254	335	268	336	360	511	295	214
4:00	235	243	320	258	323	346	490	283	205
4:10	225	233	305	247	309	332	470	273	197
4:20	217	224	290	238	298	318	452	260	189
4:30	209	216	283	229	287	306	435	252	182
4:40	201	208	274	220	277	296	420	242	176
4:50	194	201	264	213	266	286	405	234	170
5:00	188	194	256	206	258	276	392	225	164
5:10	182	188	248	199	249	266	379	219	159
5:20	176	182	240	193	242	258	368	212	154
5:30	171	176	231	187	234	250	356	204	149
5:40	166	171	223	181	228	244	346	199	145
5:50	161	167	218	176	221	236	336	194	141
6:00	156	162	213	172	215	230	327	188	137

Time (Min)	Sel. 15	Sel. 17	Sel. 18	Sel. 20	Sel. 21	Sel. 23	Sel. 24	Sel. 26	Sel. 27
1:00	920	1560	1320	970	1240	650	1820	1020	1190
1:05	849	1440	1218	895	1142	600	1680	941	1098
1:10	786	1336	1131	832	1062	557	1560	874	1020
1:15	734	1248	1056	776	992	520	1452	816	952
1:20	690	1170	990	727	930	488	1362	765	892
1:25	649	1102	932	684	875	459	1286	720	840
1:30	613	1040	880	648	826	433	1212	680	793
1:35	581	984	834	613	783	411	1146	644	751
1:40	552	936	792	582	744	390	1092	612	714
1:45	526	892	754	555	709	371	1040	583	680
1:50	502	850	720	529	679	355	992	556	649
1:55	480	816	689	506	646	339	949	532	621
2:00	460	780	660	485	620	325	910	510	595
2:05	443	748	634	466	595	312	875	489	571
2:10	425	720	609	448	572	300	840	471	549
2:15	410	694	587	432	551	289	810	453	529
2:20	394	668	566	416	531	279	780	437	510
2:25	381	646	546	402	514	269	759	422	492
2:30	368	624	528	388	496	260	736	408	476
2:35	357	604	511	376	481	252	709	395	461
2:40	345	585	495	364	465	244	681	383	446
2:45	335	568	480	352	452	236	663	371	433
2:50	325	551	466	342	438	229	642	360	420
2:55	316	534	453	334	426	223	620	350	408
3:00	307	520	440	323	413	217	607	340	396
3:10	292	492	417	306	394	205	577	322	376
3:20	276	468	396	291	372	195	546	306	357
3:30	264	444	377	278	359	186	521	292	340
3:40	251	425	360	264	346	177	496	278	324
3:50	241	408	344	254	328	170	477	266	310
4:00	230	390	330	243	310	163	455	255	297
4:10	221	374	317	233	298	156	438	245	285
4:20	213	360	305	224	286	150	420	236	275
4:30	205	347	293	216	276	144	405	226	264
4:40	197	334	283	208	266	140	390	218	255
4:50	191	323	273	201	257	134	377	211	246
5:00	184	312	264	194	248	130	364	204	238
5:10	179	302	255	188	240	126	352	197	230
5:20	173	293	248	182	233	122	341	192	223
5:30	168	284	240	176	226	118	331	185	216
5:40	163	275	233	171	219	115	321	180	210
5:50	158	267	226	167	213	112	312	175	204
6:00	153	260	220	162	207	108	303	170	198

Time (Min)	Sel. 29	Sel. 30	Sel. 32	Sel. 33	Sel. 35	Sel. 36	Sel. 38	Sel. 39	Sel. 41
1:00	1020	690	1890	1310	1120	1570	1450	1000	1480
1:05	941	637	1744	1209	1034	1450	1338	923	1366
1:10	874	591	1620	1123	960	1346	1243	857	1270
1:15	816	552	1512	1048	895	1256	1160	800	1182
1:20	765	517	1418	982	840	1178	1088	750	1110
1:25	720	486	1334	924	790	1108	1024	706	1045
1:30	680	460	1260	873	746	1046	967	667	984
1:35	644	436	1194	826	707	991	916	632	930
1:40	612	414	1134	786	672	942	870	600	888
1:45	583	393	1080	748	640	894	829	571	845
1:50	556	376	1032	714	610	856	791	545	808
1:55	532	360	986	683	584	819	757	522	772
2:00	510	345	945	655	560	785	725	500	740
2:05	489	332	907	629	538	754	696	481	710
2:10	471	318	872	605	517	724	669	461	683
2:15	453	307	840	584	498	698	644	445	659
2:20	437	296	810	561	480	672	621	428	634
2:25	422	283	782	542	463	650	600	414	613
2:30	408	270	756	524	446	628	580	400	592
2:35	395	264	732	507	433	609	561	387	573
2:40	383	258	709	491	420	589	544	375	555
2:45	371	247	686	477	407	572	527	364	538
2:50	360	244	667	463	396	554	512	353	522
2:55	350	237	648	450	384	539	497	343	507
3:00	340	230	630	437	373	523	483	333	493
3:10	322	219	601	415	354	497	458	316	470
3:20	306	207	567	393	336	471	435	300	444
3:30	292	198	540	375	320	450	415	286	423
3:40	278	188	516	357	305	425	395	273	404
3:50	266	181	493	342	293	409	378	261	386
4:00	255	173	473	328	280	393	362	250	370
4:10	245	166	454	316	270	378	348	240	356
4:20	236	159	436	303	259	362	335	231	342
4:30	226	154	420	291	250	349	322	222	330
4:40	218	148	405	281	240	336	311	214	317
4:50	211	143	391	271	232	325	300	207	306
5:00	204	138	378	262	224	314	290	200	296
5:10	197	134	366	254	217	305	281	194	287
5:20	192	130	355	246	210	295	272	188	278
5:30	185	125	343	239	203	286	264	182	270
5:40	180	122	334	231	198	277	256	176	261
5:50	175	118	324	225	193	270	249	171	254
6:00	170	115	315	218	187	262	242	167	247

Time (Min)	Sel. 42	Sel. 43	Sel. 44	Sel. 45	Sel. 46	Sel. 47	Sel. 48
1:00	980	1100	1580	1260	1380	860	1320
1:05	904	1015	1458	1163	1274	793	1218
1:10	840	943	1354	1080	1183	737	1131
1:15	783	880	1264	1008	1104	687	1056
1:20	733	825	1185	945	1035	645	990
1:25	691	776	1115	889	974	607	932
1:30	653	733	1053	840	920	573	880
1:35	619	695	998	796	872	543	834
1:40	588	660	948	756	828	516	792
1:45	560	628	903	720	789	491	754
1:50	534	600	861	691	753	469	720
1:55	511	574	824	658	720	449	689
2:00	490	550	790	630	690	430	660
2:05	470	528	758	605	662	413	634
2:10	452	508	729	582	636	397	609
2:15	436	489	702	560	613	382	587
2:20	420	472	677	540	592	368	566
2:25	405	455	655	521	571	356	546
2:30	392	440	632	504	552	344	528
2:35	379	426	613	488	534	333	511
2:40	368	413	593	473	518	323	495
2:45	356	399	576	458	502	313	480
2:50	346	388	558	445	486	303	466
2:55	337	377	543	432	473	295	453
3:00	327	367	527	420	460	287	440
3:10	309	348	499	398	436	272	417
3:20	294	330	474	378	414	258	396
3:30	280	314	452	360	396	246	377
3:40	267	300	428	344	376	235	360
3:50	256	287	412	329	360	224	344
4:00	245	275	395	315	346	215	330
4:10	235	264	380	303	332	206	317
4:20	226	254	365	291	318	199	305
4:30	218	244	352	280	306	191	293
4:40	210	238	339	270	296	184	283
4:50	203	228	328	261	286	178	273
5:00	196	220	316	252	276	172	264
5:10	189	213	307	244	266	166	255
5:20	184	207	297	236	258	162	248
5:30	178	199	288	229	250	156	240
5:40	173	194	279	222	244	152	233
5:50	168	189	271	216	236	147	226
6:00	163	184	263	210	230	143	220

Answers to Outline for Selection 31

I. The role of organization.
   A. To help identify.
   B. To help extract.

II. What is the role of outlining?

III. How is organization revealed?
   A. Through special devices.
      1. Typographical devices.
         a. Capitals.
         b. Boldface type.
         c. Italics.
      2. Rhetorical devices.
         a. Repetition
         b. Parallelism.
         c. Balance.
      3. Verbal devices.
         a. To mark transitions.
         b. To mark methods of development.
         c. To mark outline form.
   B. Through paragraph structure.
      1. Topic sentences.
      2. Supporting details.

IV. What does organization contribute?
   A. Sharpened awareness.
      1. Of main idea or thesis.
      2. Of interrelationships.
   B. Improved ability.
      1. To understand.
      2. To remember.

V. Summary of purpose or role of organization.

Key for Word Power Workouts Part A

Selection	1	2	3	4	5	6	7	8	9	10	11	12	13	14	15	16
1.	c	c	d	i	c	d	g	d	f	b	g	c	c	e	c	b
2.	g	f	e	a	e	h	d	f	c	j	e	f	i	h	d	e
3.	f	e	j	d	g	g	c	c	e	c	h	g	d	a	g	h
4.	h	j	f	e	h	a	a	i	g	d	i	i	e	i	f	f
5.	e	i	g	h	j	j	j	j	j	f	d	d	b	b	a	g
6.	i	d	h	b	f	b	e	a	d	a	b	h	f	j	h	i
7.	a	a	i	j	a	i	f	h	a	g	f	b	h	g	e	j
8.	b	b	b	c	b	e	b	g	i	i	a	j	a	c	i	a
9.	j	g	c	f	d	f	h	b	b	h	c	a	g	d	j	d
10.	d	h	a	g	i	c	i	e	h	e	j	e	j	f	b	c

Selection	17	18	19	20	21	22	23	24	25	26	27	28	29	30	31	32
1.	d	e	e	d	d	f	d	d	h	c	d	g	d	d	c	i
2.	c	g	f	f	g	e	i	e	d	e	f	j	h	f	e	f
3.	g	i	i	g	h	h	g	c	i	g	b	h	e	g	f	d
4.	f	b	g	h	f	g	h	f	a	h	g	a	g	c	g	a
5.	j	d	d	i	b	d	f	j	g	a	j	c	f	i	i	c
6.	h	h	h	b	e	c	a	a	j	j	h	i	i	b	a	b
7.	e	f	b	a	a	i	j	g	b	i	a	b	b	e	b	h
8.	a	j	a	e	j	a	c	h	c	d	i	e	a	j	h	e
9.	b	c	j	c	i	b	e	b	e	b	e	d	j	a	d	j
10.	i	a	c	j	c	j	b	i	f	f	c	f	c	h	j	g

Selection	33	34	35	36	37	38	39	40	41	42	43	44	45	46	47	48
1.	c	b	b	e	b	d	d	e	d	c	j	d	f	g	e	b
2.	d	e	d	d	g	g	i	a	f	d	f	a	g	a	c	e
3.	f	g	f	h	j	a	j	b	h	b	d	g	b	d	h	i
4.	g	a	a	a	e	f	a	c	e	g	a	f	c	f	g	h
5.	a	f	c	g	a	c	g	h	a	h	i	c	d	j	d	g
6.	i	d	g	e	h	j	h	f	j	j	c	j	e	i	i	c
7.	e	j	i	i	i	e	e	i	i	a	e	e	a	h	f	a
8.	b	c	e	b	f	i	b	d	c	f	b	b	j	b	a	d
9.	j	h	h	f	d	b	f	j	g	e	g	h	h	c	j	j
10.	h	i	j	j	c	h	c	g	b	i	h	i	i	e	b	f

Key for Word Power Workouts   Parts B & C

| Selection 1 | Selection 2 | Selection 3 |

(Part B begins with Selection 4)

C	1. preservation	C	1. harbinger	C	1. morale
	2. traumatic		2. survived		2. stabilizer
	3. avid		3. methodical		3. sonic
	4. catalyst		4. impatient		4. barrier
	5. crucial		5. bifocals		5. ego
	6. dependable		6. retort		6. sequence
	7. survey		7. plummeted		7. stall
	8. generates		8. moorings		8. bolstered
	9. potential		9. tethered		9. fluctuated
	10. indispensable		10. taffeta		10. buffet

| Selection 4 | Selection 5 | Selection 6 |

B	1. preheat	B	1. reread	B	1. procession
	2. prepare		2. reappear		2. projector
	3. president		3. return		3. prolong
	4. prefix		4. back		4. propeller
	5. before		5. again		5. forward

C	1. consolidated	C	1. sensuous	C.	1. altered
	2. hybrid		2. compadre		2. utters
	3. expedite		3. episode		3. interjected
	4. hindered		4. obligatory		4. acquired
	5. corroborated		5. salutation		5. vastly
	6. predilection		6. declarative		6. fancifully
	7. interplay		7. sibling		7. manifestations
	8. tentative		8. relic		8. invariably
	9. discrimination		9. frankly		9. nuances
	10. context		10. anonymity		10. assimilated

Selection 7	Selection 8	Selection 9
B 1. interstate	B 1. nonessential	B 1. depart
2. intermission	2. nonconformist	2. descend
3. intermediator	3. nonfiction	3. deposit
4. interrupt	4. nonsense	4. depressed
5. between	5. not	5. down

C 1. dominates	C 1. dais	C 1. media
2. abysmally	2. uninitiated	2. constraint
3. maximum	3. intents	3. retained
4. literally	4. fulsome	4. edit
5. inevitably	5. articulate	5. compelling
6. blurred	6. exhortation	6. mandatory
7. fallacious	7. sheaf	7. mastering
8. appropriate	8. lectern	8. concept
9. hypothesis	9. embodies	9. succinctly
10. terminology	10. spontaneous	10. concise

Selection 10	Selection 11	Selection 12
B 1. unusual	B 1. transatlantic	B 1. overprice
2. uncertain	2. transfer	2. overweight
3. unwise	3. transfusion	3. overcoat
4. unworthy	4. translate	4. overflows
5. not	5. beyond	5. above

C 1. minimize	C 1. cronies	C 1. status
2. plodded	2. apprehensive	2. agenda
3. reinforces	3. warped	3. dynamic
4. sliver	4. swatches	4. apocryphal
5. temporarily	5. hilarious	5. Madisonian
6. relented	6. auburn	6. gnawing
7. phenomenon	7. exuberance	7. strive
8. key	8. devote	8. sophisticated
9. impetus	9. extravaganza	9. pampered
10. initial	10. insupportable	10. presumption

Selection 13

B
1. monoplane
2. monosyllable
3. monopoly
4. monotonous
5. one

C
1. apportion
2. zeros in
3. jacket
4. concise
5. compressed
6. subsequent
7. perspective
8. veritable
9. capsule
10. technique

Selection 14

B
1. epitaph
2. epidermis
3. epilepsy
4. epidemic
5. upon

C
1. alluring
2. patronizing
3. sustain
4. auditioning
5. instinct
6. species
7. embarked
8. abyss
9. state
10. collard

Selection 15

B
1. misbehavior
2. mislead
3. mispronounce
4. mislaid
5. wrong

C
1. wary
2. aspirations
3. unique
4. genetic
5. fads
6. affable
7. anxiety
8. demonstrate
9. sadism
10. neurotic

Selection 16

B
1. compact
2. companion
3. compare
4. compound
5. together

C
1. cultivated
2. priority
3. repertoire
4. counteract
5. intervening
6. superficial
7. productivity
8. reiterate
9. snatched
10. exceptional

Selection 17

B
1. independent
2. incapable
3. informal
4. indirect
5. not

C
1. effigy
2. myriad
3. sorrel
4. paraphernalia
5. pamphlet
6. sublimely
7. listlessly
8. premier
9. intoned
10. inadvertently

Selection 18

B
1. exhale
2. exit
3. exhausted
4. explosion
5. out

C
1. cocked
2. reconstructed
3. illuminates
4. improbable
5. ruff
6. documents
7. toga
8. encounter
9. pasteurizing
10. springs

Selection 19

B
1. disagree
2. dispatch
3. disperse
4. dismissed
5. away

C
1. job
2. surpasses
3. elusive
4. sufficient
5. enviable
6. feasible
7. undigested
8. proverbial
9. versatile
10. relevant

Selection 20

B
1. adheres
2. admit
3. adjacent
4. advanced
5. to

C
1. metaphor
2. faculties
3. extermination
4. depicted
5. disapprobation
6. gross
7. discrepant
8. checkmated
9. susceptible
10. untold

Selection 21

B
1. object
2. obstacle
3. objections
4. obscure
5. against

C
1. hyperbolical
2. incarcerate
3. tortuous
4. apprised
5. variegated
6. mistral
7. unprecedented
8. intact
9. irrisistible
10. incursion

Selection 22

B
1. inside
2. insert
3. invest
4. include
5. in

C
1. subtle
2. conceited
3. emphasis
4. ambiguity
5. in-depth
6. insinuations
7. variety
8. accusation
9. inseparable
10. mature

Selection 23

B
1. subbasement
2. substandard
3. subsonic
4. subtitle
5. under

C
1. clues
2. scholarly
3. stalled
4. sustain
5. undeterred
6. seminars
7. terrain
8. vantage
9. structure
10. passively

Selection 24

B
1. connect
2. collect
3. correspond
4. conflict
5. cooperate

C
1. leitmotiv
2. tacit
3. liaison
4. acclaim
5. garnered
6. confront
7. adept
8. palpable
9. prestigious
10. converge

Selection 25

B 1. support
    2. suffix
    3. succeed
    4. suggest
    5. suspect

C 1. conservative
    2. perceptual
    3. eliminated
    4. promote
    5. latent
    6. complicated
    7. convenient
    8. contrast
    9. havoc
  10. allied

Selection 26

B 1. irradiate
    2. illuminate
    3. immigrant
    4. illustrious
    5. irrigation

C 1. fundamental
    2. deferred
    3. resist
    4. delving
    5. routine
    6. enterprises
    7. inconsequential
    8. clutter
    9. poke
  10. interim

Selection 27

B 1. accept
    2. allow
    3. oppress
    4. offend
    5. occur

C 1. synchronized
    2. therapeutic
    3. affected
    4. seeps
    5. intriguing
    6. evolved
    7. alleviate
    8. secretes
    9. diurnal
  10. vice versa

Selection 28

B 1. effect
    2. eccentric
    3. emit
    4. difficult
    5. dilapidated

C 1. relish
    2. abound
    3. transitional
    4. core
    5. conscious
    6. specialized
    7. remotest
    8. fixed
    9. nudge
  10. advantage

Selection 29

B 1. duct
    2. introduction
    3. reduce
    4. produce
    5. conduit

C 1. predicament
    2. unleash
    3. offing
    4. fallacy
    5. innately
    6. reservoir
    7. coping
    8. stultifying
    9. imprints
  10. exalted

Selection 30

B 1. prescription
    2. manuscript
    3. script
    4. subscribed
    5. describe

C 1. category
    2. evoke
    3. parity
    4. salient
    5. felicitous
    6. leverage
    7. sheer
    8. quantifiable
    9. virtually
  10. efficacy

Selection 31

B
1. posted
2. posture
3. postponed
4. deposit
5. postage

C
1. lean
2. facilitates
3. glance
4. rhetorical
5. obscure
6. chief
7. extracted
8. captured
9. subordinate
10. supporting

Selection 32

B
1. submit
2. missile
3. missionary
4. remittance
5. emitted

C
1. jangling
2. epoxy
3. chaps
4. perpetuate
5. offhand
6. dastardly
7. dissuaded
8. flinched
9. bumbling
10. slouched

Selection 33

B
1. captive
2. recipient
3. receive
4. intercepting
5. emancipated

C
1. curtail
2. rendezvous
3. senile
4. counter
5. propitious
6. irrelevance
7. connived
8. deviation
9. ostensibly
10. morbid

Selection 34

B
1. explicit
2. imply
3. deploy
4. duplex
5. reply

C
1. toll
2. released
3. culmination
4. endeavors
5. academic
6. insures
7. modified
8. utmost
9. frantic
10. pose

Selection 35

B
1. autobiography
2. bibliography
3. telegraph
4. monograph
5. graphic

C
1. metabolic
2. compulsive
3. depletion
4. malfunction
5. dilution
6. diuretic
7. imminent
8. excretes
9. insensibly
10. counterproductive

Selection 36

B
1. dialogue
2. eloquent
3. mythology
4. prologue
5. biology

C
1. circadian
2. generic
3. eons
4. extraneous
5. alleviate
6. deteriorate
7. periodic
8. incites
9. apnea
10. nocturnal

Selection 37

B 1. abstinence
2. tenant
3. detain
4. tenaciously
5. discontent

C 1. irrational
2. impersonal
3. ineptitude
4. restraint
5. renown
6. genuinely
7. voluntarily
8. outstanding
9. colleague
10. condescendingly

Selection 38

B 1. suffer
2. transfers
3. ferry
4. fertile
5. translate

C 1. radiates
2. motivated
3. ingrained
4. jeopardizing
5. halo
6. ultimate
7. components
8. engaging
9. predisposes
10. subliminal

Selection 39

B 1. defective
2. sufficient
3. defeated
4. fashioned
5. facility

C 1. trend
2. discrepancies
3. chauvinism
4. corporate
5. aspects
6. blatant
7. detrimental
8. mandates
9. deferential
10. stereotyping

Selection 40

B 1. spectator
2. respect
3. spectacles
4. aspects
5. auspicious

C 1. garret
2. ideal
3. epitomized
4. surplus
5. vocation
6. quest
7. boundaries
8. assurance
9. savored
10. trauma

Selection 41

B 1. attention
2. attend
3. tense
4. portents
5. intent

C 1. alienation
2. dogma
3. therapy
4. tempo
5. incidentally
6. compatible
7. elite
8. extensions
9. frustrations
10. deflect

Selection 42

B 1. statue
2. insist
3. stationary
4. armistice
5. assistant

C 1. criteria
2. options
3. strategy
4. objective
5. frugality
6. mobile
7. ethic
8. mentors
9. entrepreneur
10. pending

Selection 43

B
1. helper
2. youthful
3. tireless
4. lioness
5. infantile

C
1. chute
2. procedure
3. fostered
4. implications
5. pellet
6. evolved
7. instrumental
8. tidbit
9. speculates
10. operant

Selection 44

B
1. globule
2. hourly
3. returnable
4. childish
5. darken

C
1. tentacles
2. Colossus
3. contraptions
4. lethal
5. phenomenal
6. impact
7. infectious
8. ostentation
9. grueling
10. notoriety

Selection 45

B
1. grandiose
2. commendatory
3. remedial
4. picturesque
5. affectionate

C
1. menial
2. proliferation
3. thesis
4. encode
5. intuitive
6. scut
7. atrophied
8. demise
9. untrammeled
10. squelch

Selection 46

B
1. obstacles
2. persist
3. substantial
4. assistance
5. establishing

C
1. tabs
2. insatiable
3. anonymous
4. scenario
5. gamut
6. skeptics
7. huff
8. purveyor
9. cult
10. impishly

Selection 47

B
1. tends
2. extend
3. Attention
4. extensive
5. portent

C
1. synthesized
2. banning
3. benign
4. disrupt
5. propellant
6. affected
7. incentives
8. ensure
9. inert
10. vaporize

Selection 48

B
1. conduct
2. reduce
3. produce
4. educated
5. conducive

C
1. noxious
2. spectral
3. profligate
4. impermeable
5. affluence
6. festering
7. gargantuan
8. dilemma
9. brazenly
10. indiscriminate

Key for Words in Isolation Vocabulary Test

1. c	6. a	11. e	16. e	21. c
2. a	7. b	12. a	17. e	22. a
3. a	8. c	13. c	18. c	23. d
4. b	9. b	14. c	19. d	24. a
5. e	10. c	15. a	20. b	25. d

COMPREHENSION CHECK QUESTIONS

Selection	1	2	3	4	5	6	7	8	9	10	11	12	13	14	15	16
1.	b	d	a	d	c	b	b	d	c	c	a	c	c	b	a	a
2.	b	c	d	c	a	a	c	a	b	d	c	a	d	c	d	b
3.	d	b	d	c	b	c	a	c	d	a	d	c	b	c	d	a
4.	a	c	a	d	b	b	b	b	a	b	b	b	d	a	c	b
5.	d	c	b	c	d	a	b	d	a	c	c	c	b	b	b	c
6.	c	c	c	a	c	d	a	c	c	a	a	d	a	d	d	d
7.	b	b	c	a	d	a	c	b	d	d	d	a	b	d	b	b
8.	d	b	a	d	a	d	a	c	b	b	c	d	d	a	d	c
9.	c	d	b	d	c	a	d	a	c	a	b	a	c	c	b	d
10.	b	b	c	b	d	c	c	d	c	c	a	c	c	a	a	d

Selection	17	18	19	20	21	22	23	24	25	26	27	28	29	30	31	32
1.	b	a	a	c	b	b	d	d	a	a	c	a	d	d	a	c
2.	c	c	d	b	a	c	c	a	c	b	b	b	a	b	b	a
3.	c	d	d	d	c	c	a	b	d	d	d	c	c	c	a	d
4.	a	b	c	a	d	a	b	c	c	b	a	c	b	a	b	c
5.	c	c	c	b	a	c	c	c	b	b	c	b	c	d	a	d
6.	c	b	d	d	b	b	d	c	a	b	d	b	c	c	a	c
7.	a	a	c	a	a	d	a	a	a	a	a	d	a	c	a	b
8.	d	d	b	c	d	c	b	c	a	d	c	c	d	b	b	a
9.	b	c	b	b	c	b	b	a	d	c	a	b	b	d	a	d
10.	d	c	a	c	b	d	b	a	c	b	b	c	b	d	a	a

Selection	33	34	35	36	37	38	39	40	41	42	43	44	45	46	47	48
1.	c	b	a	c	d	d	c	b	b	b	a	c	c	a	b	b
2.	a	c	b	a	d	b	a	c	b	d	d	a	d	d	a	d
3.	d	a	a	d	a	c	a	a	a	c	a	d	a	c	d	a
4.	b	c	b	b	b	a	c	a	b	a	c	b	a	c	c	c
5.	d	d	c	d	a	b	b	b	c	c	d	d	d	a	c	d
6.	b	b	d	d	a	a	d	b	b	b	d	b	b	b	a	b
7.	d	c	b	a	b	d	c	c	c	b	d	b	d	b	c	d
8.	d	b	c	b	d	c	a	a	a	c	a	c	a	a	a	c
9.	a	a	b	c	b	b	b	d	d	a	c	c	c	c	c	c
10.	b	a	a	a	a	c	d	d	c	d	c	b	c	d	b	d

Acknowledgments

p. 17 From *All I Really Need to Know I Learned in Kindergarten* by Robert L. Fulghum. Copyright © 1986, 1988 by Robert L. Fulghum. Reprinted by permission of Villard Books, a Division of Random House, Inc.

p. 23 Excerpt from *Yeager An Autobiography* by General Chuck Yeager and Leo Janos. Copyright © 1985 by Yeager, Inc. Used by permission of Bantam Books, a division of Bantam, Doubleday, Dell Publishing Group, Inc.

p. 39 "How to Write a Personal Letter" by Garrison Keillor. Copyright © 1988 by International Paper Company. Reprinted by permission of International Paper and Garrison Keillor.

p. 47 From *Are You Listening* by Ralph G. Nichols and Leonard A. Stevens. Copyright © 1957, renewed 1985 by McGraw Hill Book Co. Reprinted by permission of Curtis Brown, Ltd.

p. 61 "How to make a speech" by George Plimpton from "Power of the Printed Word" series. Reprinted by permission of International Paper.

p. 69 "How to Get Your Point Across in 30 Seconds—Or Less" by Milo Frank. Copyright © 1986 by Milo Frank. Reprinted by permission of Simon & Schuster, Inc.

p. 95 From *A Preface to Politics* by David F. Schuman with Bob Waterman. Copyright © 1986 by D. C. Heath and Company. Reprinted by permission of the publisher.

p. 109 Excerpt from *Love and Marriage* by Bill Cosby, copyright © 1989 by Bill Cosby. Used by permission of Doubleday, a division of Bantam, Doubleday, Dell Publishing Group, Inc.

p. 115 From *Introductory Psychology* by Morris K. Holland. Copyright © 1981 by D. C. Heath and Company. Reprinted by permission of the publisher.

p. 131 From *Lincoln* by Gore Vidal. Copyright © 1984 by Gore Vidal. Reprinted by permission of Random House, Inc.

p. 179 "How to Read a Difficult Book" from *Great Ideas from The Great Books* by Mortimer J. Adler. Copyright © 1961, 1963 by Mortimer J. Adler. Reprinted by permission of Pocket Books, a division of Simon & Schuster, Inc.

p. 185 Story by Hilary Richardson Bagnato from *The Rotarian*, April 1989. Reprinted by permission of *The Rotarian* and the author.

p. 201 From *How To Get Control of Your Time and Your Life* by Alan Lakein. Copyright © 1973 by Alan Lakein. Reprinted by permission of David McKay Co., a division of Random House, Inc.

p. 207 "Guiding Light" by Hal Hellman from *Psychology Today*, April 1982. Copyright © 1982. Reprinted by permission of the Julian Bach Literary Agency, Inc.

p. 221 Text by Bill Moyers from *Family Weekly*, December 27, 1981. Reprinted by permission of Bill Moyers.

p. 227 "Creativity in the Advertising Mix" by Burt Manning. Reprinted by permission of the author.

p. 243 Selected excerpt from "The Dumbest Antelope" from *The Night The Bear Ate Goombaw* by Patrick F. McManus. Copyright © 1989 Patrick F. McManus. Reprinted by permission of Henry Holt and Company, Inc.

p. 253 "Mrs. Packletide's Tiger" by Saki in *Short Stories*, 1976. Published by Viking Penguin, Inc.

p. 269 "The Wonders of Water" by Jane Brody. Reprinted from *Jane Brody's Nutrition Book* by Jane Brody by permission of W. W. Norton & Company, Inc. Copyright © 1981 by Jane E. Brody.

p. 275 "Can't Get a Good Night's Sleep?" Reprinted with permission from *Changing Times* Magazine, © Kiplinger Washington Editors, Inc., April 1977. This reprint is not to be altered in any way, except with permission from *Changing Times*.

p. 293 "How to Get the Job You Want" by Dr. Joyce Brothers from *Parade Magazine*, November 16, 1986, pp. 4–6. Reprinted by permission of Dr. Joyce Brothers.

p. 301 From *Management* by Jerry Kinard. Copyright © 1988 by D. C. Heath and Company. Reprinted by permission of the publisher.

p. 319 From *A Preface to Politics* by David F. Schuman with Bob Waterman. Copyright © 1986 by D. C. Heath and Company. Reprinted by permission of the publisher.

p. 327 From *Business* by Leon C. Megginson, Lyle R. Trueblood, and Gayle M. Ross. Copyright © 1985 by D. C. Heath and Company. Reprinted by permission of the publisher.

p. 335 From *Introductory Psychology* by Morris K. Holland. Copyright © 1981 by D. C. Heath and Company. Reprinted by permission of the publisher.

p. 343 From *The American Pageant* by Thomas A. Bailey and David M. Kennedy. Copyright © 1987 by D. C. Heath and Company. Reprinted by permission of the publisher.

p. 351 "Next" by Isaac Asimov from *P/C Computing*, September 1988, pp. 241–242. Reprinted by permission of Isaac Asimov, President of Nightfall, Inc.

p. 357 "The Future Shock's Doc" by Nancy Spiller published in *American Way*, September 1, 1988. Reprinted by permission of the author, a Los Angeles based writer.

p. 365 "Deadly Danger In a Spray Can" by Michael D. Lemonick from *Time*, January 2, 1989. Copyright © 1988 The Time Inc. Magazine Company. Reprinted by permission.

p. 373 "A Stinking Mess" by John Langone from *Time*, January 2, 1989. Copyright © 1988 The Time Inc. Magazine Company. Reprinted by permission.